Youth Ministry

ENCYCLOPEDIA

by Lyman Coleman

SERENDIPITY HOUSE / BOX 1012 / LITTLETON, CO 80160   800-525-9563

Contents

104 WAYS TO INVOLVE KIDS

55 EXERCISES TO GET ACQUAINTED

12 CONVERSATIONAL QUESTIONNAIRES

12 QUESTIONNAIRES ON PARABLES

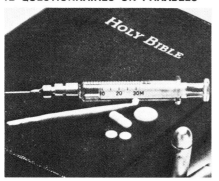

12 QUESTIONNAIRES ON LIFE OF CHRIST

12 QUESTIONNAIRES ON CHARACTER

"We loved you so much that we were delighted to share with you not only the gospel of God but our lives as well, because you had become so dear to us."

1 Thessalonians 2:8

8 Assumptions Behind the Serendipity Group Model

1 WE are created in the image of God and endowed with His own potential.

2 This POTENTIAL can best be realized through Jesus Christ, in the company of a supportive Christian community.

3 To become a truly SUPPORTIVE CHRISTIAN COMMUNITY we need to get to know one another in depth, and this takes time, effort, and a common commitment to life together.

4 Personal GROWTH begins with inner change—as we respond to the invitation of God for newness of life.

5 The HOLY SPIRIT has endowed us with SPIRITUAL GIFTS for ministering to others within our supportive community, and through the community to the church and world at large.

6 SCRIPTURE is the living account of God's redemptive activity, and the best guide to His will for right now.

7 Spiritual WHOLENESS includes our whole being—our emotions, relationships, values, and lifestyles.

8 CELEBRATION happens naturally and spontaneously when we are set free in a supportive Christian community to discover and express the beautiful persons we are in Christ.

Youth ministry is . . .

people . . . . not programs

relationships . . . . not religion

Christ . . . . not creeds

a new	not a tired
radical	old
life-changing	gutless
personal	religious
faith . . . . tradition

Youth are looking for a choice, not a compromise.

7

Go heavy on Group Building at first!

As the Good Book says, "There is a time for everything." And in youth ministry, there needs to be a time for:
□ *Content:* Spiritual Formation
□ *Group Building:* Becoming a Christian Community
□ *Service:* Reaching Out to Others

But the twelve-month cycle of a youth program needs to be carefully tuned to the "seasons" of "sowing and reaping." First of all, let's agree that a balanced youth program needs the three elements: (1) Content--learning what the Christian faith is all about; (2) Group Building—becoming a caring, Christian community; and (3) Service—reaching out to others.

The trick is in knowing *how* to plan a full year's program to accomplish these three needs. Some youth groups have built their program around the premise that great content will create a caring group of kids, but this does not always happen. Other youth groups are built around mission projects, assuming that kids who are involved in helping others will experience community in the process, but this does not necessarily follow.

So what do you do to bring these three

elements together? We like to describe our yearly model for a youth program as a ribbon cake, where you get more of GROUP BUILDING in the fall . . . and slowly increase the CONTENT and OUTREACH after the group has started to experience the closeness of a caring community. (See the diagram.)

We talk a lot about the principles behind group building on the next few pages, and most of this Encyclopedia is designed for creating small group sessions where the emphasis is on becoming a caring community by getting to know one another.

The 6 Training Sessions for Building a Youth Ministry Team on pages 207-235 goes into greater detail on the philosophy of this model of youth ministry.

The important thing to understand here is the fact that GROUP BUILDING in a youth program is not supposed to take the place of CONTENT or SERVICE. Rather, it is to enable the youth to integrate CONTENT into their lives and want to REACH OUT to others *because* of the closeness they have felt as a group.

	SEPT	OCT	NOV	DEC	JAN	FEB	MAR	APR	MAY	JUN
1. CONTENT/SPIRITUAL UNDERSTANDING										
2. GROUP BUILDING/BECOMING A CHRISTIAN COMMUNITY										
3. SERVICE/OUTREACH/EVANGELISM										

WINTER AND SPRING

As the youth group moves into the winter and spring quarters, you would want to increase the amount of time spent in the youth meetings on discussions of faith and outreach. And by the end of the school year, you would have spent just as much time on CONTENT and OUTREACH as you would have spent on GROUP BUILDING. BUT YOU WOULD BRING IN THESE ELEMENTS WHEN THE GROUP IS READY, NOT BEFORE.

This Encyclopedia is basically a recipe book for cooking up your own Group Building menus—putting together a delectable mix of Games to start off the youth meetings, Communication Exercises to get the youth into small groups for sharing, and Bible Studies that let the kids talk about their own life stories through the stories in Scripture.

This Encyclopedia does not provide help on catechesis or religious instruction which we assume your church is already doing well for your youth. Neither does this Encyclopedia offer anything in the way of outreach options, assuming that your church is already moving in this direction. (Although we have found that a youth group where there is a lot of caring and loving is one of the best ways to attract kids.)

If you are going to take seriously our model for youth ministry, you may want to plan a training event for the youth staff and counselors—described on pages 191-195. And if you are planning a Weekend Retreat or Weeklong Camp where Group Building is major, you will find further suggestions on pages 197-205.

This Encyclopedia is designed for youth workers who understand our basic philosophy and are willing to take the time to build their own program with these simple tools. If you understand the basic philosophy, this Encyclopedia will give you a lot to work with.

1. CONTENT/SPIRITUAL UNDERSTANDING

2. GROUP BUILDING/COMMUNITY

3. SERVICE/OUTREACH/EVANGELISM

C-Groups--where relationships come together

Specifically, what does Group Building mean and how do you go about this in a youth group? If you can understand this, you can use this Encyclopedia like a cookbook . . . and cook up your own group-building designs.

Group Building means the process of becoming a caring, Christian community, where kids can *feel* a sense of belonging, love, acceptance and forgiveness—a spiritual community of strugglers on their way to becoming the people of God. We call this "place of belonging" a C-Group.

We recommend that the entire youth group be divided into smaller clusters of 4 to 7 kids, plus a counselor who is three or four years older. Part of every youth meeting would be given over to C-Groups—the same group for a 7-week period. Then, divide the groups for another 7-week period. This way the entire group will get to know each other over the year.

The best way to explain what happens in a 7-week sharing period is to think of a baseball diamond—with the goal of the small group to reach Home Plate together. But to get to Home Plate, the group must go through three levels of sharing, like the three bases of a ball diamond.

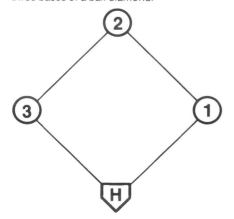

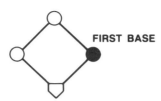

FIRST BASE

HISTORY GIVING

In the first three or four times together, the C-Groups concentrate on sharing their "story" with one another: who they are, where they have come from, their likes and dislikes, values and what they want to do with their lives.

The Communication Exercises on pages 52-68 (with the First Base Ball Diamond in the top margin) are designed for this kind of "get acquainted" period for C-Groups. Also, the first six Questionnaires in the Yellow, Red, Blue, and Green Bible studies (with the First Base Ball Diamond in the top margin) are designed for this group time.

Look for the First Base Ball Diamond. This monogram will tell you if we feel this exercise or Bible Study is suitable for getting acquainted in C-Groups. Do *not* use a Second or Third Base exercise in the first few times that the group gets together.

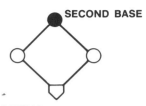

SECOND BASE

AFFIRMATION

After a group has gotten to know one another, the C-Group should spend a session or two in feedback—but keep the feedback on the positive side. Give the group members a chance to share what they like about each other, where they identified with each other's "story," the beautiful things they see in one another, and how they have contributed to each other's lives.

The Communication Exercises on pages 69-76 (with the Second Base Ball Diamond in the top margin) are designed for this kind of affirmation sharing. Also, the Bible Study Questionnaires in the Yellow, Red, Blue, and Green sections (with the Second Base Ball Diamond in the top margin) are designed for this sharing.

Remember to check the Baseball Diamond. Do *not* use one of these exercises until the group members have had a chance to get to know one another and hear each other's "stories."

THIRD BASE

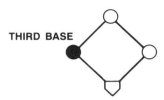

GOAL SETTING

Goal Setting is another way of saying "need sharing"—where I *need* to change some things in my life; where I *need* the help, strength, forgiveness, and support of God and his community.

The Communication Exercises on pages 77-79 (clearly marked with a Third Base Ball Diamond) are designed to get into this kind of sharing in C-Groups that have gotten to know each other over several weeks. Also, the Bible Study Questionnaires in the Yellow, Red, Blue, and Green sections (with the Third Base Ball Diamond) are designed for these purposes.

Need-sharing in a C-Group that has taken the time to get to know one another is very natural and safe—where a level of trust and confidence has been built up over the weeks. Need-sharing where the kids do *not* know each other, or where there is *not* a level of trust and confidence can be quite dangerous. Again, look for the Baseball Diamond markings.

KOINONIA
HOME PLATE

The word "koinonia" is a Greek word in the New Testament that means a depth spiritual community, centered around Jesus Christ and the "body ministry" of the Holy Spirit. It is the thing that happened to the disciples of Jesus when they gathered in the Upper Room after the ascension of Christ to care for each other, to share their stories, pain, struggles, doubts, fears and failures. They were probably the most battered, broken, and bruised people that the church has ever known.

But something happened to them as they told their "stories" to one another. They found out that they were not alone. They started to reach out, care, touch, pray and celebrate with one another.

This is what Home Plate is all about. It happens when a small group of kids agrees to stick together for 7 weeks, walk through each others' "stories," affirm each other's strengths, and minister to one another as they share their needs. It is the miracle of Pentecost that can happen when people commit themselves to one another and to God.

QUESTIONS AND ANSWERS

1. *What is a C-Group?* A small caring unit with 4 to 7 kids plus a counselor inside of the larger youth group.
2. *What do they do?* The C-Group meets together for 30 to 45 minutes at the close of every youth meeting to share and pray for one another.
3. *How do they get into sharing?* Two pass-outs from this Encyclopedia are given out for discussion: (a) a get acquainted exercise (pages 51-83) and (b) a Bible Study (pages 85-187).
4. *Who is the leader of a C-Group?* A person from the Youth Ministry Team who has been through 6 sessions of training (pages 207-235).
5. *What else does a C-Group do besides share and pray?* The C-Groups are put together in teams for all of the games and relays at the beginning of the youth meeting.
6. *How long does a C-Group last?* The group stays together from 7 to 13 weeks in order to get to know one another in depth. (See the Baseball Diamond illustration.)
7. *What happens if a new person comes into the youth group?* The C-Groups are urged to bring their friends to the group to fill the "empty chair"—the symbol that there is always room for one more.
8. *What happens if a C-Group gets over 8?* The C-Group is split into two groups of 4 each and a new leader from the Youth Ministry Team is given one of the groups.
9. *Why do you split up C-Groups after 7 to 13 weeks?* In order for the kids in the bigger youth group to get to know each other.
10. *Where do you get your leaders?* They are recruited from the age group above—college age to help with the High Schoolers, and Senior Highs to help with the Junior Highs.

Youth Meetings that do it all!

**5:00
MEAL**

**5:30
FUN GAMES—ALL TOGETHER**

Ask one or two parents to bring enough food for a hearty but inexpensive meal, such as spaghetti and a tossed salad, or sloppy joes. Ask the kids to bring $1.50 to cover the cost and give the money to the parents.

The meal not only brings the kids together, but also serves as a buffer for anyone who is a little late. And it gets the parents involved.

Use paper plates and cups that can be quickly discarded and serve in the parking lot or a fellowship hall where it will not matter if you spill something.

Choose three or four games each night to start off the youth meeting with some energy-releasing, side-splitting, relationship-building fun.

Start with a large crowd game from the Crowd Breakers, Elimination Games or Outdoor or Indoor Sporting Events on pages 18-29. Then, break into the C-Groups that will be sharing together later on and run one or two Team Relays, Scavenger Hunts, Quizzes or Concentration Games (pages 30-45).

Then, slow down the hyperactivity with the kids sitting down for a skit or stunt . . . or something to turn down the throttle (pages 40-47).

Remember, the game time is part of the "group building" process. Choose games

that help the kids to get to know each other, to laugh with each other and laugh at the counselors in a healthy sort of way.

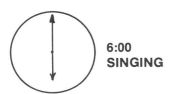

6:00 SINGING

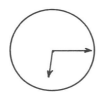

6:15 C-GROUPS

6:45 WRAP UP/TALK

Settle down a little more with a few songs from a songbook that includes choruses. Ask the kids that can play the guitar, drums, or something crazy to bring their instruments.

Start off with a rowdy chorus and end up with something mellow. Remember, the songs set the stage for the sharing time.

Divide into the small groups that will be sticking together for seven weeks. Each group should be about 4 to 7 kids, plus a counselor that is 3 or 4 years older than the kids. That means that the seniors in high school could be counselors for the junior high kids, and college-age young adults could be counselors for senior high kids.

Ask all counselors to go through the training program (on pages 207-235) and attend a planning breakfast with the youth leader every week—to discuss the Communication Exercise (page 51-83) and the Bible study (pages 85-187) you will be using for the C-Group sharing.

Close the sharing in the C-Groups with prayer.

Don't laugh—but the new thing the counseling profession is telling us that kids are looking for is a strong, spiritual faith! Not a bunch of pious talk—or a lecture about how bad they are.

Kids are searching for the kind of LIFE that Jesus offers. Give it to them straight. Short. In their own words.

Stick to the Bible passage that they have already discussed. Maybe share some of your own responses to the questionnaire.

And somewhere along the line, give the kids a chance to turn over the ownership of their lives to Jesus Christ—the only person who can make sense out of the world we are in.

Kids will respect this kind of 5-minute presentation . . . and thank you for it.

13

Putting a meeting together

Now that you have our model for a youth meeting, it is a simple matter of sitting down with your Youth Ministry Team (if you don't have one, see pages 207-235) and putting the program together. You ought to meet with your Youth Ministry Team once a week anyway for prayer and support. It doesn't have to be long—30 minutes for breakfast is enough—but it should be every week.

Check out the sample of a youth meeting agenda on the next page. You need to fill in this kind of agenda including: (a) Meal, (b) Games, (c) Songs, (d) C-Groups, and (d) Talk.

MEAL

Who are you going to ask to fix the meal? One parent for the meat and another for the salad. Make the menu simple, but ample. (Kids are hungry.) Spaghetti. Sloppy joes. Hot dogs. Punch or some "mystery" drink . . . like "bug juice."

Ask the kids to bring $1.50 to cover the cost and give this money to the parents.

Invest in some paper plates and cups that can be thrown away.

GAMES

Start off with some large crowd breakers that involve the entire group, like dodge ball, Hungarian baseball, etc. Try to work off about 50% of the group's energy with these games.

Then break into the C-Groups that you will be using for sharing the Bible study and do some relays, team competitions, etc., that make the C-Groups work together— with the counselors of the C-Groups as the team captains.

Finally, pick a game that lets the kids sit down and slow down with an up-front skit, stunt, contest, competition, etc., by the counselors or the captains of each C-Group or one kid from each C-Group as the

"contestant." You will find all of these games in the section on pages 17-49.

SINGING

While the kids are still laughing about the skit or stunt, pass out song sheets and start with a rousing chorus or two. Then slow down the pace with something more mellow.

If one or two of the kids are learning guitar, ask them to help out with the music . . . with one of the counselors doing the leading. Or get four or five kids (like the typical football jock) who knows nothing about music to "lead" the songs. Sometimes kids will sing for one of their "own" better than some professional that nobody knows.

On the mellow song, if it is appropriate, you might ask the kids to reach out and touch or put their arms around each other in a big "football huddle."

And close with a simple prayer . . . "for the time to follow."

C-GROUPS

Divide the entire youth group into small groups and keep the same groups together

for 7 to 13 weeks so that they can "go around the bases of the Ball Diamond" together.

Put a trained leader from the Youth Ministry Team in charge of each C-Group. (See the training program on pages 207-235.) The C-Group leaders should be at least three or four years older than the kids and committed to the youth program and to Christ. (You should be recruiting and training people for your Youth Ministry Team all of the time . . . and using those who are just starting out for the games, music, meals, etc., until they are ready to be given a group to lead.)

The sharing in the C-Groups should be based on *two* pass-outs from this manual— which you are free to photocopy for this occasion. The first pass-out should be picked from the Communication Games on pages 51-83. And the second pass-out should be picked from the Yellow, Red, Blue, or Green questionnaires.

In the first few sessions, make sure that you pick exercises with a FIRST BASE indication on the Baseball Diamond in the top margin. In the next two or three sessions, choose exercises with a SECOND BASE indication in the Baseball Diamond, and in the later sessions of the C-Group, use the THIRD BASE Baseball Diamond markings. (Read and re-read the philosophy of the Baseball Diamond on pages 10-11).

Keep the C-Groups small—4 to 7 kids per group. BUT ASK EACH C-GROUP TO KEEP AN "EMPTY CHAIR" FOR NEWCOMERS THROUGHOUT THE TIME. When the C-Group reaches 8 kids, divide the C-Group into 2 groups of 4 each . . . and bring in another counselor from the Youth Ministry Team for the extra C-Group. This way you can keep multiplying with the "empty chair" but not make the C-Groups so large that some of the kids don't have a chance to participate . . . AND THE NAME OF THE GAME IN A C-GROUP IS PARTICIPATION!!!

YOUTH MEETING AGENDA SAMPLE

Time	Event	Person(s) in Charge	Equipment	Area
5:00	Meal	Mrs. Brown Mrs. McGilichutty	Spaghetti Tossed salad	Outside patio
5:30	Games (10 min.) Tetherball	Bill Smith	Newspaper on rope	Ball field
	(15 min.) Hungarian Baseball	2 team capt.s	Soccer ball	Ball field
	(15 min.) Little Nemo-skit	4 kids 2 counselors	Sheet Shaving cream 2 pr. shoes Lipstick 2 shirts Powder 2 pr. shorts Shaving razor	Inside
6:15	Singing	Bob - guitar Mary - guitar	Mike Songbooks	Inside
6:30	C - Groups	Counselors	20 copies. Values Auction Strengths Bible Study	Groups
6:45	Talk (5 min.)	Pastor Bob	"God don't Make no Junk"	Inside - all together

TALK

The last few minutes of the session should be with all of the C-Groups back together for a Wrap Up or Talk.

The best talks are often from the Youth Ministry Team who have never shared their "faith" before . . . and simply tell the kids "how they came to know God through Jesus Christ in a personal way." No sermons! No guilt trips. Just a simple "witness" from someone that the kids know and respect . . . about his or her own personal faith. (If you have trouble getting volunteers for the talk, ask the counselor on the Youth Ministry Team who is most afraid to "go first." The talk should be about 5 minutes—*never* more than 10 minutes.

EQUIPMENT AND ASSIGNMENTS

When you have finished with the agenda go back over the schedule with the Team and divide up the chores.

☐ Who is going to get the meal set up?
☐ Who is going to get all of the athletic equipment?
☐ Who is going to get the songbooks or song sheets?
☐ Who is going to photocopy the pass-outs for the C-Groups?
☐ Who is going to get the pencils, paper plates, balloons, and all of the other "little" things that ruin youth meetings if you forget them?

Group Games

FOR STARTING OFF YOUTH MEETINGS

Crowd Breakers

PASS THE BALLOON

Give each C-Group a large balloon. When the whistle blows, start passing the balloon around the group. When the whistle blows again, whoever is holding the balloon gets a penalty:

☐ First penalty: you must stand up and sit down before you can pass the balloon.

☐ Second penalty: you must stand up and turn around before you can pass the balloon.

☐ Third penalty: you must stand up, turn around, laugh like a hyena, flap your arms like a bird, and sit down before you can pass the balloon.

Pass out a balloon to each group. When the whistle blows, start passing the balloon. When the whistle blows again, the person holding the balloon is penalized. Keep track of your penalties.

(Leader: vary the time between whistles to add tension and excitement).

CLUMPS

This game may be used for as many as 1000. Everyone crowds to the center with arms at sides. They are instructed to keep moving, but crowd toward the center. They must keep their arms at their sides. The leader blows a whistle or foghorn to stop all movement, and immediately yells out a number. If the number is 4, for instance, everyone must get into groups of 4, lock arms, and sit down. Leaders then eliminate all those not in groups of 4. This process is repeated, with different numbers each time, until all have been eliminated.

AUTOGRAPH PARTY

This is a great crowd breaker for parties or socials. Type up a copy of the list below for everyone in the group; however, no two lists should be in the same order unless the group is very large. The idea is to have everyone doing something different at the same time. Also, you are not able to tell who is winning until the game is over. The winner is the first one to complete all ten things on his list *in order*. Anyone who will not do what someone asks him to do is automatically disqualified.

1. Get ten different autographs. First, middle, and last names. (On the back of this sheet.)
2. Unlace someone's shoe, lace it, and tie it again. (Not your own.)
3. Get a hair over six inches long from someone's head. (Let them remove it.)
4. Get a girl to do a somersault and sign her name here. _____
5. Have a boy do five pushups for you and sign his name here.

   _____
6. Play "Ring Around the Rosy" with someone and sing out loud.
7. Do twenty-five "jumping jacks" and have someone count them off for you. Have that person sign here when you have done the stunt.

   _____
8. Say the "Pledge of Allegiance" to the flag as loudly as you can.
9. Leapfrog over someone five times.

KNOTS

Knots is a game that gets people together by getting them apart. About a dozen players are needed to tie on a good one.

To form the knot, stand in a circle, shoulder-to-shoulder, and place your hands in the center. Now everybody grab a couple of hands. If you want to get out of this, make sure that no one holds both hands with the same person or holds the hand of a person right next to them. It might take a bit of switching around to get the knot tied right. (If you have too much trouble getting this part together, you might want to quit before you try getting it apart!) Now untie the knot.

CLOTHESPINS

Give everyone in the group six clothespins. On GO each player tries to pin his clothespins on the other players' clothing. When you have put your six clothespins on other people, try to place any clothespins anyone has placed on you on someone else. At the end of the time limit (3 minutes), the person with the fewest clothespins is the winner.

BEAN BLITZ

Equipment: An envelope with twenty beans for each person.

Give an envelope with 20 beans in it to each person. Ask people to circulate around the room offering to someone else (one at a time) the chance to guess the number of beans in your closed hand. You can put as many or as few beans in your hand as you wish. You say to the person you approach "Odd or Even." If the person guesses correctly, this person gets the beans. If this person guesses incorrectly, this person must give you the same number of beans in your hand. A time limit is set—5 minutes—and the person with the most beans at the end wins. When your beans are all gone, you are out.

BALLOON STOMP

Everyone receives a balloon and a piece of string. Each person blows up the balloon *completely* and ties it to his ankle with the string. (If the balloon is not full of air it won't pop.) Working individually or as a C-Group team, try to stomp on the other balloons without getting your balloon stomped on.

AMOS MOSES SHUFFLE

If you can get your hands on the "Amos Moses" record by Jerry Reed, here is a series of motions that fit the music:
- ☐ Right foot forward and back
- ☐ Left foot forward and back
- ☐ Right foot to side and back
- ☐ Left foot to side and back
- ☐ Right foot behind and back
- ☐ Left foot behind and back
- ☐ Turn right (to side) and repeat

COORDINATION CLAP

This is a crowd breaker that you can use anytime, as many times as you want. It is always fun, gets good laughs, and involves everyone. The procedure is very simple. You cross your hands in an up-and-down manner (vertical), and the group must clap every time your hands cross in the middle. If your hands stop and do not cross, then the audience must not clap. That is basically it. The fun is when you fake the group out by almost crossing your hands but stopping just before they do. Go fast, slow, and point out people who goof it up by giving them a penalty of some kind, such as a "hot seat." You may also keep it up and when anyone goofs, they are out of the game. Keep going until there is only one person left, and give him a prize.

LINE UP

Equipment: A room that can be darkened.

The object of this exercise is to line up according to shoe size without talking — *in the dark*. Turn out the lights and quickly form a single line, moving people around until you think you have everyone lined up according to shoe size. Then, turn on the lights and see how you did.

Another way to line up is according to height.

KIDS' CHARACTER NAME GUESS

Equipment: Individual stick-on name tags with the names of Disney characters or other characters out of children's literature, such as those given below.

To begin, stick on the back of everyone a different Disney character. The object of the game is to try to guess what Disney character you have on your back. You do this by asking questions from others in the room that can be answered "yes" or "no." For instance, "Is my character an animal?"

On the word GO, everyone mills around, asking questions of others in the room. You can ask only ONE question of a person before going to another person. (The person you ask should also have the chance to ask you one question about their character.) After the exchange, each person moves on to ask a question of another person.

Here are some possible names: □ Dumbo □ Tigger □ Bambi □ Peter Pan □ Pluto □ Jiminy Cricket □ Anastasia □ Goofy □ Captain Hook □ Love Bug □ Sleeping Beauty □ Piglet □ Christopher Robin □ Prince Charming □ Winnie the Pooh □ Pinocchio □ Thumper □ Eyore □ Fairy Godmother □ Cinderella □ Snow White □ Dr. Doolittle □ Kermit the Frog □ Miss Piggy □ Paddington □ Garfield, □ Mickey Mouse □ Snoopy □ Bashful □ The Cat In the Hat □ Pink Panther □ Oscar □ Captain Kangeroo □ Mister Rogers □ Mister Greenjeans □ Darth Vader □ E.T. □ Superman □ Tarzan □ Dorothy/Wizard of Oz □ The Cowardly Lion □ Bigfoot □ Little Red Riding Hood □ The Cat in the Hat/Dr. Seuss □ Smurfette □ Charlie Brown □ Woodstock □ Beetle Bailey □ Peppermint Patty □ Linus □ Big Bird

NOSE TO NOSE/BACK TO BACK

Have everyone stand in the center of the room. Blow a whistle and call out either: *Nose to nose* . . . or *Back to back.* Everyone quickly finds a partner and stands with their partner accordingly.

Blow the whistle again and call out the instructions. Everyone must find a new partner and assume the position you called out. For greater excitement, speed up or slow down the cadence . . . and repeat the same instructions two or three times in a row.

LET'S GET ACQUAINTED

The following list should be printed up and given to each person in the group. The idea is to fill in each blank on your sheet with someone who fits the description. The first person to get all his blanks filled, or the one who has the most at the end of the time limit is the winner. The sample list below is only a suggested list. Be creative and come up with some of your own. This is a good way for people to get to know each other a little better.

Find someone who uses Listerine

Find someone who has three bathrooms in his house

Find someone who has red hair

Find someone who gets hollered at for spending too much time in the bathroom

Find someone who has been inside the cockpit of an airplane

Find someone who plays a guitar

Find someone who likes "frog legs"

Find someone who has been to Hawaii

Find someone who uses your brand of toothpaste

Find a girl with false eyelashes on

Find a guy who has gone water skiing and got up the first time

Find someone who knows what "charisma" means

Find someone who is on a diet

Find a girl who uses a Lady Remington Shaver

Find a guy who has a match with him

Find someone who has his own private bath at home

Find someone who didn't know your last name

Find someone who has a funny-sounding last name

Elimination Games

TETHERBALL CONTACT DROPOUT

Leader sits on ground or floor and swings a tetherball violently overhead like a lariat as close to ground as possible. Players join around in a circle within range of circling tetherball. When leader says "go," all players must move within radius of tetherball circle and jump the ball and rope as it circles under them. If player is touched or knocked down that player must drop out of competition until a single winner is declared. If player jumps back out of range of the tetherball once leader says "go," that player has committed a foul and must drop out until a new game is started. This is an excellent coed game with lots of physical activity. Start a new game as soon as a winner is declared.

SPUD

All players are numbered consecutively. One player throws ball high in the air and calls a number. Person with that number catches the ball and cries, "Spud." Other players have been running away, but must stop and stand still when catcher cries out. If person with number called catches the ball before it hits the ground, he may take three steps toward any other player. He then tries to hit the player with the ball. If he does, player receives an "S." If he misses, the thrower gets an "S." When a player receives S, P, U, D, he is out.

DODGE BALL

Ten to 15 players on a side, volleyball.

One team forms a circle while the opposing players scatter inside. Players forming the circle throw the ball and attempt to hit the players inside the circle. Players inside the circle may dodge any way they choose, but they cannot leave the circle. A player who is hit by the ball is eliminated from the game. Scoring: The time required to eliminate all the players of each team is determined. The winning team is the one for which the greater time was required to eliminate.

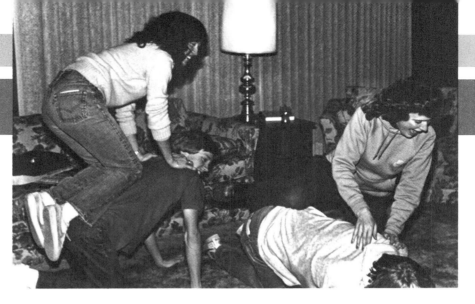

MUSICAL HATS

Give a hat to everyone in the room. Ask them to put it on and stand in a circle. This game is played like "musical chairs," but instead of a missing chair, there is a missing hat.

When the whistle blows, everyone starts walking in a circle. With their right hand ONLY, they grab the hat on the head of the person in front of them and place the hat on their head. When the whistle blows again, the person without a hat on their head is OUT.

The object of the game is to keep a hat on your head by grabbing the hat on the head of the person in front of you and putting it on your head.

You cannot use your left hand. You cannot hold your hat on your head. All you can do is take the hat off of the head of the person in front of you and put their hat on your head.

Now, to start, get into a circle. Turn right . . . and start walking. (Leader: Remove one hat from the group after each round so that there is always one hat less than people. After each round, ask the person without a hat to step out).

SHUFFLE YOUR BUNS

Arrange chairs in a circle so each person has a chair. There should be two extra chairs in the circle. Each person sits in a chair except for two people in the middle who try to sit in the two vacant chairs. The persons sitting on the chairs keep moving around from chair to chair to prevent the two in the middle from sitting down. If one or both of the two in the middle manage to sit in a chair, the person on their right replaces them in the middle of the circle and then tries to sit in an empty chair.

BIRDIE ON THE PERCH

Split into 2 groups. One group forms a circle facing out. The other group forms a circle around the first circle. Pair off—one person from the INNER circle with one person from the OUTER circle—making partners. At the whistle, the INNER and OUTER circles move in opposite directions.

When the whistle blows a second time, the people in the OUTER circle kneel *where they are* on one knee . . . and their partner from the INNER circle runs from wherever they are and "perch" on their partner's knee. THE LAST "couple" to perch is OUT.

The second round begins with the whistle. Circles move in opposite directions. When the whistle blows, the OUTER circle kneels *where they are* and their partners in the INNER circle run and perch on their knees. The last couple to perch is OUT. Repeat this procedure until a winning couple is determined.

ANATOMY SHUFFLE

This game is similar to "Birdie on the Perch." The group pairs off and forms two circles, one inside the other. One member of each couple is on the inside circle, the other is in the outside circle.

The outer circle begins traveling in one direction (clockwise), and the inner circle goes in the opposite direction (counter-clockwise). The leader blows a whistle and

yells out something like "Hand, ear!" On this signal, the inner circle group must find their partners and place their hand on their partner's ear. Last couple to do so is out of the game. The leader calls out all sorts of combinations as the game progresses, such as:

> "Finger, foot"
> "Thigh, thigh"
> "Elbow, nose"
> "Nose, shoulder"
> "Head, stomach"
> "Nose, armpit"

The first thing called is always the inner group's part of the body, and they must find their partners, who stand in one position (they cannot move after the whistle blows) and touch their part of the body to the second item called on the partner. The last couple to remain in the game wins.

TOUCH

The leader yells out the name of an object and all the participants run to that object, touch it, and then return to their original place (in line). Objects such as wood, paint, glass, door, grass, tree, me, book, etc., can be called. Participants are not permitted to use any objects they are wearing, but they can use what others in the group have on them. After the group has warmed up you can eliminate the last one to return to their spot till you have only one remaining.

WATER BALLOON RUGBY

Equipment: 20 large rubber balloons filled with water.

This is the English equivalent of our football, with a new twist. Instead of using a rugby ball, you will have balloons filled with water.

Make two teams. Use football ground rules. Four downs to make a touchdown or "lose the ball" to the other side. First team starts on their own 20 yard line. Offense can lateral the ball as many times as they wish. Play is stopped when a runner with the ball is tagged by an opposing player . . . OR if the balloon pops.

Have plenty of balloons filled with water ready to put a new "ball" in play when one pops.

Keep the sidelines tight to force the offense to go up the middle with lots of laterals.

COUPLES' SOFTBALL

This is an excellent game for teenage, coed camp or retreat recreation fun. The girl must hold onto a boy at all times (hands, shirttail, belt, etc.). If she loses contact during a play (pitching, running, catching, sliding, etc.), the play is no good. The boy and girl alternate on times at bat. This is on the honor system. Every other inning the girl does the fielding, pitching, and catching while the boy hangs onto her. The only time it is legal not to be holding onto one's partner is when he (or she) is at bat. At this time, the partner must stand halfway between home plate and first base ready to grab hold as partner runs by provided he (or she) hits the ball fairly. Except for these rules, the game is played according to regular softball rules.

MOON BALL

Divide the group into two teams. Establish two goals and start in the middle. The first team to get the ball across the opposite goal line wins.

HUNGARIAN BASEBALL

Equipment: One soft soccer ball or volley ball.

This game is played like "kick baseball" except with these two changes. (1) When the ball is kicked by the first "batter," the entire team that is "up to bat" forms a conga line (with hands on the waist) and runs around the pitcher and back to home plate, and (2) the team that is "in the field" must retrieve the ball and line up behind the pitcher and pass the ball back to the pitcher *under their legs.* The team that completes the process first either scores or makes an "out."

Three "outs" retires the side. Foul balls don't count.

STOP BALL

Organize two teams with not over ten players on each. The fielding side scatters over the playing area, while the side at bat lines up single file. One player of the fielding side lobs the ball to the head man in the single file line. This player hits the ball with his fist, then runs around his teammates, who remain in single file. The fielding team side scurries to line up in single file behind whichever player succeeds in fielding the ball. When the line is completely formed, the ball is passed overhead, from the first player to the last, each player handling the ball in turn. As it reaches the last person in line, all yell "STOP." The batter halts immediately—his side scores one point for each time he completely circled his line. The fielding side now becomes the batting side, and the game continues. Several games may go on simultaneously in the same playing area. Variations of the game can be played—like kicking the ball for younger children; like not passing the ball overhead and when fielding team lines up, all shout, "Stop."

WATER BALLOON TOSS

Group is divided into pairs. Each pair is four or five yards from the next. (For explanation, think of players in pair numbered "one" and "two.") All ones face the same direction. Twos face ones starting toe to toe. All ones are given a balloon filled with water. On "Go," ones hand balloon to twos who take one step backward. They hand balloon back to ones who take one step backward. Now balloon must be tossed. When a player catches the balloon, he takes one step backward. Winning team is team farthest apart when all balloons have burst, or the last person to toss the balloon wins for his team.

COCK FIGHT

Designate a circle within which the group has to stay. All participants stand on one leg, holding the other foot with one of their hands. At a signal, participants try to push everyone else out of the circle with their body (not their free hand). Winner is the last one inside the circle.

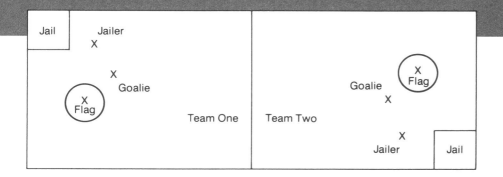

Jail · Jailer X

X
Goalie

X
Flag

Team One

Goalie
X

X
Flag

Team Two

X
Jailer · Jail

CAPTURE THE FLAG

Team 1 is on one side of the field, and Team 2 is on the other side. The idea of the game is somehow to capture the flag, located in the other team's territory, without getting tagged (or tackled, clobbered, etc.). Once you cross over the line in the middle of the field, you can be tagged, and sent to "jail," which is set up behind each team back by the flag. However, if you are in jail, one of your teammates can free you by getting to the jail without getting tagged, and then he can tag you, which frees you. You both get a free walk back to safety. Each team gets one "goalie" who watches the flag from a distance of about ten feet away, and also a "jailer," who guards the jail. The idea is to work out some strategy with your teammates to rush the flag, or in some other way, "capture the flag."

FLAMINGO FOOTBALL

Equipment: Soft rubber football and big yard.

Announce that you are going to play "tackle football." The rules are the same except for this one exception. The guys over age 12 must hold their left foot with their right hand at all times, like a "chicken fight." They must run, pass, hike, catch, and even kick on one foot. There will be 5 minute quarters and a 2 minute half.

FRISBEE FOOTBALL

This game is a mixture of Frisbee and lacrosse. All that is needed is a playing field, a Frisbee, and from 10 to 75 players. Goals are set up on opposite ends of the field, two markers about ten feet apart. Divide up into two teams. Each team selects goalies, and perhaps other positions such as defense, offense, forward, middle, back, etc. The two teams then line up on opposite ends of the field and the Frisbee is placed in the middle. On the starting whistle, players run for the Frisbee, and the first to get it may pass it to

any other player on his team. When a player catches it, he may run with it, pass it, or down it, which is a "stop." (To down it, he simply falls on it.) Any player carrying the Frisbee may be "tagged" by a member of the other team and must then surrender the Frisbee to him immediately. (Referees should make judgments on this.) If a player downs the Frisbee before being tagged, he can then stand up and throw it to any other player on his team without interference. However, once the Frisbee is thrown, it may be intercepted. Also, a person downing the Frisbee cannot score after downing it. Goals are scored by throwing the Frisbee between the goal markers.

Note: This can also be played with a balloon filled up with water. If the balloon breaks, the other team gets possession with a new balloon.

WATER BALLOON FOOTBALL

Fill balloons with water and place in a large tub near the playing field. Each team lines up fairly close for the "kickoff." With one balloon, toss it to the opponent. He may run with it until it bursts. Each play, a new, filled balloon is used. The playing area is smaller than a football field. No tackles, but when balloon bursts, the down is over. You may run or pass. If you pass, the receiver must at least touch the balloon for a completion. Use your own ground rules for this hilariously wet activity.

WORM RACE

Four to eight persons per team (girls with skirts not eligible). The team sits in a straight line. Each person wraps their legs around the person in front of them. Only the player in the front of the line may allow his feet to touch the ground. Finish line is only ten feet, but entire worm must cross the line.

AMOEBA

Divide into teams and simply tie a rope around the team at their waists. To do this, have the team bunch up as close together as they can, and hold their hands up in the air while you tie the rope around them. After they are tied, they can race to a goal and back. Unless they work together and cooperate as a team, they will go nowhere. This is a good fun game for camps and outdoor activities.

KICKBALL

Nine to 20 on a side, soccer ball and bases, 45 feet between bases, 30 feet from pitcher's box to home plate.

The pitcher rolls the ball to the batter who kicks it. Put-outs are made by: (a) batter kicking three fouls; (b) fielder catching any fly ball; (c) the ball beating the runner around the bases to home plate. After kicking the ball, the runner circles the bases. The runner must make a home run. On a fair ball not caught on the fly, the fielder throws the ball to the pitcher who then throws to either the first or third baseman. The ball then must reach home via the first, second, and third basemen in that order or via the third, second, and first basemen. Each baseman must be standing on his base before he can relay the ball to the next base. Three outs constitute an inning and nine innings a game. Scoring: If the batter succeeds in beating the ball around the bases, he scores a run for his team. Variations: (1) This game may be played in an identical manner except that the ball is put into play by the pitcher tossing the ball to the batter who hits it with his fist or forearm. The pitcher must deliver the ball with an underhand throw. (2) The ball may be played by placing it on home base and kicking it by the batter from that point. The above rules apply. (3) Do not count fly ball caught as an out but rather play it as any fair hit ball. (4) The game may be played according to softball rules.

Indoor Sports

BLIND VOLLEYBALL

Divide the players into two equal groups. The two teams then get on different sides of a volleyball court and sit down on the floor in a row, as in regular volleyball. The "net" should be a solid divider that obstructs the view of the other team, such as blankets hung over a regular volleyball net or rope. The divider should also be low enough that players cannot see under it. Then play volleyball. Use a big, light plastic ball instead of a volleyball. Regular volleyball rules and boundaries apply. A player may not stand up to hit the ball. The added dimension of the solid net adds a real surprise element to the game when the ball comes flying over the net.

EXPANDABLE HOPSCOTCH

This is a grown-up version of the old child's game of hopscotch. Secure small-size carpet remnants from any carpet store (they usually charge 10 - 25¢ for each one). These are the hopscotch squares. The game is played as usual, except that the squares are spaced further and further apart as the game progresses until the players are jumping several feet between squares. It's good competition and is great for laughs.

PING-PONG FOOTBALL

Decorations are up to you. The ping-pong table is the football field. With string or masking tape, line off the table as you would

a football field. Even decorate the end zone. For goalposts, straws stuck in clay with the crossbar fastened with pins.

Each team sits alternately around the table. The middle man at each end of the table (goal) is on the offensive, while the two on the outside are defensive.

With a ping-pong ball on the 50-yard line, the referee blows the whistle. Everyone, with hands under the table, and chin on the table, blows the ball toward the opponent's goal. If the ball falls off the table, place it where it fell off and continue. Score 6 points for every touchdown. If you want to, extra points can be tried by someone "kicking the ball" through the goalpost with his finger.

Five-minute quarters, substitutions, and cheering sections enhance the enthusiasm.

BROOM HOCKEY

This game may be played with as many as 30 or as few as 5 per team, but only 5 or 6 are actually on the field at one time from each team. Two teams compete by (at a whistle) running out onto the field, grabbing their brooms and swatting a volleyball placed in the center through the opposite goal. Each team has a "goalie," as in ice hockey or soccer, who can grab the ball with his hands and throw it back onto the playing field. If the ball goes out of bounds, the referee throws it back in. The ball may not be touched with hands, or kicked; but only hit with the broom. Score 1 point for each time the ball passes between the goal markers.

For a team with 30 members, for example, have them number off by sixes, which would give you 6 teams of 5 members each. Let all the "ones" play a 3-minute period, then the "twos," etc.

LINE PULL

Divide the group into two equal teams. The teams then face each other, by lining up on two sides of a line drawn on the floor. The object of the game is to pull the other team onto your side of the line. You cannot move behind your side of the line farther than three feet, and you must try to reach out and grab someone on the other side of the line without stepping over the line. Once you are over the line, you are automatically a member of that team and then you must try to help pull your former team over the line. At the end of the time period, the team with the largest number wins.

SNATCH

This is a good game for campus or outdoor events, and is best used with junior highs. The group is divided into two teams each lined up behind its goal line 20-30 feet apart. A towel tied in the middle is placed at a point halfway between goal lines. Each player is given a number. The two teams are numbered from opposite ends of the line.

The leader calls out a number. The player on each team having that number runs to the center and tries to snatch the towel and return to his goal without being tagged by the other person. Each successful return gains one point for the team.

ROUND TABLE PING-PONG

Up to approximately twenty persons may play. One person picks up paddle at each end of the table. Other players line up behind these two facing clockwise around the table. One person serves, drops paddle on table, and moves around the table clockwise as next person picks up paddle and prepares to return ball. Continue rotating until someone misses. Player missing drops out of game.

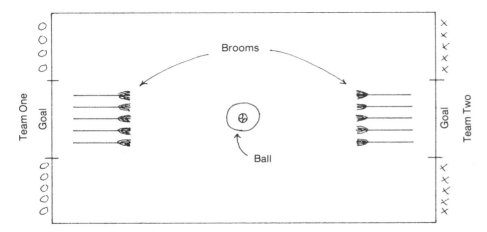

SUITCASE RELAY

Divide the group into equal teams—as many boys as girls. Give each team a suitcase. In each suitcase is a lady's dress and a man's suit—complete with shirt and tie. On the word GO, a *first* couple (boy and girl) from each team must run with their suitcase to the opposite end of the room, open the suitcase, and put on everything in the suitcase—the boy putting on the lady's dress and the girl putting on the man's suit. Then they carry their suitcase back to the starting line. Undress. Put the clothes back into the suitcase and hand the suitcase to the *next* couple. The first team to complete the relay wins.

HAPPY HANDFUL RELAY

This relay may be easily adapted for indoor or outdoor use. Assemble two identical sets of at least 12 miscellaneous items (i.e., 2 brooms, 2 balls, 2 skillets, 2 rolls of bathroom tissue, 2 ladders, etc.) Use your imagination to collect an interesting variety of identical pairs of objects. Place the two sets of objects on two separate tables.

Line up a team for each table. The first player for each team runs to his table, picks up one item of his choice, runs back to his team, and passes the item to the second player. The second player carries the first item back to the table, picks up another item, and carries both items back to the third player. Each succeeding player carries the items collected by his teammates to the table, picks up one new item and carries them all back to the next player. The game will begin rapidly, but the pace will slow as each player decides which item to add to a growing armload of items. It will also take increasingly longer for one player to pass his burden to the next player in line.

Once picked up, an item may not touch the table or floor. Any item which is dropped in transit or transfer must be returned to the table by the leader. No one may assist the giving and receiving players in the exchange of items except through coaching. The first team to empty its table wins.

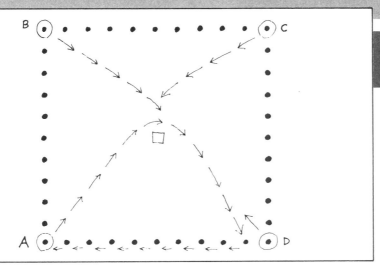

SQUARE RELAY

Eight to twelve people are seated in chairs without arms on each side of a square. There is one chair in the center of the square. (The circled dots in the diagram are the leaders of the sides.)

At a signal each leader hurries to the center chair and goes around it and on to the last chair on his side (follow on the diagram the route of A). The last chair is vacant because as soon as the leader left his place, everybody on his side slid up one chair. Thus number two is now number one. As soon as number one sits down, number two hurries around the middle chair while his side does the sliding act again, leaving the last chair vacant for number two. Now number three is on his way. There is a constant running and sliding. The side that has the original leader back in position and everybody seated in the order in which they began wins.

Now play it again with this variation: Give the leader on each side a ball or some other object. When he sits down in the last chair he passes the ball down the line to the first one waiting to run. This one cannot run until he gets the ball. Each man on the side must handle the ball. The procedure is the same as above. The only difference is that the one occupying chair number one cannot leave until he gets the ball.

BALLOON POP RELAY

Divide your group into teams. The teams line up single file at a starting line. A chair is placed about 30 feet away. Each team member has a deflated balloon. One at a time, kids run to the chair, blow up the balloon, tie it, pop it by sitting on it, and go to the end of the team line. First team to pop all of its balloons wins.

FILL THE MAT RELAY

Each team is given two mattresses on which to perform. A description is called out, then on the starting whistle each team begins to fulfill the description. First team to accurately fulfill this description is the winner. Suggested descriptions:

- ☐ 8 players standing shoulder to shoulder, facing in alternate directions
- ☐ 10 players in one huge pyramid (pyramid must remain standing)
- ☐ 4 people standing on their heads
- ☐ 10 contestants lying in a circle with feet together and holding hands like a huge wheel
- ☐ 8 people lying side by side with heads and feet in alternate directions
- ☐ 2 piles of 4 players each
- ☐ 6 players sitting on each other's laps
- ☐ entire team in a "Rube Goldberg machine" with all parts interconnected and moving

SUPER SACK RELAY

Divide into teams with 10 people on each team. Have a brown paper bag for each team with the following items in each:

- ☐ jar of baby food
- ☐ Green onion
- ☐ Can of cola (warm)
- ☐ Raw carrot
- ☐ Piece of cream cheese (wrapped in waxed paper)
- ☐ Box of Cracker Jacks
- ☐ Peanut-butter sandwich
- ☐ An orange
- ☐ An apple
- ☐ A banana

On signal, the first member of each team runs to his bag and must eat the first item he pulls out. Sponsors should make sure items are satisfactorily finished before the person goes back and tags the next member of the team. First team to finish its sack wins.

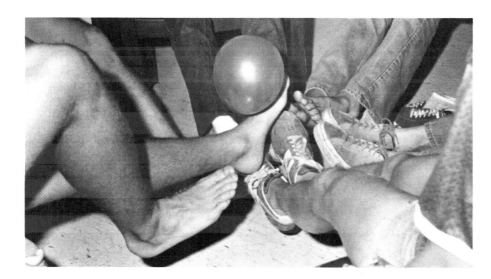

WATER BALLOON OVER AND UNDER

Form two lines. Everyone is one arm's length behind each other. Have several balloons filled with water. Using the old over-under relay, (First person passes balloon over her head, second person passes balloon under his legs, etc.) pass a water-filled balloon over, then under to the back of the line. This person rushes to the front of the line and begins the process again. If the balloon bursts, supply the team with another balloon where it burst. Continue until the first person comes to the front again.

PASS THE FEETBALL

Give each group a large balloon. Blow up the balloon to the size of a watermelon.

By groups, sit in a circle with your feet in the middle. On the word go, pass the balloon around your group, using only your feet. (If it touches your hands, you have to start over.) The first group to pass the balloon *five* times around their group wins.

SCRABBLE

Here is a new way to play this game. Each C-Group is a team and given a portion of the room to spell words by quickly lying on the floor in the correct spelling of a word. BEGIN with a letter of the alphabet, such as "O" or "A." Then, move on to two-letter words, such as "AT" or "AS." Finally, if you have enough people in each C-Group, attempt some three-letter words, such as "SOX" or "ROT." You need a large room for this game and a stepladder so that you can see from overhead. The first team to correctly spell the word—lying on the floor—WINS.

FULL DRESS

Lots of fun! Have a complete change of clothes for each team. At each team member's turn, he runs down to where the clothes are, puts them all on, and then takes them off. The team whose members finish first, wins. When choosing clothing for this relay, be sure it is big enough for everyone.

LEAPFROG RELAY

Equipment: Starting line and finish line made out of a rope.

Choose 4 people from each team. Line up behind starting line. On the word GO, first person leans over. Second person leapfrogs over first person and leans over. Third person leapfrogs over first two people and leans over. Fourth person leapfrogs over first three people and leans over. Then, first person leapfrogs over the other three, etc. . . . until you reach the finish line.

INNER TUBE RELAY

This relay can be run in two ways: (1) with truck-size inner tubes, two people must get inside the inner tube—back to back or (2) with regular car inner tubes, one person must crawl through the tube at the end of the field and return. You need inner tubes for each C-Group.

PAPER CUP—WATER PITCHER RELAY

Form relay lines. Give each participant a clean paper cup. Place two pitchers of water at destination of each relay line. A judge at each station. On word "go" first person runs down, fills paper cup with water, runs back to starting point and drinks it. Next person repeats. Winner is relay line emptying pitcher of water first. Good game as a break in active evening for thirsty players.

ELECTRICITY

Divide the group into two equal groups. Have each group sit in a line, holding hands, with their backs facing the other group. A leader at one end flips a coin. It if is heads, the two students at the end send a signal down the line by squeezing the person's hand next to him. When the person at the other end gets his hand squeezed he grabs the towel that is sitting between him and the end person on the other team. The team that grabs the towel first wins. If the coin comes up tails, then nothing is supposed to happen. Sometimes one of the teams will jump the gun and end up grabbing the towel even though it came up tails.

THREAD THE NEEDLE

For this game you will need two table knives (the old-fashioned kind that had a "neck" between the blade and the handle) and two balls of string (medium weight).

Divide the group into two teams. The teams start at exactly the same time to . . . "thread the needle" (the knife with the end of the string tied tightly to the neck of the knife) down through their shirt and one pants leg (or . . . their blouse and skirt or shorts etc.). This person then passes the "needle" on to the person behind him to do the same and on down to the end of the line. Each team member is constantly busy, for he is continually feeding "thread" (the string) along the way, so that there is enough thread to connect the entire team.

When the last person has "threaded the needle," he then begins the process of "unthreading the needle"! This is done by pulling up on the string and getting the "needle" (knife) up, through, and out of his slacks and shirt (or whatever!). This takes constant teamwork, for when "unthreading the needle," each team member works to pass the slack in the string along so at the end, the first person in line has the string in a neat ball again. And the team has been able to complete the whole procedure without the "thread" becoming detached from the "needle" at any given time!

The fun part of the game is to try in every way to make it a speedy relay. The fun mounts as members help teammates along yet keeping the "thread" from getting knotted, the "needle" from getting stuck, etc.

This game has proven to be an excellent, exciting game for junior-high-age boys and girls through older adults.

Scavenger Hunts

PERSONAL SCAVENGER HUNT

In this scavenger hunt each C-Group is to find the item you call out and bring it to the center. Each C-Group appoints a captain who is responsible for getting the item to the center of the room. Start off by awarding one point for the first round . . . and double the points each round . . . so that the more difficult items get more points: For instance:

☐ For 1 point: A picture of George Washington (a dollar bill)
☐ For 2 points: A 20¢ stamp—used
☐ For 4 points: A sock with a hole in it
☐ For 8 points: 4 different-color hairs—tied end to end
☐ For 16 points: A love letter
☐ For 32 points: One guy dressed with 4 shirts and 8 socks
☐ For 64 points: The entire C-Group enclosed in a rope of socks tied together

For even more points, you may want to add more impossible tasks, such as "your counselor" carried bodily to the center, two people in one shirt, one person with everyone's socks, belts, and watches, etc.

GROUP SCAVENGER HUNT

Equipment: Whatever is in your wallet, purse or pockets.

This game is played like an "old-fashioned" scavenger hunt, except this time the teams have to produce the items from things they have in their possession.

One person acts as the referee in the center of the room. Each team sits in a cluster, equidistant from the referee in the center. The referee calls out an item, such as a shoestring . . . and the first team to bring this item to the referee in the center of

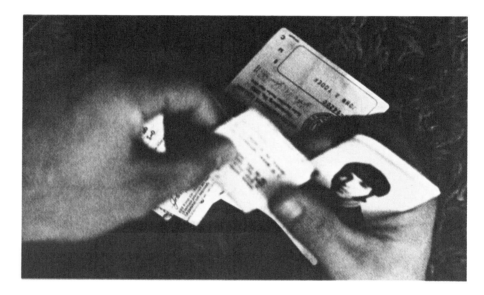

the room is the winner. Points are awarded to the team based on the "difficulty factor" in obtaining the items. The referee keeps score and periodically announces the score. (If one team is ahead, the referee can equalize the score by awarding a few extra points for the next item.)

Here is a list of items and suggested points. Call out one item at a time. For 1000 points, the first team to bring to the referee a:

☐ sock with a hole in it
☐ picture of Thomas Jefferson (on 25¢ piece)
☐ something that smells
☐ guy with lipstick on
☐ baby picture
☐ love letter
☐ dirty comb
☐ seal of the United States (dollar bill)
☐ used ticket
☐ 1982 dime

For 2000 points, the first team to bring to the referee:

☐ eight shoestrings tied end to end
☐ three shirts on one person backwards and buttoned up
☐ 89¢ in change
☐ three different colored hair tied together
☐ four shoes that total 29 in shoe sizes . . . tied together

For 3000 points, the first team to bring to the referee:

☐ two people inside one shirt . . . all buttoned up
☐ one person with 4 belts, 3 shirts, and 8 socks on
☐ first team to line up in a row according to shoe size

For 5000 points, the first team to bring to the referee:

☐ the whole team surrounded by a rope made out of socks

MAGAZINE SCAVENGER HUNT

Divide into C-Groups and give each group several old magazines. Then, give each group a list of various items to be found in their search, such as pictures (airplane, flower, etc.), words (Coke, love, etc.) or names of famous people. When they find an item on their list, tear it out. The object is to find as many items on the list as possible in the time allowed. At the end of 10 minutes, have each group count up the number of items.

Another way to play this game is to call out a word or picture and the first group to bring this item to the center is the winner.

CRAZY SCAVENGER HUNT

Here's a fun variation of the old scavenger hunt. Give each team a list of crazy names (such as the following sample list) and the kids have to go out and collect items that they think best fit the names on the list. For example:

☐ A P B J
☐ Zipper zapping shoestring fuse
☐ Idaho
☐ Tweed
☐ Snail Egg
☐ Chicken Lips
☐ Will be

☐ Pine Needle Bushing Brush
☐ Snipe
☐ Piano Key Mustache Waxer
☐ Yellow Grot Grabber
☐ Portable Electric Door Knob Kneeler
☐ Thumb Twiddly Dummer
☐ Thingamabob
☐ An Inflatable Deflater
☐ Galvanized Ghoul Gooser

A panel of judges can determine the winners based on each team's explanation of how their "items" fit the various descriptions on the list.

COUNSELOR FASHION SHOW

Hold a "far-out" fashion show—with your counselors modeling some "way-out" clothes. Collect some outrageous outfits—underclothes, high fashion, formal wear, bathing suit—maybe some "mock" teenage fashions. The MC should run the fashion show just like a Paris Original Exhibition or Miss/Mr. America Contest. Have the kids vote on various awards.

PAPER AIRPLANE CONTEST

Everyone makes their own paper airplane. While they are doing that, draw in place a large dartboard in the middle of the room. The inside circle is worth 20 points, middle circle 10, and the outside circle is worth 5. Each person gets a chance to throw his/her airplane three times. The one with the most points wins.

COMMUNICATION

Divide into C-Groups. Station one half of each C-Group at opposite ends of the room. On the word GO, one person from each C-Group is given an envelope with a message in it. This person opens the envelope, reads the message, wads it up, and throws it away. This person then *runs* to the next person (opposite end of room) and whispers the message. Then the second person runs back to the next person and whispers the message and so on until the last person runs to the supervisor and whispers it to him. The team closest to the original message wins. Accuracy, not time, is most important, but they must run. Sample message: "Mrs. Sarah Sahara sells extraordinary information to very enterprising executives."

JOKE CONTEST

See who can come up with the "World's Worst Joke." Give the kids a chance to

"enter" a joke . . . and have the "judges" decide. For instance:

1. What do you get when you put soap suds on the stove?
2. Why did the chicken cross the road?
3. A line of rabbits was crossing the field. They all took one hop backward. What is this called?
4. What's black and white and red all over?
5. What did the big balloon say to the little balloon?
6. What was the elephant doing on the highway?
7. Why did the farmer go over his field with a steamroller?
8. What did the goat say as he ate a reel of film?
9. What happens to frogs when they double park?
10. What's worse than a giraffe with a sore throat?

Answers to Jokes

1. Foam on the range.
2. To see a man laying bricks.
3. A receding hare line.
4. A chocolate sundae covered with ketchup.
5. My pop is bigger than your pop.
6. About two miles an hour.
7. He wanted to raise mashed potatoes.
8. "I liked the book better."
9. They get toad away.
10. A hippopotamus with chapped lips.

BODY PAINTING

Ask a guy from each C-Group to volunteer as the models for a body-painting contest. The rest of the C-Group are the designers. They must create a huge hat to fit over the shoulders of their model—covering up the head and arms. Then, on the bare chest of the guy, they have to draw two eyes, a nose, and a mouth—using the natural "features" on his chest for starters. Then, cover the hips with a coat or sheet to appear like shoulders.

Give each C-Group 5 minutes to create their "body painting" before the "judging" by someone for the most creative sculpture.

For paint, you can use liquid shoe polish, wide felt-tip pens, or washable poster paint and brushes.

CONCENTRATION

Gather about twenty objects and put them on a tray. When you are ready to play uncover the tray in front of the group. Give everyone 2 minutes to memorize what is on the tray. Then take it away and pass out paper and pencils. The group will have five minutes to write everything down they remember that was on the tray. After that bring the tray back so they can see how accurate they were. The one who had the most correct answers wins.

SCULPTURING

Get together in C-Groups. Inside C-Groups, pair off in twos. One person is modeling clay and the other person is the artist/sculptor.

Round 1: The leader calls out a word and the artist in the twosome has 10 seconds to mold his/her partner into this word. Then the leader will scream "Freeze," and the person who is the modeling clay must "freeze" in the position they are in. (Leader: start out with some easy feelings such as: fear . . . joy . . . tension . . . rejection.)

Round 2: Get together in fours: Two people are modeling clay and the other two are the artists. The leader now calls out relational words and give the two artists/sculptors 10 seconds to mold their "modeling clay" into these relationships. Then the leader screams "Freeze" and the modeling clay people "freeze" as a statue in this relationship. (Here are some relational words to call out: trust . . . distrust . . . confrontation . . . affirmation.)

Round 3: Get the entire C-Group together. This time, everyone is modeling clay, as well as the artist/sculptor. Somehow, you must quickly decide on the meaning of the word and sculpt yourselves into this word. You will have 30 seconds. Then the leader will scream "Freeze" and you are to freeze in position. (Leader: start off with a word like . . . Rube Goldberg machine. Yell "Freeze" and comment on their sculptures. Then call out . . . "Christian community" and give them 30 seconds to sculpt what this means.)

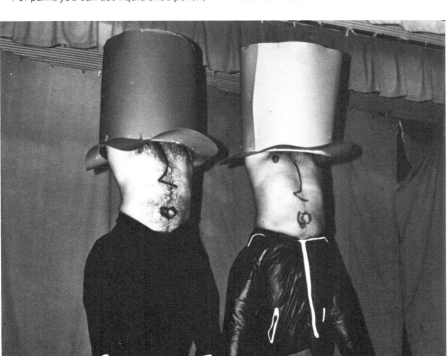

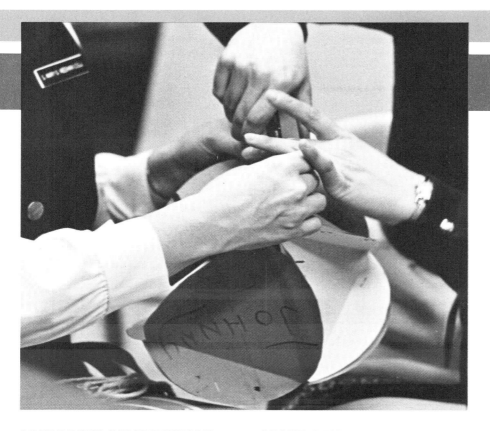

HUMAN MACHINE

The group is to create a human machine in which each person becomes a part and a sound, linking into the total group by way of physical contact.

If there are fewer than 20 in the class, the class should work together to create one machine. If there are more than 20, the class should gather together in groups of eight—by combining two or three groups from the previous exercise.

A person can be a piston that goes up and down (raise and lower hands) or a gear that goes round and round (move arms in circular motion). The challenge is to come up with original and creative motions that utilize more than one arm or leg and to assume a creative position that permits great flexibility.

When everyone has started his own motion, the challenge is to somehow interlink his part of the machine to the other parts to form a unit of gears, pistons, wheels, etc.

All the while, each part of the machine is to create a sound that is consistent with its action and which somehow harmonizes into the total to form a symphony of sound.

The whole experience need not last more than a minute or two. It will have served its purpose by simply loosening up the class.

(Note: If you have two or three persons in the group who are natural "hams" it would be helpful to have them put on a demonstration!)

COMMUNITY CONSTRUCTION

In groups of 4's assume that you can create a new church and community for your area. Consider the master plan for the community as well as the architectural design for the church.

In brainstorming fashion, decide what the community should look like—the roads, the shopping center, schools, neighborhoods—whatever should be in an ideal community. Share resources and come up with ideas to meet your needs and those of the people living around you.

Focus on the kind of church you would want in this community—the building, with the arrangement of the sanctuary, educational rooms, etc. Don't worry about matters of tradition, negative reactions or cost.

Put everything into the model that you feel is important, leave everything out of the building that you feel is unimportant.

GROUP BANNER

Each group of eight makes a banner with materials from a paper sack. In the sack are: one balloon, four different colors of tissue paper, a strip of white wrapping paper six feet long, and some masking tape. Your group decides upon a theme that expresses what you are experiencing together. You work out the design with the materials available and hang the banner on the wall.

CHUBBY BUNNY

This is a marshmallow-eating contest. Ask one person from each C-Group to enter the contest. The object is to see how many marshmallows one can stuff into his or her mouth and still say "chubby bunny." Start by giving each person ONE and asking them to say "chubby bunny." Then, keep adding and asking them to repeat "chubby bunny" until someone is the winner. THE RECORD is 27 marshmallows. See if you can get someone to beat this.

50s DRESS UP CONTEST

Announce a week ahead of time a prize for the best 50s outfit and award something crazy for the best-dressed. Call upon some of the parents who grew up in the 50s to judge the contest. This is a great beginning for a parent-kid night.

To add to the fun, ask two or three "experts" from the 50s era to be judges and give out some prizes for the winners of various divisions: "The Charmin Toilet Paper Award" for the "Most Touching Outfit," etc.

LITTLE NEMO AND LITTLE NEMA

This is the old ventriloquist act in reverse. Instead of one person playing two roles, you have two people playing one role: (1) one person providing the head and legs (with their arms) and (2) the other person (behind the sheet) providing the arms.

For this skit, you need (a) two kids to play the boy and (b) two kids to play the girl. The second person stands behind the first person and reaches his or her arms around (under the sheet) to be the arms of the first person.

In addition, two others stand by as assistants to provide the materials and provide coaching.

AS THE SCENE OPENS: The scene takes place in Little Nemo's bathroom for the guy and Little Nema's bathroom for the girl.

The coach for the guy asks Little Nemo: "You've got this hot date with Nema tonight. Do you think you ought to shave?" (Hand him the shaving cream . . . and then a bladeless razor.)

At the same time, the coach for the girl asks Little Nema: "You've got this date tonight with Nemo. Do you think you ought to fix your face?" (Hand her some rouge, lipstick, and powder, etc.)

The coaches keep asking questions, such as: "What do you think you ought to wear," etc., and giving them stuff to put on. Keep coaching with questions until the couple meet each other—with a big kiss.

For even more fun, have a girl play the second person (behind the sheet) for Little Nemo and a guy play the second person (behind the sheet) for the girl. This will not only look weird, but will also provide a lot of laughs as they start to make up, get dressed, etc.

SONG CHOREOGRAPHY

This activity will help a small group work together on a project that is "group building" for themselves and entertaining for others in the class.

Prepare beforehand slips of paper with song titles. For example: (a) *Old MacDonald Had a Farm,* (b) *I've Been Working on the Railroad,* (c) *My Bonnie Lies over the Ocean,* (d) *Clementine,* (e) *Yankee Doodle,* (f) *O Susanna,* (g) *Dixie,* (h) *Blow the Man Down,* (i) *In the Good Old Summertime,* (k) *Home, Home on the Range* and (l) *When the Saints Go Marching In.*

Gather the following props: broom, mop, bucket, an old sheet or blanket.

Give one slip of paper to each group and show them the props they will be able to use.

All the groups are to quickly create a choreography or musical drama—or comedy—out of their song titles using the four props in any way they like.

After 5 or 10 minutes, call everyone together. Then, one by one, have each group put on its act before the entire class.

The competition will be judged on the basis of originality, the best use of props, and the overall production.

MOVIE SKIT

This skit takes place in a movie theater. One person enters, sits down, and gets absorbed in the movie—totally absorbed. Another person enters and sits beside the first person. The second person tries to get the attention of the person absorbed in the movie. He taps ... whispers ... nudges ... but nothing works. Slowly, he starts to take things out of a paper sack and tries to distract this person by chomping ... squirting shaving cream, powder ... anything!

To add a little "junior high" humor, announce that the two are junior highs. The movie is ..., the first guy is ..., and the second person is ... (some girl in the youth group). The "girl" is really a boy dressed like a girl—trying to "make a pass" at the guy.

Have two C-Group leaders play the part of the two "junior highs." If one is "a girl," dress this person like a typical "junior high"—going to the movies to find "a guy."

41

Quizzes/Guessing Games

WHAT'S THE PRODUCT?

Beforehand think of twenty well-known advertising slogans. When you are ready to play the game, read most of the slogan, leaving off the name of the product it is promoting. The participants have to supply the name. The player with the most right answers wins.

☐ Reach out and touch someone (Bell Telephone)
☐ Things Go better with (Coke)
☐ Gentle but effective (EX-Lax)
☐ Everything you want and a little bit more (Safeway)
☐ Oh what a feeling (Toyota)
☐ When you care enough to send the very best (Hallmark)
☐ You've come a long way, baby (Virginia Slims)
☐ The friendly skies (United Airlines)
☐ Just one look. That's all it took (Mazda)
☐ When _____ talks, people listen (E. F. Hutton)
☐ Don't leave home without it (American Express)
☐ Let the good times roll (Kawasaki)
☐ Takes a lickin' and keeps on tickin' (Timex)
☐ Leave the driving to us (Greyhound)
☐ Has a better idea (Ford)
☐ You've got a lot to live (Pepsi)
☐ Put a tiger in your tank (Exxon)
☐ We try harder (Avis)
☐ I can't believe I ate the whole thing (Alka Seltzer)
☐ You're in good hands (Allstate)
☐ Think small (Volkswagen)
☐ Put the snap, crackle, pop into your life (Kelloggs)
☐ Life is too short not to go first class (Mercedes-Benz)
☐ We do it all for you (McDonalds)
☐ What the big boys eat (Wheaties)
☐ We treat you right (Dairy Queen)
☐ Because time goes by (Kodak)

MURDER

This is a great indoor game. Place a number of slips of paper in a hat. There should be the same number of slips of paper as there are players. One of these slips of paper has the word "detective" written on it, and another has the word "murderer" on it. The rest of them are blank. Everyone draws a slip of paper from the hat. Whoever drew the word "detective" announces himself, and it is his job to try to locate the murderer, who remains silent.

The detective leaves the room, and the room is darkened. All the players mill about the room and the "murderer" silently slips up behind someone and very quietly whispers, "You're dead," in his ear. The victim counts to three, screams, and falls to the floor. The lights are turned on and the detective reenters the room. He then may question the players for one minute or so and tries to guess the identity of the murderer. If he is correct, the murderer becomes the detective, and a new murderer is selected (by passing out the slips again). During the questioning, only the murderer may lie. All others must tell the truth, if they saw anything.

DUCKIE WUCKIE

Everyone sits in a circle on the floor with one person standing in the middle. The person in the middle is blindfolded and given a rolled-up newspaper. Then spin this person around while everyone else changes places. The blindfolded person finds a lap by using the end of the newspaper. This person then sits in the lap and says, "Duckie Wuckie." In a disguised voice the person being sat upon responds with "quack-quack." The blindfolded person tries to guess the identity of the voice (who the person is). If he/she is wrong, this blindfolded person is led to the center of the group and spun around again for another try. If this person is right in their guess, this person gets to exchange places with the person they guessed.

WHAT IS IT?

Select 20 objects from around the house. Wrap them in cloth—any old scrap will do—and attach numbers to each. Players try to figure out what each object is, writing their answers on paper and pencils you provide. The one with the most right answers wins. Objects like candy, bar of soap, nutcracker, etc., work well.

MATCH GAME

This is an indoor game that is quite simple and easy to play. Distribute a list similar of the following to each person:

1. Donut
2. The colonel
3. A famous band
4. Looks like a foot
5. Headquarters
6. A stirring event
7. The end of winter
8. A pair of slippers
9. Pig's retreat
10. An old beau of mine
11. The peacemaker
12. There love is found
13. Cause of the Revolution
14. Glass of water
15. A place for reflection
16. The reigning favorite
17. A morning caller
18. Seen at the ball game
19. Messenger
20. Fire when ready
21. Drive through the wood
22. Bound to shine
23. Life of China
24. Top dog
25. My native land

Next, place various articles on a table or around the room that will match the "clues" given in the first list. For example, the corresponding items for the preceding list would be:

1. The letter "o" on a card
2. Kernel of corn
3. Rubber band
4. Ruler
5. Pillow
6. Spoon
7. Letter "r"
8. Two banana peels
9. Writing pen
10. Old ribbon bow
11. Pair of scissors
12. Dictionary
13. Tacks on tea bags
14. Blotter or sponge
15. Mirror
16. Umbrella
17. Alarm clock
18. Pitcher
19. Penny (one sent)
20. Match
21. Nail
22. Shoe polish
23. Rice
24. Hot dog
25. Dirt

Of course, you may think of many more besides these. The winner is the person who can correctly match up all the items in the shortest time. To make the game harder, place twice as many items on the table than you have clues for.

THIRD DEGREE

The leader divides the group into two teams, one composed of FBI members, the other of spies. Each spy is given a card bearing one of the instructions listed below, each spy receiving a different instruction. The FBI members then take turns asking questions of specific spies, calling out the name of each spy before asking the question. The FBI members may ask as many questions of as many or as few spies as they decide, and may ask any questions they wish (except about the instructions the spies were given). Each spy must answer each question asked him, but always in the manner described on his card. Whenever a spy's instruction is guessed correctly by an FBI member, that spy is eliminated from the game. The questions continue until all the spies' instructions are guessed correctly. If a spy gives an answer without following his instructions, he is eliminated.

Scores are kept on individuals rather than teams. The winning spy is the one who has the most questions asked him before his instructions are guessed correctly. The winning FBI member is the one who guesses correctly the most number of instructions. (An FBI member may make a guess at any time, whether it is his turn to ask a question or not.)

1. Lie during every answer.
2. Answer each question as though you were (name of leader).
3. Try to start an argument with each answer you give.
4. Always state the name of some color in each answer.
5. Always use a number in your answers.
6. Be evasive—never actually answer a question.
7. Always answer a question with a question.
8. Always exaggerate your answers.
9. Always pretend to misunderstand the questions by your answers.
10. Always scratch during your answers.
11. Always insult the questioner.
12. Always begin each answer with a cough.
13. Always mention some kind of food during each answer.

Concentration Games

RHYTHM

Everyone in the room numbers off in a circle (1, 2, 3, 4, etc.) with the #1 guy in the end chair. The "rhythm" is begun by the #1 guy and everyone joins in by first slapping thighs, clapping hands, then snapping right-hand fingers, then snapping left-hand fingers in a continuous 1-2-3-4-1-2-3-4-1-2-3-4, etc., motion at a moderately slow speed. (It may speed up after everyone learns how to play.) The real action begins when the #1 guy, on the first snap of the fingers, calls out his own number, and on the second snap of the fingers, calls somebody else's number. For example, it might sound something like this: (slap) (clap) "ONE, SIX!" and then the number six guy (as an example) might go: (slap) (clap) "SIX, TEN!" and then the number ten guy would do the same thing, calling out someone else's number on the second finger snap, and so on. If anyone misses, he goes to end and everyone who was after him before moves up one number. The object is to eventually arrive at the number one chair.

CATEGORIES

This game is played exactly like rhythm. But instead of having number, you follow the category . . . whatever the person ahead of you called out.

To begin, everyone (a) slaps their knees and (b) claps their hands. Then, when you snap your right fingers and then your left fingers, the leader says "cate-gory" (in two syllables).

Then the next person in the group (going clockwise) calls out a particular "cate—gory," such as "vege—tables" or "auto—mobiles" or "movie—stars" or "opera—singers."

Then, *without breaking the rhythm:* (a) slap, (b) clap, etc. . . . the next person (going clockwise) must call out something within this "cate—gory," such as (for automobiles) "Chev—rolet" or "Dat—sun" or "Olds—mobile."

If you cannot think of something in the "cate—gory" when it comes your turn, you can change the "cate—gory" by calling out "cate—gory." And the next person in the group must change the "cate—gory" to something else WITHOUT BREAKING THE RHYTHM, such as "football players." And the next person must come up with a football player in this NEW cate—gory without breaking the rhythm, etc.

THUMPER

This game is played exactly like rhythm. But instead of a number, each person creates a "sign"—such as (a) picking your nose, (b) scratching your head, (c) moving like a baboon, etc. Everyone thinks up their own "sign" and shows this "sign" to their group.

Then, on the word GO, you begin the rhythm: (a) slap your knees once, (b) clap your hands once, etc. Then, instead of snapping your right fingers, the #1 person (c) shows his/her "sign" . . . and then (d) someone else's "sign."

Then, you repeat the rhythm: (a) slap your knees, (b) clap your hands . . . and (c) the person whose "sign" was shown proceeds to repeat his/her "sign" and (d) shows someone else's "sign."

In other words, instead of saying *your* number and then *someone else's* number, you show *your,* "sign" and then *someone else's* "sign." The object is to keep the rhythm.

To begin, everyone slaps their knees and claps their hands. Then, the C-Group leader will give his/her "sign" and someone else's "sign."

CHARADES

This crowd breaker is great for a C-Group to compete against other C-Groups. Before the session, prepare a set of 8 stick-on name tags for *each* C-Group. The name tags can be: movie stars, well-known athletes, comic strip or fictional characters—anyone that can be easily and quickly portrayed, such as:

- ☐ Liberace
- ☐ Jimmy Carter
- ☐ Raquel Welch
- ☐ Lady Godiva
- ☐ Romeo and Juliet
- ☐ Three Little Pigs
- ☐ O. J. Simpson
- ☐ John Denver
- ☐ The Dallas Cowboys

While the Leader is explaining the directions, have two helpers go to the C-Groups and put the name tags on each person——a different name tag for everyone in the group.

On the word GO, one person in *each* C-Group turns around and lets the others in the C-Group see the name tag on his or her back. Then, the others start acting out (in silence) this character until the person can guess who it is.

Then the second person in the C-Group turns around and lets the others see the name tag. The others act out this character until the person can guess who it is, etc., until everyone in the group has guessed. The first C-Group to guess all the characters wins.

ONE FROG

Work together by C-Groups on this mathematical riddle about ten frogs in a pond. Starting with *one* frog, go around your C-Group and have each person add to the riddle:

- ☐ First person: *"One frog"*
- ☐ Second person: *"Two eyes"*
- ☐ Third person: *"Four legs"*
- ☐ Fourth person: *"In the pond"*
- ☐ Fifth person: *"Kerplunk"*
- ☐ Sixth person: *"Kerplunk"*

Then, you move to *two* frogs and double everything—just like two frogs:

- ☐ Next person: *"Two frogs"*
- ☐ Next person: *"Four eyes"*
- ☐ Next person: *"Eight legs"*
- ☐ Next person: *"In the pond"*
- ☐ Next person: *"In the pond"* (you need two "in the ponds" for two frogs)
- ☐ Next person: *"Kerplunk"*
- ☐ Next person: *"Kerplunk"*
- ☐ Next person: *"Kerplunk"*
- ☐ Next person: *"Kerplunk"*

The object of the game is to count up to *ten* frogs without making a mistake. IF ANYONE IN YOUR GROUP MAKES A MISTAKE, YOU MUST GO BACK TO "ONE FROG" AND START OVER.

The first C-Group that gets to *ten frogs* stands up and cheers.

MOTORBOAT

Make believe your C-Group is a motor. See how much speed you can achieve. At the word GO, the first person turns his head to the right, saying the sound for the specified motor; then the next person turns his head to the right, repeating the sound, etc. The first group to finish the number of laps should clap.

- ☐ Round One: *Go-carts* . . . for five laps . . . and the sound is "putt."

- ☐ Round Two: Motorcycles . . . for seven laps . . . and the sound is "rrrrrrr.___
- ☐ Round Three: Racing cars at the Indianapolis Speedway . . . for twenty laps . . . and the sound is "zoooooommmmmmm."

BUZZ-FIZZ

Sit with your team in a circle. Try to count up to 50 as fast as you can, but instead of saying "five" or any multiple of "five," say "BUZZ." Instead of saying "seven" or any multiple of "seven," say "FIZZ."

For example, each person, in turn around your team, will sound off with "one," "two," "three," "four," and the next person will say "BUZZ"; the next person "six" and the next person "FIZZ," etc.

If the number is a multiple of "five" and "seven," say "BUZZ-FIZZ." If you make a mistake, start over. The first group to reach 50 WINS.

THIS IS A CUP! A WHAT?

In your C-Groups, pass two objects around your group at the same time in *opposite* directions.

- ☐ A pretty paper cup
- ☐ A round rubber balloon

On the word GO, the person holding the two objects turns to the person on the right, hands this person the cup, and says, *"This is a pretty paper cup."* The person on the right replies: "A what?" And the first person answers: "A pretty paper cup!"

Then the second person hands the cup to the person on the right and says: "This is a pretty paper cup!" The third person replies: "A what?" The second person, in turn, asks the first person, "A what?" And the first person answers the second person, "A pretty paper cup" . . . and the second person answers to the third person, "A pretty paper cup," etc.....

Now, while the "pretty paper cup" is going in the right direction, the first person starts the "round rubber balloon" in the left direction by saying to the person on the left, "This is a round rubber balloon." And the second person on the left responds, "A what?" And the first person answers, "A round rubber balloon."

In other words, the response "A what?" must come back to the first person *each* time . . . and the answer, "A pretty paper cup" . . . or "round rubber balloon" must be repeated back *each* time down the line.

When the balloon has gone all the way around the group, the last person in the group should sit on it . . . until it pops.

On the word GO, the person holding the two objects starts the "pretty paper cup" to the right . . . and the "round rubber balloon" to the left. And each time, the "A what?" must come all the way back to the first person.

TRUST WALK

Pair off with someone you don't know very well. One person keeps his eyes closed while the other leads him around the room, in the hall and even outside for 5-10 minutes. Ask questions to stimulate the imagination, such as, "What does this texture make you think of?" "What kind of music comes to your mind now?" "What does this remind you of?" "Do you feel safe?" Reverse roles and go for another trust walk.

Take a couple minutes to fill out the questionnaire. Partners share their answers and explain the reasons behind them.
1. How would you describe the inner feelings that you had on the trust walk?
2. What was the most significant moment for you during your blind walk?
3. How would you describe your partner if your only experience with him was the trust walk?
4. What did you discover about yourself during this time?

TRUST FALL

This is especially good with this session on friendships IF it is followed up with a discussion in the C-Groups with the question at the close.

With your C-Group form two lines facing each other with your arms stretched out in front of you. One person stands on a table (or other object) about three feet off the ground. The person standing on the object falls backward into the arms of the group. The person falling must keep his *body stiff* and arms by his side.

If your group feels comfortable with it, have the platform a little higher than three feet from the ground. Note: practice this with your leaders to determine if it is safe before trying it with your kids.

After one or two in each group have tried it, sit down together and discuss: "How did it feel to trust someone completely?"

HANDS

Form a circle with everyone's hands stretched toward the center. Then with each hand grab someone else's (making sure not to hold both hands of the same person or the person next to you). After everyone is connected—untangle! Don't give up; it is possible! Be careful not to let go of anybody's hands. After you untangle, try it again without talking.

STAND UP

Sit on the ground with your partner, backs together, feet in front of you, and arms linked. Then try to stand up *together.* After you succeed add another twosome and try again. Keep adding people until your whole group is trying to stand together.

COORDINATED JUMP

This is "jump rope" . . . group-style. Have the entire youth group get in a circle. Arms over the shoulders. On the word GO, see if everyone can jump (feet off the floor) at the same instant.

Once you have mastered this, try jumping with an imaginary rope . . . which a person in the middle of the group swings by slowly spinning a pointer around the group. Then, reverse . . . and reverse again.

If you want to use an actual rope, this is okay too.

TWISTER

Mark off the tile floor with masking tape like a huge "Twister" board and have everyone in the youth group get on the "board." Spin the color wheel just like in the game and call out the color.

Everyone must put a foot or hand on this color. Then, spin the color wheel again and call out another color . . . and everyone must get a foot or hand on this color while keeping their other foot or hand on the first color.

Anyone who falls off balance or cannot keep a foot or hand on all of the colors is out.

MY GRANDMOTHER'S TRUNK

This game is best done sitting in a circle. Someone starts by completing this sentence with an object that begins with the letter A, "My grandmother keeps _____ in her trunk." The next person completes the sentence repeating the A word and adding a word that starts with B. This continues around the circle, each person repeating what the others said and adding another with the next letter of the alphabet. Anyone who blows it is eliminated.

MIRROR

In twos: One person puts his hands up, fingers out—like he was standing in front of a mirror. His partner is this mirror. Whatever the person does with his hands, the mirror does . . . exactly.

To begin, pair off and decide who is the "leader" and who is the "Mirror." On the word GO, the leader proceeds to hand-dance and the "mirror" follows. Then, after 30 seconds, call time and reverse the roles.

SHOULDER RUBDOWN

Stand. Turn right and rub down the shoulders of the person in front of you.

This is a good exercise in the middle of a talk, between group sharing experiences or when you move from groups back into the larger group.

It only takes 30 seconds, but it gives a brief moment to break the tension and prepare for the next thing in the program.

TRIANGLE SLAP DOWN

Divide the class into groups of three and let each trio slap down each other in rotation.

One person in each group should bend over, letting his hands fall free toward the ground and keeping his knees straight. The other two people should stand on either side of him and lay their hands on his back. Then, in perfect rhythm they should slowly start to pat his back, starting at the shoulders and moving down to the hips and back again. After a few seconds, they are to increase the tempo and intensity until they are vigorously patting. Then they are to slow the tempo and gradually diminish the patting until their hands are gently resting again on the back.

After about 45 seconds, slap down the second person—and then the third.

The important thing to keep in mind is rhythm and control. Try to get all of the same groups to start and finish at the same time.

(Note: The leader should demonstrate the procedure with a group in front so that everyone knows exactly what to do.)

47

Dogpatch Olympics

Here's a chance to put on an international Olympic Track Meet with each C-Group or team entering every event.

Create a huge scoreboard or have someone on the Youth Team with a "used car salesperson's" gift of blarney to announce the events and keep score. (Of course, if you have to rig the rules to keep the score close, that is all part of the fun.)

The more you can do to build enthusiasm the better — cheerleaders, T-shirts, team names, etc.

The more participants in each even the better. For instance, don't settle for one entry per team in the "three-legged race." Ask the whole team to line up in relay fashion . . . or have one pair run to one end of the field and another pair return to the "finish line."

Here are some possible events. You can add or substitute depending upon your equipment and the size of the teams.

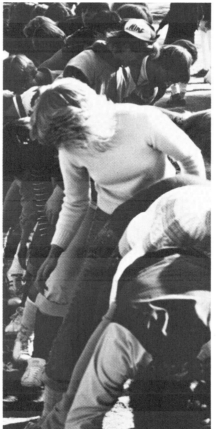

RELAYS

1. Three-legged race (two people with one leg each in a sack or tied with a T-shirt).
2. Wheelbarrow race (two people with one carrying the feet of the other). Person in front carrying the baton (toilet roll) in mouth.
3. Back-to-back race (two people tied together with T-shirt or with a balloon between their backs).
4. Balloon hop (one person with large blown-up balloon between legs).
5. Piggyback races (girl on the back of a guy).

FIELD EVENTS

1. The Javelin (plastic straw).
2. The Shot (whiffle ball).
3. Football Kick (Nerf ball).
4. The Discus (paper plate).

SPECIAL EVENTS

1. Amoeba Race (whole team inside of a rope made out of their socks). Only one person on the team can have their eyes open and this person must shout directions to the rest of the team on how to overcome the "obstacles" on the field, such as trees, hedges, etc.
2. Over-and-Under Relay (with balloons filled with water). Each team lines up in a straight line. The lead person passes the balloon over the head. The next person under the legs, etc. The last person runs to the head of the line and passes the balloon over the head, etc. . . . until the original "lead" person reaches the end of the line and returns the balloon to the front.
3. Through the Legs Relay (with soccer ball). Each team lines up in a straight line. The soccer ball is passed under the legs and the last person in line runs to the head of the line and starts the ball under the legs again. When the original lead person rotates to the end of the line and returns the ball to the front, this team wins.
4. Tricycle Relay (with real tricycle).

5. Counselor Carry Relay (with the team carrying their counselor any way they can to the finish line).
6. Tug of War (over a mud hole).
7. Egg Toss (with real eggs). In pairs, line up with partners one foot away from each other. The egg is tossed from one partner to the other. Then both partners take one step backward and the egg is tossed again between partners. Then each couple takes another step back and tosses the egg again, etc. When an egg breaks, that couple is out. The last remaining couple is the winner.

Communication Exercises

FOR BUILDING RELATIONSHIPS

How do you say "hello"?

THE BAG THAT'S ME

Create a paper sack collage out of newspaper or magazine tear-outs. Paste on the outside of the paper sack any tear-outs that symbolize how you appear on the *outside*. Put inside of the paper sack any symbols that reveal who you are on the *inside*.

Spend about 10 minutes tearing out things from a magazine—words, photographs, slogans—anything that reminds you of yourself. Then take about 5 minutes pasting your tear-outs on the outside or inside of your paper sack. Finally, get together with a small group and explain your "bag."

In your small group, let each person explain the outside of his/her "bag" first. Then go around a second time and let each person take two things from the inside of the bag and explain.

SHOW AND TELL

Create an exciting pictorial description of your life out of magazine or newspaper tear-outs: pictures, words, symbols, slogans—anything that reminds you of who you are. Title your creative masterpiece: "My Self Portrait."

First leaf through a magazine and tear out the pieces. Then make a name tag with the tear-outs and wear it around your neck like a medallion.

FRONT SIDE: Who I am on the outside
- ☐ **My interests / likes**
- ☐ **Things that turn me on**
- ☐ **Pastimes / good times**

BACK SIDE: Who I am on the inside
- ☐ **My hopes and dreams**
- ☐ **Things I think about**
- ☐ **Feelings about myself**

MY ROUTINE

Get together with one other person (that you do not know very well) and explain this self-profile. Then let your partner respond, using the PARTNER RESPONSE.

Finally, take your partner, get together with two others, and introduce your partner with the half-finished sentences under PARTNER INTRODUCTION.

MY DAILY ROUTINE

1. **I usually wake up around....**
2. **I start the day by....**
3. **For breakfast, I usually eat....**
4. **My most creative time in the day is....**
5. **I really get "turned on" by....**
6. **When I feel "low," I....**
7. **I enjoy reading....**
8. **The people I enjoy being around are....**
9. **My favorite pastime is....**
10. **I usually get to bed around....**

YOUR PARTNER'S RESPONSE

1. **I wish we had more time to talk about....**
2. **We have a lot in common in our....**
3. **I really liked what you said about....**
4. **I was surprised by your....**

INTRODUCING YOUR PARTNER TO GROUP

1. **My partner's daily routine is like....**
2. **My partner would be good at....**
3. **My partner reminds me of _____ in the TV/movies.**
4. **If my partner was in a circus, he/she would be the....**

WALLET SCAVENGER HUNT

Take 5 minutes and find the following items in your wallet or purse. Then get together with your small group and have each person share the first item. Go around again on the second item, etc., until you have gone through all the items.

ITEMS TO FIND:

Something that . . .
1. I have had a long time
2. I like to do
3. I am very proud of
4. reveals a lot about me
5. reminds me of a beautiful experience
6. gives me concern/worry
7. I prize the most

GROUP INVENTORY

In your group of 4, hurriedly come up with the TOTAL of these items in your group.

_____ different states you have lived in

_____ houses you have lived in

_____ pictures of guys you have on you

_____ pictures of girls you have on you

_____ love letters you have on you

_____ speeding tickets you have received
          (minus 5 points each)

PERSONAL HABITS

Put a dot on the lines below—somewhere between the two extremes—to indicate how you see yourself. Then get together with your small group and explain where you put the dots and why.

I SEE MYSELF SOMEWHERE IN BETWEEN:

ON HOUSEWORK
Eat off the floor   Where's the floor
Felix Unger (The Odd Couple) _____Oscar Madison

ON COOKING
Every meal is an act of worship   Make it fast and hold the frills
Julia Child _____Ronald McDonald

ON DRIVING
Get out of my way   Better late than never
Johnny Rutherford _____Officer Bob (Driver's Ed Instructor)

ON KEEPING TRIM AND FIT
Workout every morning   I love chocolate anything
Jane Fonda _____Fat Albert

ON SHOPPING
Shop all day for a bargain   Buy only the best
Secondhand Rose _____Alexis (Dynasty)

ON EATING
You are what you eat   Eat, drink, and be merry
Health-nut Ewell Gibbons _____Junk food Johnny

ON SAVING
Last of the big spenders   Mattress stuffer
Diamond Jim _____Ebenezer Scrooge

ON CLOTHES
I don't feel dressed without a fur   Give me my old grubbies anyday
Madonna _____Bruce Springsteen

MR/MISS AMERICA CONTEST

Put a dot on the lines below—somewhere between the two extremes—to indicate how you see yourself. Then get together with your small group and explain.

IN A BATHING SUIT

Men: Mr. America————————————————Don Knotts

Women: Cristie Brinkley ————————————Olive Oyle

IN FORMAL EVENING CLOTHES

Men: Prince Charles ————————————Crocodile Dundee

Women: Joan Collins ————————————Mary Poppins

IN CONVIVIALITY (CHARM)

Men: Ronald Reagan ————————————Rodney Dangerfield

Women: Linda Evans————————————Joan Rivers

IN COORDINATION

Michael Jordan————————————————Chevy Chase

IN MUSICAL ABILITY

Lionel Richie ————————————————Edith Bunker

IN ACTING ABILITY

Tom Cruise ————————————————Mr. T

BUMPER STICKERS

If you could put two bumper stickers on your car—one on the front bumper and the other on the back bumper—what would you choose? One could be just for fun, but the other should be something you believe in strongly. If your particular bumper sticker is not listed here, add it at the bottom.

- ☐ I may be slow, but I'm ahead of you.
- ☐ One nuclear bomb can ruin your whole day.
- ☐ Shop til you drop.
- ☐ My other car is a Mercedes Benz
- ☐ Don't laugh. It's paid for.
- ☐ Save water—shower with a friend.
- ☐ Stop pollution. Ride a horse.
- ☐ I finally got it all together—but I forgot where I put it.
- ☐ I'm already distressed.
- ☐ Keep America beautiful—eat your beer cans.
- ☐ If you are out of work and hungry, eat an environmentalist.
- ☐ Don't bug me. I'm peddling as fast as I can.
- ☐ Driver in love—stops at all full moons.
- ☐ If you're rich—I'm single.
- ☐ Go ahead and hit me, I need the money.
- ☐ Have you hugged a musician today?
- ☐ If you don't like the way I'm driving, stay off the sidewalk.
- ☐ I can't be overdrawn. I still have checks.
- ☐ This is not an abandoned car.
- ☐ I am the guy your mother warned you about.

FIGHT TRUTH DECAY: READ THE BIBLE!

Where have you been?

THOSE WERE THE DAYS

Form a double circle—with the inside circle facing out and the outside circle facing in—like a square dance double-circle. The outside circle rotates to the right every 2 minutes and picks up on the next question with new partners.

To begin, allow each person one minute to give an answer to the first question to the person opposite them. Then call time and have the outside circle rotate one person and start on the next question.

In 32 minutes, you have covered all of the questions and met 16 different people.

I REMEMBER . . .
1. my favorite TV program as a kid
2. my best subject in school
3. my first pet
4. the chore I hated to do
5. my first big trip or vacation
6. my favorite room in the house
7. the time I played hookey from school
8. the fun thing we did as a family
9. the person who helped me with my homework
10. the thing I wanted to be when I grew up
11. my hero at age 12
12. the first time I got kissed (outside the family)
13. the tower of strength in our family
14. my mother's favorite food or dessert
15. my first job
16. the time I got into trouble in school

MY WORLD

Put the symbols below on the map. Then get together with your small group and explain where you put each symbol. If there is a good "story" connected with one of the events, take time to tell the "story."

B = where I was *born*
P = where my *parents* grew up
V = most memorable *vacation*

H = my dream *honeymoon* spot
L = where I would choose to *live*
M = the area I see like *myself*

55

MY CHILDHOOD TABLE

With your small group, reminisce about the year you were 9 years old. If you have time, have everyone share the first question. If you don't have time, have one person in the group answer the first question; the next person the second question, etc.

1. Where were you living?
2. What was your house like?
3. What was your bedroom like?
4. What was your favorite hiding place?
5. What was your favorite TV/radio program?
6. At the supper table, where did you sit?
7. What was the conversation like at the table?
8. Who was the "warm" person for you at the table?
9. What were the "happy times" at this table?
10. How did your family praise you? And for what?
11. Who did you look up to at this table?
12. What was so special about this person?
13. How did your family deal with problems at this table?
14. If you could change one thing about this table, what would it be?
15. In what way has your childhood table affected the person you are today?
16. What would you like to keep from your childhood table for your children?

MY COAT OF ARMS

Fill in the coat of arms below. Then get together with one person and explain your answers to your partner. Let your partner "feed back" to you responses to the half-finished sentences below the coat of arms. Finally, join together with another twosome and let each person introduce his/her partner to the foursome, using the half-finished sentences under INTRODUCTION.

MY FULL NAME	
Two strengths my father gave me (like courage and sense of humor)	Two strengths my mother gave me (like kindness and devotion)
Two issues I feel strongly about (like women's lib and abortion)	Two people (outside my family) I admire (like Ralph Nader and Martin Luther King)
A strong influence in forming my own moral values (like my uncle or coach)	A color that would best express my value system now (like light green, symbolic of spring)

FEEDBACK: (From your partner)
1. I appreciate what you said about...

2. I was surprised to hear you say that ...

3. The thing I appreciate about you is ...

4. I hope we have a chance to talk more about ...

INTRODUCTION: Finish these sentences about your partner in a group of 4.
"From the little I know about my partner, I would guess that he/she ..."
1. would have voted for _____ in the last Presidential election.
2. listens to radio station _____ most of the time.
3. buys his/her clothes from _____ most of the time.
4. looks forward to the TV program _____ every week.

How are you doing?

MUSIC IN MY LIFE

Put a dot on the lines below—somewhere between the two extremes—to indicate how you are feeling right now about each area in your life. Then get together with your small group and explain where you put the dots and why.

In my personal life, I'm feelin' like . . .

Danger Zone _____Footloose

In my family life, I'm feelin' like . . .

Papa Don't Preach _____The Sound of Music

In my work, school or career, I'm feelin' like . . .

Take This Job and Shove It _____Everything's Coming Up Roses

In my spiritual life, I'm feelin' like . . .

Mickey Mouse Disco _____Hallelujah Chorus (Messiah)

In my close relationships, I'm feelin' like . . .

Nowhere Man _____Power of Love

As I look at my immediate future, I'm feelin' like . . .

State of Confusion _____Dancing on the Ceiling

TURKEY FEELINGS

Read over the poem below and think about the three half-finished sentences at the close. Then get together with your small group and share the first sentence. Go around again on the second sentence, etc.

Turkey Feelings

Lord, am I an eagle or a turkey?
I have all the markings of an eagle,
    but I can't fly.
High places that you promised are out of
    reach for me.
I spend my days here in the valley,
    watching the eagles soar overhead
    higher and higher
And all I do is flap my wings
    and pretend.

Tell me, God, if you made me like an eagle,
    why can't I fly?

If I were to compare my life to an eagle or turkey, I would be . . . .

I get "turkey feelings" especially when . . . .

When the turkey feelings come, I find it helpful to . . . .

57

PHYSICAL CHECK-UP

In each category circle the condition where you are at the moment. Then, with your small group, share two categories: (a) Where you are closest to EXCELLENT and (b) Where are you closest to DANGEROUS.

	EXCELLENT	GOOD	FAIR	POOR	DANGEROUS
SMOKING	Never smoked or have stopped smoking	Less than 10 cigarettes per day, not inhaled	Less than 10 cigarettes per day, inhaled	10-19 cigarettes per day	20 or more cigarettes per day
TRIMNESS	Lean	Slightly overweight	Moderately overweight	Considerably overweight	Greatly overweight
PHYSICAL ACTIVITY	Consistently active daily (equivalent to 2-5 miles daily)	Moderately active daily (equivalent to 1.5-2 miles daily)	Some exercise (equivalent to 1-1.5 miles daily)	Seldom exercise (equivalent to .5-1 miles daily)	Sedentary (less than .5 miles daily)
NON-PRESCRIPTION DRUGS	Only on doctor's orders and never mixed with alcohol	Used occasionally for short periods only, alcohol not used at same time	More frequent use for long periods; no alcohol used at same time	Used frequently; mixed with alcohol	Continually used; mixed with alcohol
TRANQUILLITY	Generally relaxed, able to relieve stress by exercise or recreation	Generally relaxed; sometimes able to relieve stress	Moderate degree of stress	Easily stressed; not able to relieve stress or sleep it off	Continually stressed

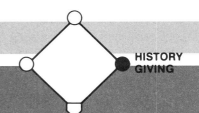
MENTAL ATTITUDE

Circle a number below to indicate how you would evaluate your mental attitude for each statement. Then get together with your small group and explain what you circled and why.

In all honesty, how do I think of myself right now? (circle a number in each category)

I PUT MYSELF DOWN   –5 –4 –3 –2 –1   0   1   2   3   4   5   **I BUILD MYSELF UP**

I am not OK. God goofed when he made me. I'm no good and never will be.

God don't make junk. I am a beautiful person. There ain't nothing gonna change that.

SELF-DEFEATING ATTITUDE   –5   –4   –3   –2   –1   0   1   2   3   4   5   **SELF-CONFIDENT ATTITUDE**

I don't want to try, because I know before I start I'm gonna fail. I'll never make it.

I can do anything through Christ who gives me his strength. Failure only makes me try harder.

STRESS TEST

Take a moment and determine your stress level right now, based on a chart developed by Dr. Richard Rahe. If you score more than 150 points on this scale in the last six months, you are probably under a lot of stress right now.

EVENT	STRESS POINTS
Death of spouse	100
Divorce	73
Marital separation	65
Jail term	63
Death of close family member	63
Personal injury or illness	53
Marriage	50
Loss of job	47
Marital reconciliation	45
Retirement	45
Health problem of family member	44
Pregnancy	40
Sex difficulties	39
Gain of new family member	39
Business readjustment	39
Change in financial state	38
Death of a close friend	37
Change in line of work	36
Increased arguments with spouse	35
Large mortgage taken out	31
Foreclosure of mortgage or loan	30
Change in work responsibilities	29
Son or daughter leaving home	29
Trouble with in-laws	29
Major personal achievement	28
Wife starting or stopping work	26
Change in living conditions	25
Revision of personal habits	24
Trouble with boss	23
Change in work hours	20
Change in residence	20
Change in school	20
Change in recreation	19
Change in church activities	19
Change in social activities	18

HISTORY
GIVING

What do you think I would say?

LET'S PRETEND

When you answer the four questions below, make three of your answers TRUE and one of your answers FALSE. Then ask the small group to guess which of your answers was a lie.

IF I COULD

1. Marry a famous movie star, I would marry . . . .

2. Have my dream car, I would choose . . . .

3. Be in a circus, I would be a . . . .

4. Live in any part of the world, it would be . . . .

BACK TO BACK

Sit back to back with another person and try to guess how this person would answer the quiz below. Then turn around and check your guesses. For every correct guess, you get 10 points. Remember, you are guessing about your partner.

My partner is someone who has:

Y	N	1. kissed before asking
Y	N	2. never used an outhouse
Y	N	3. chewed tobacco
Y	N	4. sneaked out of church
Y	N	5. stolen a watermelon
Y	N	6. eaten raw oysters
Y	N	7. stayed up all night
Y	N	8. never milked a cow
Y	N	9. streaked in public
Y	N	10. stolen a road sign
Y	N	11. danced the twist
Y	N	12. won something on TV
Y	N	13. pulled false fire alarm

QUIZ SHOW

Give the others in your small group a chance to guess what your answer would be before you explain on the quiz below. For every right guess, they get 10 points. The person in your group with the most points after you have completed guessing about each other wins.

Let one person go through the quiz and the others guess after each question. Then move on to the next person and let the others guess.

IF I HAD TO CHOOSE . . .

FROM THESE MOVIES
a. musical comedy   c. love story
b. horror film   d. western

ONE NEW THING FOR MY ROOM
a. waterbed   c. Great Books set
b. exercise machine   d. expensive stereo

SOMETHING FOR MY CAR
a. crushed velvet decor
b. wide tire / mags
c. full stereo system
d. Fuzzbuster

A PLACE TO EAT OUT
a. crowded disco
b. intimate cafe
c. expensive restaurant
d. fast food

A SPECIAL EXOTIC FOOD
a. frogs legs
b. sweet bread
c. snails / escargot
d. Rocky Mountain oysters

SOMEONE FOR A DATE
a. enjoys talking
b. would spend the most
c. likes doing crazy things
d. likes popcorn and TV

THE TOP OF THE LINE IN ANYTHING
a. socks   c. shoes
b. underwear   d. suit / dress

FISHBOWL

On a blank slip of paper jot down five clues about your identity—based on the way you see yourself. Then have everyone in your group fold his/her slip of paper and put it into the center of the group.

Stir up the slips of paper and have someone draw one slip and read the five clues. Then let everyone in the group try to guess who this person is.

After everyone has guessed ask this person to "reveal" themselves and explain.

Then draw another slip of paper and repeat the process.

If I had to describe myself as a:

1. kind of dog
2. automobile: year / model / color
3. kind of music
4. animal in the zoo
5. TV or movie character

CLUE

Write your name on a slip of paper and put the slip into the center of the group. Deal a slip of paper to each person. (If you get your own name, ask for a reshuffle.)

Have someone explain what the person on his/her slip of paper would do in the following three situations. Then let everyone guess who this person is. When everyone has guessed, reveal who the person is.

Continue until everyone has been covered.

IF THIS PERSON WERE IN THESE SITUATIONS, WHAT WOULD THEY DO?

1. If they lost a dime in a pay toilet, this person would. . . .
2. If it were half-time at a football game, this person would. . . .
3. If this person were in a circus, this person would probably be the. . . .

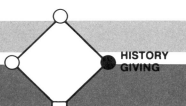

What are you into?

TAKE YOUR CHOICE

In your small group, let one person read and explain his/her choice for the first situation. Then let the next person take the next situation, etc., until you have worked through this quiz.

FOR A ROOMMATE
____someone neat
____someone friendly
____someone with your moral values

FOR A POLITICAL SCIENCE TEACHER
____someone who shared your moral values
____a radical with off-the-wall ideas
____went by the book

IF A PERSON DID NOT AGREE WITH YOU
____be up-front about it
____don't discuss it
____give in to make him or her happy

WHO WOULD YOU GO TO WITH A PROBLEM
____former prostitute
____dishonest politician
____self righteous person

WHICH JOB WOULD YOU CHOOSE
____dull job with good pay and security
____exciting job with low pay and little security
____self-employed in your chosen field with no security

WHAT IS MORE IMMORAL
____premarital sex
____choosing a job just for money
____putting your parent in a nursing home

HOW WOULD YOU LIKE PEOPLE TO THINK OF YOU
____someone who was a success
____someone who loved people
____someone who lived life to the fullest

HOW WOULD YOU LIKE TO DIE
____prolong life with support systems
____die naturally in hospital with good care
____die at home without medical care

ALADDIN'S LAMP

You have found Aladdin's magic lamp. As you rub it, a genie appears and grants you three wishes. Look over the list below and pick the three wishes you would want most. Then get together with your small group and explain.

____HIGH-PAYING JOB: never have to worry about bills again

____ONE ABIDING FRIENDSHIP: a friend who will stick with you forever

____STRESS-FREE LIFE: a life free of struggle and strife, tension and pain

____TRAVEL: an all-expenses-paid trip around the world

____CLOSE FAMILY: a family bond that is lasting, secure, and affirming

____GOOD HEALTH: long life full of vitality and well-being

____WORLDWIDE RECOGNITION: success and fame in your chosen field

____HAPPINESS: a life full of joy and fulfillment

____WEALTH: a vast fortune to spend any way you want to

____CONTRIBUTION: a chance to make a contribution to mankind

____DIRECTION NOW: to know what you want to do with the rest of your life

____A SATISFYING FAITH: a fulfilling spiritual life

PREFERENCES

If you had your choice what would you choose from the list below? When you have finished the quiz, get together with your small group and let the first person explain his/her choice on the first preference. Then let the next person take the next item, etc., until you have gone through the list.

For more fun, let the others in your group guess before you explain your answer.

I PREFER (choose one in each category)

staying up late . . . . getting up early
Bach . . . . Lionel Richie
fast-food drive-in . . . . elegant restaurant
drumstick . . . . breast
going out to the movies . . . . curling up with a book
playing touch football . . . . armchair quarterback
cabin in the mountains . . . . cottage by the sea
sports clothes . . . . grubbies
soap opera . . . . news
rodeo . . . . symphony
lots of friends . . . . one close friend

I WOULD CHOOSE

life of ease . . . . life of surprises
easy but boring course . . . . hard but fascinating course
sit on the bench of a winning team . . . . play every game on a losing team
inherit a million to enjoy . . . . make a million to give away
a job with lots of challenge/no security . . . . a job with lots of security/no challenge
a cheap but lengthy vacation . . . . a short but luxury vacation
live close to parents . . . . see parents once a year
live in retirement community . . . . move in with my children

MY RISK QUOTIENT

Take the quiz and mark your score on the line below. Then get together with your small group and explain where you scored.

You can disagree with the scoring method if you wish. The test is just to get the conversation started.

If I lost my way, I would:
- a. **stop and ask directions**
- b. **check the map**
- c. **keep driving on my hunch**

On the menu, I look for something
- a. **familiar — I know I like**
- b. **special — a little different**
- c. **I have never tried before**

In playing Monopoly, I usually
- a. **play it safe/hide money under table**
- b. **hang loose/save a little back**
- c. **go for broke/gamble everything**

In dating, I would prefer:
- a. **someone I know I like**
- b. **someone I'm not sure about**
- c. **blind date**

I would prefer to make:
- a. **an "A" in a snap course**
- b. **a "B" in a so-so course**
- c. **a "C" in a tough, demanding course**

On choosing a job, I would prefer:
- a. **a boring job with security/benefits**
- b. **an interesting job with some security**
- c. **free lance with no security**

I would prefer to
- a. **inherit a million and enjoy it**
- b. **make a million and spend it**
- c. **make a million and leave it all behind**

SCORING: Give yourself 1 point for every "a;" 2 points for every "b;" and 3 points for every "c." Then circle the total on the line below to get your risk quotient.

PLAY IT SAFE   TAKE A CHANCE
7 8 9 10 11 12 13 14 15 16 17 18 19 20 21

TV AUCTION

You've just turned on the TV and discovered the auction of a lifetime. You have $1,000 to bid on all of the items below. Decide on 5 items that you would like to have from this list and divide the $1,000 between these 5 items. Jot down the amount you would bid in the left column under BUDGET for the 5 items. Remember, the total for all 5 items cannot exceed $1,000.

BUDGET

_____ VACATION: All-expenses-paid vacation for two (including air travel) to Disneyland.

_____ SUBSCRIPTION: A year's membership in the dating computer-bank, guaranteeing the "perfect" date every weekend.

_____ HEALTH CLUB: Lifetime membership to European health spa, guaranteed to build up your sagging muscles.

_____ SKIING EXTRAVAGANZA: One month each year of skiing in Vail, Colorado, and the use of your own condo.

_____ HASSLE FREE YEAR: A solid year of no hassles at home with your parents/kids/brothers or sisters.

_____ CLASSIC CAR: Vintage Masserati automobile to add a touch of class to your driving style.

_____ SEASON TICKETS: Your favorite pro team—box seats—plus club card to the players' lounge.

_____ TIME OFF: Six months off to do the special things that you've never had time to do.

_____ WORLD PEACE: A seat on the U.N. Security Council to work for world peace.

_____ SCHOLARSHIP: A full scholarship to return to college and prepare for your dream career.

_____ RETIREMENT: A paid-up retirement plan to solve all of your future financial worries.

_____ HAPPINESS: One year of happiness when everything seems to go your way.

FANTASY TRIP

Pair off and interview your partner as though you were a TV talk show interviewer, like Johnny Carson. Then let your partner interview you.

IF YOU COULD PLAN YOUR OWN FANTASY TRIP . . .

1. Where would you like to go?
2. Outside your family, who is one other person you would like to invite along?
3. How would you like to travel?
4. What book would you like to reread on your trip?
5. If you could stop off for a side trip, what would it be?
6. How would you spend most of your time?
7. At night, what are some special things you would like to do?
8. While you are away, what are some things in your life that you would want to reevaluate?
9. Before you returned, what letter would you like to write?

ONCE-IN-A-LIFETIME PARTY

Guess what! You're going to have a party— for yourself. A once-in-a-lifetime party for the reunion of old friends and special people who have made your life full. If you had an unlimited budget, what would you plan?

Get together with one other person and plan your party, using the interview questions below.

1. Invitation list: who would be invited?
   - ☐ Close friend in your childhood
   - ☐ Favorite teacher/coach
   - ☐ Person who influenced you spiritually
   - ☐ Person who stood by you
   - ☐ Significant person in your life now
2. Place: where would you hold the party?
3. Entertainment: what would you have for music/entertainment?
4. Decorations: how would you decorate?
5. Toasts: what would you give in the way of gifts or toasts to each guest?

Where do you stand?

LAY IT ON THE LINE

Put a dot on each line below—somewhere between the two extremes—to indicate where you stand on each issue. Then get together with your small group and explain where you put the dots.

ON RESPECT FOR TRADITIONAL VALUES
Mass every morning   Nothing is sacred
Lee Iacocca _____ John DeLorean

ON POSSESSIONS
I like livin' this way   My treasure is in heaven
Liberace _____ Mother Teresa

ON MONEY
Money can buy anything   The love of money is the root of all evil
J. R. Ewing (Dallas) _____ St. Paul

ON FEMINISM
A woman's place is in the home   Being a mother is second class
Phyllis Schlafly _____ Gloria Steinem

ON LAW AND ORDER
Lock the "critters" up   Empty the jails
Lyndon LaRouche _____ Allen Ginsberg

ON POLITICS
Apple pie, motherhood and America   Let's take God out of America
Ronald Reagan _____ Madelyn Murray O'Hare

ON REALITY
The wonderful world of   It's been real
Walt Disney _____ John Lennon

ON WELFARE
It is nothing but communism   Give 'em anything they want
John Birch _____ Ted Kennedy

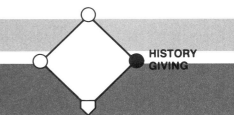

WHAT WOULD I DO?

Check YES, NO or MAYBE on each situation in the quiz. Then get together with your small group and explain.

If you don't know each other very well, form a double circle—with the inside circle facing out and the outside circle facing in—each person facing another on the opposite circle.

Take two minutes with the person you are facing and explain your responses to the first question. Then have the outside circle move one person to the right and explain your answer to the next question to your new partner. Call time and have the outside circle rotate again.

After 32 minutes the outside circle will have rotated 16 times and gotten to know 16 people.

I AM SOMEONE WHO WOULD:

YES	NO	MAYBE	
☐	☐	☐	1. allow my children to drink as teenagers.
☐	☐	☐	2. drive a gas-guzzler car if I could afford it.
☐	☐	☐	3. let my children decide if they want to attend church.
☐	☐	☐	4. defy the law if I thought it was unjust.
☐	☐	☐	5. vote to legalize marijuana.
☐	☐	☐	6. take someone off welfare who refused to work.
☐	☐	☐	7. marry someone of another race if I loved him/her.
☐	☐	☐	8. drive with a suspended license.
☐	☐	☐	9. send my kids to a private school if I could afford it.
☐	☐	☐	10. stick to my values even if it means that my children leave home.
☐	☐	☐	11. speak up in class if I disagree with my teacher on morals.
☐	☐	☐	12. support the contras in Nicaragua
☐	☐	☐	13. give my kids more freedom than I had.
☐	☐	☐	14. lobby for a gun control law.
☐	☐	☐	15. allow my kids to "live together" before marriage in my home.
☐	☐	☐	16. live with my kids when I retire.

FIRE DRILL

Your house is on fire. You have only 5 minutes to run through the house and collect the most important possessions (assuming the people and pets are safe) in your house. Jot down *specifically* what you would grab, such as your stamp collection, your Ocean Pacific T-shirt, your autographed album of the Michael Jackson concert, etc.

Then, beside your list, jot down the following symbols next to the appropriate items.

Remember, be specific. Very specific. Run through every room in your house . . . including the garage. What would you try to save???

$	=	cost more than $100
D	=	still owe on this item (debt)
*	=	first thing I would grab
S	=	sentimental value because it was a gift
X	=	could get along without if necessary
T	=	source of tension right now
F	=	important to the family
N	=	necessary to go on with my life

MY VALUE SYSTEM

How do you see your values in comparison to other people? Circle the person or thing that comes the closest to your own values at the moment. Then get together with your small group and compare results.

I SEE MY MORAL VALUES MORE LIKE

Archie Bunker	"Meathead"
Hollywood	Omaha, Neb.
Dan Rather	Chevy Chase
Sat. Night Live	Little House on Prairie
Wall St. Journal	Rolling Stones
Unfinished Symphony	New Wave
Good Housekeeping	Playboy
Used car salesman	Scout den mother
Ralph Nader	Ronald Reagan
Billy Graham	Billy Carter

INFLUENCE ANALYSIS

When it comes to making decisions, who influences you the most? In each area check one or two of the major influences. Then get together with your small group and compare notes.

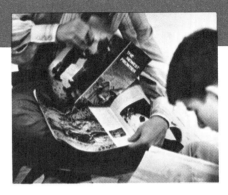

	Parents	Friends	TV	Mate	My ideas
___ Tastes in clothes					
___ How to use spare time					
___ Music/entertainment					
___ Reading matter					
___ Lifestyle					
___ Moral issues					

NEWSPAPER/MAGAZINE SEARCH

Leaf through a daily newspaper or a weekly news magazine and jot down a list of the 5 or 6 headlines that are a major concern to you at the moment. Then code the headlines by jotting down in the margin the following symbols where they apply:

? = an issue I am still undecided about
40 = an issue when I reach 40, but not now
P = an issue when I become a parent, but not now
C = a major issue because of my commitment to Christ

SYMBOLS	HEADLINES

INSURANCE APPRAISAL

You want to insure *everything* of value in your life. You contact the one insurance company in the world that will insure everything—*everything*. Together, you go over the list below and place a value; that is, how much you want to insure each item on the list for.

NOW, HERE'S THE CATCH: (1) you *must* insure everything on the list, and (2) the grand total cannot exceed $1000. This means that you may have to go back and devalue your stereo system to only $50 when you are all through . . . so that your grand total comes out to $1000.

$_____ **My stereo and record collection**

$_____ **My closest friend**

$_____ **My car/motorcycle/bicycle**

$_____ **Peace and harmony at home**

$_____ **Starting position on my team**

$_____ **Popularity with my group**

$_____ **Time off every weekend**

$_____ **A chance to make a contribution to mankind**

$_____ **Assurance of a job when I graduate**

$_____ **Guarantee my driver's license will not be revoked**

VALUES AUCTION

Today, the following items will be auctioned. You are invited to submit a bid in writing for any item you want . . . BUT YOU ONLY HAVE $1,000 TOTAL to spread over *all* the items.

Read over the list. Select the items you want. Jot down in the margin the amount you want to bid on these items—such as $50 for the first item. Remember, you only have $1,000 total to spread over *all* the items you want. For more fun, run an old-fashioned auction.

MY BUDGET		MY WINNING BID
$ _____	1979 Silver Corvette in perfect condition	$ _____
$ _____	Season tickets for my favorite pro team	$ _____
$ _____	Pioneer Quadraphonic Sound System	$ _____
$ _____	One year of no hassles with my parents/kids	$ _____
$ _____	One deep abiding friendship	$ _____
$ _____	Six months off to do anything I want	$ _____
$ _____	Date with Miss America / Mr. America	$ _____
$ _____	Fastest car in my town	$ _____
$ _____	Complete new outfit (latest fashion)	$ _____
$ _____	Winter vacation with friend in Hawaii	$ _____
$ _____	Super Bowl tickets for 10 years	$ _____
$ _____	Be on Johnny Carson show	$ _____

What do you see in me?

PERSONALITY HATS

If you could pick hats for the persons in your small group—to fit their personalities as you see them—which hat would you pick for each person? Think of the others in your small group as your read over the hats and jot down their names next to the hats that you feel would fit them.

Then ask one person in your group to sit in silence while the others explain which hat they picked for this person. Then ask the next person to sit in silence, etc.

_____ **AFRICAN SAFARI PITH HELMET** for the lion-hunting, adventure seeker.

_____ **COLORFUL EASTER BONNET** for the extravagant, effervescent party girl.

_____ **LEOPARD FUR HAT** for the radical chic—furry, svelte and seductive.

_____ **SWATHED COWL** for the mysterious, elusive, alluring woman of good taste.

_____ **WIDE-BRIMMED PICTURE HAT** for the graceful, garden-party host.

_____ **PEEK-A-BOO VEIL** for the provocative, secretive, espionage agent on the prowl.

_____ **MEXICAN SOMBRERO** for the happy-go-lucky, easy-going romantic.

_____ **DON QUIXOTE'S GOLDEN HELMET** for the eccentric, knight-errant who sees beautiful things in others.

_____ **WEATHERED COWBOY HAT** for the hard-driving, big-hearted tough hombre.

_____ **DR. SEUSS HAT** for the mischievous, surprising improper professor.

_____ **DASHING CAVALIER'S HAT** for the gallant, chivalrous amorous consort.

_____ **WORLD WAR I AERO SQUADRON'S CAP** for the perennial fight pilot, complete with all the medals.

_____ **LEPRECHAUN'S HAT** for the whimsical, playful, mischief maker.

_____ **FIREMAN'S HELMET** for the thrill-seeking, fire-chasing kid.

_____ **COONSKIN CAP** for the wild, adventurous, daring frontiersman.

_____ **SANTA CLAUS CAP** for the jovial, jolly, rollicking tease.

_____ **PAPER PARTY HAT** for the fun-loving, childlike life of the party, complete with horn.

_____ **STRAW CARIBBEAN HAT** for the enchanting, exotic world traveler.

_____ **FLOPPY-MOPPY ALL-PURPOSE HAT** for the individualist who is careless of public opinion.

_____ **OLD-FASHIONED SUNBONNET** for the warm, homey, bread-baking prairie girl.

LUV BUG

What contribution has each person in your small group made to your group and your own life personally? Read over the parts of the car below and jot down the names of your group members next to the part that best explains the contribution each person has made.

Then ask one person to sit in silence while the others explain where they have jotted down this person's name. Repeat the process for each person in your group.

_____BATTERY: a dependable "die-hard"—provides the "juice" for everything to happen.

_____SPARK PLUG: Ignites the air and gas. Makes sure there is "fire," even on cold mornings.

_____OIL: "The razor's edge" to protect against engine wear-out, longer mileage, and lubrication for fast moving parts.

_____SHOCK ABSORBER: Cushions heavy bumps. Makes for an easy, comfortable ride.

_____RADIO: The "music machine," making the trip fun and enjoyable. Adds a little "rock and roll" and a good time.

_____MUFFLER: Reduces the engine roar to a cat's "purr," even at high speeds over rough terrain.

_____REFRESHMENT BAR: The extra touch of "class," providing just the right combination of tonic and refreshment for the long journey.

_____ROLLS ROYCE FRONT: The outrageous, slightly incongruous touch to keep "herbie" from being ordinary.

_____TRANSMISSION: converts the energy into motion, enables the engine to slip from one speed to another without stripping the gears.

_____GAS: liquid fuel that is consumed, giving away its own life for the energy for propulsion.

_____WINDSHIELD: Keeps the vision clear, protects from debris and flying objects.

CRYSTAL BALL

Below is a series of crazy forecasts. Try to match the people in your group to something that they will be or accomplish in their lifetimes. Write their initials next to the forecast.

THE PERSON IN OUR GROUP MOST LIKELY TO:

_____ be the first woman to win at the Indianapolis 500

_____ be the used car salesman of the year

_____ rise to the top in the diplomatic corps

_____ win the lottery

_____ replace Ahmad Rashad on Monday Night Football

_____ write a best selling novel about their own love life

_____ be a world famous hairdresser

_____ make a fortune in pay toilet rentals

_____ become Joe Namath's understudy for women's panty hose

_____ become an underworld detective

_____ become a lobbyist for recycling cemetery lots

_____ start a gossip column for the love-lorn

_____ get busted for skinny-dipping in Rockefeller Plaza

_____ open a charm school for Hells Angels alumni

_____ be a double agent for the ERA

_____ skateboard across the country

_____ discover a new use for underarm deodorant

_____ become a soap opera celebrity

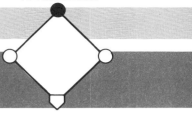

MUSICAL INSTRUMENTS

Think of the others in your small group as musical instruments in an orchestra (or a band). Jot down the names of your group members next to the instruments that explain their personality . . . or the contribution they have made to your group.

Then ask one person to sit in silence while the others explain where they jotted down this person's name. Then let another person sit in silence while you "affirm" this person, etc.

_____ ANGELIC HARP: soft, gentle, melodious, wooing with heavenly sounds.

_____ OLD-FASHIONED WASHBOARD: authentic, non-conforming, childlike, and fun.

_____ PLAYER PIANO: mischievous, raucous, honky-tonk—delightfully carefree.

_____ KETTLE DRUM: strong, vibrant, commanding when needed but usually in the background.

_____ PASSIONATE CASTINET: with Spanish fervor, stormy, wild, seductive—with rose in mouth.

_____ STRADIVARIUS VIOLIN: priceless, exquisite, soul piercing—with the touch of the master.

_____ FLUTTERING FLUTE: tender, lighthearted, wide-ranging, and clear as crystal.

_____ SCOTTISH BAGPIPES: martial, visceral, moving—distinctive and unmistakable.

_____ SQUARE DANCE FIDDLE: folksy, down-to-earth, toe tapping—sprightly and lighthearted.

_____ ENCHANTING OBOE: haunting, charming, disarming—even the Cobra is harmless with this sound.

_____ MELLOW CELLO: deep, sonorous, compassionate—adding body and depth to the orchestra.

_____ PIPE ORGAN: grand, magnificent, richly endowed—versatile and commanding.

_____ HERALDING TRUMPET: stirring, lively, invigorating—signaling attention and attack.

_____ CLASSICAL GUITAR: thoughtful, contemplative, profoundly entertaining, and entertainingly profound.

_____ ONE-MAN BAND: Harmonica in mouth. Accordion in hands. Noisy drum on rear end.

_____ COMB AND TISSUE PAPER: makeshift, original, uncomplicated—homespun and creative.

_____ SENUOUS TROMBONE: warm, rich, swinging—great in solo or background support.

SAY IT WITH FLOWERS

Below is a list of flowers, shrubs, and trees that you might find in a botanical garden. Think of the people in your group as you read over the list and pick one for each person in your group. Jot down their name next to the item that you feel is close to the individual's personality.

_____ **BURSTING SUNFLOWER:** exuberant, effervescent, giver of sunshine and nourishing seeds with all sorts of energy.

_____ **SHY, DELICATE VIOLET:** sensitive, refreshingly natural—often found along the beaten path—a traveler's delight.

_____ **WILD ROSE:** untamed, unpretentious, rambling, flourishing along country lanes and unexpected places.

_____ **STURDY, DESERT CACTUS:** with unbelievable tenacity to overcome adverse elements—giving natural beauty to the desert.

_____ **GLORIOUS EASTER LILY:** dramatic, symbolic of resurrection and new life, of hope and courage.

_____ **WHITE DAISY:** bright, happy, with a quiet fragrance—innocent and irresistible. A harbinger of love.

_____ **GIANT CORSAGE CHRYSANTHEMUM:** bold, vivid, bursting with inner beauty—extravagant and outrageous.

_____ **TALL MAJESTIC OAK:** stalwart, deep-rooted, rough-textured on the outside, strong on the inside. Endures raging storms.

_____ **ROYAL PALM TREE:** complete with succulent coconuts—found along shorelines of exotic islands.

_____ **CHRISTMAS TREE:** radiant, life-sharing, joy-giving—brightly decorated, childlike and exciting.

_____ **YEAR-AROUND EVERGREEN:** consistent, never-changing—able to thrive in rocky soil and harsh, cold environments.

_____ **HARDY BUTTERCUP:** modest, unassuming, old-fashioned, enduring, and very special.

_____ **COLORADO ASPEN:** shimmering, vivacious, colorful, found in the high country—brilliant and gloriously alive.

_____ **GRAPEVINE:** source of joy, gaiety, vitality, and life. Lives only to give itself away.

JOB PLACEMENT

Congratulations. Everyone in your group is out of work and you are asked to assign each one a new career. Write each name next to the career you would match with that person's personality.

Then have one person sit in silence while the others explain what job they picked for this person. Repeat this procedure until you have covered everyone in your group.

_____ **SPACE ENVIRONMENTAL ENGINEER** in charge of designing the bathrooms on space shuttles.

_____ **SCHOOL BUS DRIVER** for junior high kids in New York City (no earplugs allowed)

_____ **WRITER** of an ''advice to the lovelorn'' column in Hollywood, California.

_____ **SUPERVISOR** of a complaint department for a large automobile dealership and service department.

_____ **ANIMAL PSYCHIATRIST** for French poodles in a fashionable suburb of Paris.

_____ **RESEARCH SCIENTIST** studying the fertilization patterns of the dodo bird—now extinct.

_____ **SAFARI GUIDE** in the heart of Africa for wealthy widows and eccentric bachelors.

_____ **PEE WEE LEAGUE BASEBALL COACH** in Mudville, Illinois. Last year's record was 0 and 12.

_____ **TOY REPAIRMAN** for toyland during the Christmas holidays.

_____ **MANAGER** of your local McDonalds during rush week with 20 teen employees.

_____ **AEROBIC DANCE INSTRUCTOR** at the Jolly Time Mental Health Center for overweight grandparents.

_____ **LIBRARIAN** for the Walt Disney Hall of Fame memorabilia.

_____ **CURATOR** for the wax museum of Indian artifacts in Juno, Alaska.

_____ **HEAD COUNSELOR** of Camp Runamuck Nudist Colony.

_____ **TRAP SHOOT MANAGER** for the CIA special weapons firing range.

_____ **JELLY BEAN TASTER** for Ronald Reagan.

_____ **MANICURIST** in the birdhouse of the San Diego Zoo.

BROADWAY SHOW

How would you go about casting a Broadway show with the talent in your group? Jot down the name of each group member next to the role you see this person filling.

     Then have one person sit in silence while the others explain their choice for this person. Then ask another person to sit in silence while you explain your choice for this person, etc.

_____ **PRODUCER:** typical Hollywood business tycoon; extravagant, big-budget, big-production magnate in the David O. Selznik style.

_____ **DIRECTOR:** Creative, imaginative brains behind the scene; perfectionist, big-spender, unpredictable genius.

_____ **HEROINE:** beautiful, captivating, seductive, everybody's heartthrob, defenseless when men are around, but nobody's fool.

_____ **HERO:** tough, macho, champion of the underdog, knight in shining armor, Mr. Clutch in the John Wayne mold, always gets his man.

_____ **COMEDIAN:** childlike, happy-go-lucky, outrageously funny, covers up a brilliant interior with the carefully tailored "dim" exterior.

_____ **CHARACTER PERSON:** one-of-a-kind eccentric, rugged individualist, outrageously different, colorful, adds spice to any surrounding.

_____ **FALL GUY:** studied, nonchalant character, who wins the hearts of everyone by being the "foil" of the heavy characters.

_____ **TECHNICAL DIRECTOR:** the genius for "sound and lights," complete with beard, tennis shoes, "off the wall" T-shirt and jogging shorts.

_____ **COMPOSER OF LYRICS:** Communicates in music what everybody understands, heavy into feelings, moods, outbursts of energy and emotion.

_____ **PUBLICITY AGENT:** Mafia leader turned Madison Avenue executive, knows all the angles, good at one-liners, a flair for "hot" news.

_____ **VILLAIN:** The "bad guy" who really is the heavy for the plot, forces others to think, challenges traditional values; out to destroy "clichés," shallow morality, and plastic conformity.

_____ **AUTHOR:** shy, aloof, eccentric person, very much in touch with himself, sensitive to people, puts into words what others only feel.

_____ **STAGEHAND:** supportive, behind-the-scenes person who makes things run smoothly; patient, stable, unflappable.

MY GOURMET GROUP

Here is a chance to pass out some much deserved praise for the people who have made your group something special. Put down the name of each group member next to the delicacy that person has added to your group.

Then let one person sit in silence while the others explain where they put this person's name. Repeat this process for each person.

_____ **CAVIAR:** that special touch of class, aristocratic taste, that has made the rest of us feel like royalty.

_____ **ARTICHOKE HEARTS:** tender, delicate, succulent, disarmingly vulnerable, that has whetted the appetite for heart-felt sharing.

_____ **IMPORTED CHEESE:** distinctive, tangy, mellow with age, with a special flavor all its own, that brings depth to any meal.

_____ **VINEGAR AND OIL:** tart, witty, dry, a rare combination of healing ointment and pungent spice to add "bite" to the salad.

_____ **FRENCH PASTRY:** tempting, irresistible, "crème de la crème" dessert, the connoisseur's delight for topping off a meal.

_____ **PHEASANT UNDER GLASS:** wild, untamed, totally unique, a rare dish for very special people who appreciate original fare.

_____ **CARAFE OF WINE:** sparkling, effervescent, exuberant, and joyful; outrageously free and liberating to the rest of us.

_____ **ESCARGOT AND OYSTERS:** priceless treasures of the sea once out of their shells; succulent, delicate, and irreplaceable.

_____ **FRESH FRUIT:** vine-ripened, energy-filled, absolutely fresh, invigorating—the perfect treat after a heavy meal.

_____ **CANDELABRA:** soft light, jeweled excellence, the special atmosphere for splendor and romance.

_____ **PRIME RIB:** stable, brawny, macho, the generous mainstay of any menu, juicy, mouth-watering "perfect cut" for good nourishment.

_____ **MEDITERRANEAN DANCING:** tempestuous, untamed, spontaneous, high-stepping entertainment to cheer the soul.

_____ **ITALIAN ICE CREAMS:** colorful, flavorful, delightfully childlike, non-fattening, the unexpected surprise in our group.

CHOOSING PARTNERS

If you could choose someone in your group as your partner for the situations below, who would you choose? You can use a person's name only once so pick the best spot for each person.

     Then let one person sit in silence while the others explain where they put this person's name. Then take another person and have the others explain their choices for this person, etc.

_____ **ENDURANCE DANCING contest at the Astrodome**

_____ **SCUBA DIVING in the Caribbean with the Jacques Cousteau crew**

_____ **MONDAY NIGHT FOOTBALL "color" announcer with you**

_____ **EXECUTOR for my estate**

_____ **GOSSIP COLUMN research associate**

_____ **BODYGUARD for me in the event I strike it rich**

_____ **SANCHO for the next "windmill" you decide to chase**

_____ **SPACE SHUTTLE flight to Mars**

_____ **BEST MAN or MAID OF HONOR at my wedding**

_____ **TRAPEZE ACT for the Barnum and Bailey Circus**

_____ **HOT TUB demonstration at the Home Show**

_____ **HANG GLIDING off the Palisades**

_____ **AUTHOR of my biography**

_____ **SURF BOARD doubles championship in Hawaii**

GOAL SETTING

Where are you going?

FUNNY FACES

Fill in the funny faces below to indicate how you are responding to these "calls" in your life right now. For example:

 Whatever you say, Lord.

 Let me think about it, Lord.

 Wish you hadn't asked.

 The call to make Jesus Christ the Lord of my life.

The call to reach out to my friends who need God.

 The call to share my special gifts with his community.

The call to really serve God in my career, whatever it is.

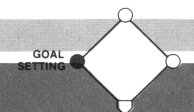

THINGS GO BETTER WITH LOVE

REDECORATING MY LIFE

If you could put a poster in every "living space" in your house, what poster would you choose for each area? Match the poster with the living spaces below. Then, in your small group, explain your selections and why.

____TV room
____office/study
____bedroom
____family room
____game room
____magazine rack
____garage
____checkbook
____kitchen
____hope chest
____workbench
____safe
____hideaway

1. All things are possible through Christ.
2. Winning isn't everything. It is the only thing.
3. If you're not good to yourself, I can't be.
4. When God closes a door, another one opens.
5. Love is patient and kind.
6. You can see my value system here.
7. Keep within your heart a place where dreams can grow.
8. I believe in the sun, even if it does not shine.
9. I would if I could, but I can't so I won't.
10. I have tried so hard to become what I ought to be that I forgot what I am.
11. Fragile: handle with care.
12. I don't need a great deal of love but I need a steady supply.
13. Take life one day at a time.
14. Prayer changes things.
15. Lord, make me an instrument of your peace.
16. Keep your mind with all diligence, for out of it are the issues of life.
17. I am easy to please as long as I have things my way.
18. Lord, protect me from myself.
19. Give to the world the best that you have, and the best will come back to you.
20. The power of God is at work here.

CAUTION
human beings he
HANDLE WITH CA

PRESCRIPTIONS

If you had to write a prescription for yourself right now, what would you write? Check "✓" two on the list below and add one more for your spiritual life at the bottom.

Rx ☐ **IF LONELY:** Hug 3 people per day or as needed.

Rx ☐ **IF TIRED:** Go to bed early. No *Johnny Carson* for 3 weeks.

Rx ☐ **IF LETHARGIC:** Walk 3 miles per week; "stop and smell the roses."

Rx ☐ **IF DEPRESSED:** Visit an old friend; reminisce about the good ole days. Read a good book and take yourself "out" for dinner.

Rx ☐ **IF OVERLOADED:** Take 1 day off to reorder priorities; cut back on your schedule and spend 2 nights at home each week.

Rx ☐ **IF OVERSTRESSED:** Take Vitamin B complex; drink fresh orange juice; jog 1 mile per day.

Rx ☐ **IF OVERWEIGHT:** Cut back on sugar, white flour, and all snacks; do 3 pushups daily—away from the table.

Rx ☐ **IF BORED:** Volunteer some time to the hospital, little league, or local nursing home. Find someone who needs you.

Rx ☐ **IF HYPERACTIVE:** Run around the block until your socks stink. Volunteer your time to preschool for a month.

Rx ☐ **IF INSECURE:** Talk to your pastor— he probably is too.

Rx ☐ **IF BUMMED OUT:** Take a walk around the park; pick flowers and speak to two people about the weather.

Rx ☐ **IF FRUSTRATED:** Enroll in an aerobic dancing class and sweat it out.

MY OWN OBITUARY

If you could write your own obituary, what would you want to have said about you? Fill in the typical obituary form below. Then, in your small group, read your obituaries to each other and discuss.

Yours truly, died last night at his home. Yours truly will always be remembered as a person who . . .

Yours truly was dedicated to . . .

At the time of death, yours truly was engaged in . . .

The funeral will be held at . . .

Yours truly has requested this song to be sung at the funeral . . .

In lieu of flowers, yours truly has requested that a fund be set up for . . .

WANT AD

This is a fishing expedition for clues into the thing God might be calling you to do . . . or the career you would be happiest in. Take a few minutes to fill in the questionnaire and code your responses.

Then get together with one other person and let this person listen while you walk through your "résumé."

CLUES TO MY CALLING

Five things I am good at:

Five things that turn me on:

Three jobs I have enjoyed:

Three issues/causes that concern me:

One dream that keeps recurring:

CODING: Go back over the list of things and jot down these symbols where they apply:

- **P** = **involve other people**
- **A** = **done alone**
- **$** = **can be money-making**
- **L** = **could enjoy the rest of my life**
- **S** = **restores my life spiritually**
- **C** = **has career possibilities**

DECODING INTERVIEW: Get together with one other person and interview each other with these questions—one at a time.

1. **What did you find out about yourself in this exercise?**
2. **What do your skills and interests indicate you would be happy doing?**
3. **How could you go about getting involved in these areas of interest?**
4. **If you knew that you could not fail, what would you like to try?**
5. **What is keeping you from this?**

MY BUDGET

Take a moment and make two budgets. In the first column, jot down what you spend now—per month. In the second column, put down the percent (%) this would be of the total budget. (Divide the total into the amount.)

If you are the wage earner for the family, make a family budget. If you live with your folks, fill in only those areas you spend money on.

	PRESENT BUDGET	PERCENT OF BUDGET
Shelter (house, apartment)	$_____	_____%
Food (when you eat at home)	$_____	_____%
Food (for eating out)	$_____	_____%
Clothes	$_____	_____%
Car: payments/insurance/gas	$_____	_____%
Telephone/Utilities	$_____	_____%
Insurance: life/fire/medical	$_____	_____%
Taxes/Social Security/etc.	$_____	_____%
Entertainment/Movies/Sports	$_____	_____%
Vacation/hobbies	$_____	_____%
Education/Self-improvement	$_____	_____%
Church/Charity	$_____	_____%
Savings/Investments	$_____	_____%
Emergency Fund	$_____	_____%

How did it go?

KOINONIA

CHILDREN'S ZOO

Visit this adorable, petting, children's zoo. Choose an animal for yourself that sort of endears itself to you, particularly since being in this course. In fact, the animal might reveal what this group has meant to you . . . or how your outlook on life has changed since being in this group.

_____CUDDLY BOA CONSTRICTOR: Because I would like to wrap up this whole group and take you home with me.

_____PLAYFUL PORPOISE: Because you have helped me to find a new freedom and a whole new world to play in.

_____COLORFUL PEACOCK: Because you have told me that I am beautiful, and I have started to believe it, and it is changing my life.

_____SAFARI ELEPHANT: Because I have enjoyed this new adventure and I am not going to forget it . . . or this group. Can hardly wait for the next safari.

_____LOVABLE HIPPOPOTAMUS: Because you have let me surface and bask in the warm sunshine of God's love.

_____BLACK PANTHER: Because you have helped me to look very closely at myself and see some of the spots . . . and you have told me it's OK to be this way.

_____DANCING BEAR: Because you have taught me to dance in the midst of pain, and you have helped me to reach out and hug again.

_____ROARING LION: Because you have let me get down off my perch and roll in the grass, and not even worry about my mane.

_____WILD EAGLE: Because you have helped to heal my wings, and taught me how to soar again.

_____TOWERING GIRAFFE: Because you have helped me to hold my head up and stick my neck out, and reach over the fences I have built.

_____ALL-WEATHER DUCK: Because you have taught me to enjoy the weather (even on rainy days) and to celebrate the hard times like a duck in a storm.

_____OSTRICH IN LOVE: Because you have loved me so much that I have taken my head out of the sand, and found a whole new reason for living.

PROJECTION

Take a moment to look back over the time since you have been in this course. Fill out the questionnaire about your experience . . . and the next steps in your life.

1. **Five years from now, I will probably remember this course as:** (circle one)
   a. a lot of fun
   b. the beginning of something new
   c. a turning point in my life with God
   d. a waste of time
   e. don't know yet

2. **The high point in this course for me has been the:**
   a. study of Scripture
   b. times of prayer together
   c. finding out that I am not alone
   d. taking a hard look at my lifestyle
   e. listening to each other
   f. feeling like someone really cared
   g. realizing that happiness can be mine

3. **The biggest change that has occurred in my life during this course has been:**
   a. reordering my priorities
   b. affirming myself as a person of worth
   c. getting a handle on my walk with God
   d. seeing the world as God sees it
   e. believing that I can make a difference
   f. learning how to laugh at my problems
   g. a healthy sexual revolution in me
   h. healing some broken relationships that I thought were over
   i. cutting out the excess baggage in my life
   j. learning how to love

4. **If I am going to move on in my spiritual growth, I need:**
   a. a lot more personal discipline
   b. support from others
   c. a group like this to belong to
   d. a deeper faith
   e. a better understanding of Scripture

APPROPRIATE HOMES

Reflect back over the experience you have had with this group and pick a "living environment" that would best express what has happened in your life during this time. Choose the home below that best "fits" the new YOU.

____**SLEEPING BAG:** Because you have helped me to get back to simple things, a simple lifestyle—wide open to the outdoors, the stars, smelling flowers and listening to the birds again.

____**GLASS HOUSE:** Because you have let me be open and free—to look out at the world around, get rid of my rocks, and enjoy life—to let the sun shine in.

____**MEDIEVAL CASTLE:** Because you have helped me to dream again—of noble causes, chivalry, honor, and valor—even take on the dragons.

____**SWISS FAMILY TREE HOUSE:** Because you have helped me to rebuild my family, work together, see the inner strength in the others and accept the situation as a new challenge.

____**GREENWICH VILLAGE APARTMENT:** Because you have helped me to know myself, be myself, celebrate the "wild, way-out" side of me as a gift of God, to care less about conformity and "measuring up" to other's expectations.

____**LOG CABIN:** Because you have affirmed my pioneering spirit that strikes out into unknown expeditions, "homesteading" new frontiers in my spiritual journey.

____**SOUTHERN MANSION:** Because you have helped me to accept gracious living, culture, relaxing with a mint julip while at the same time calling forth the rebel spirit within me.

____**WINNEBAGO CRUISER:** Because you have released in me a desire to travel the "back roads" and rediscover my heritage—the old watering places of my childhood and the simple joys of life.

____**EIGHT-PERSON TENT:** Because I want to share more of my life with the rest of you. We have become a family together, and there is so much more we can share.

____**HOUSEBOAT:** Because you have started me on a life cruise into new uncharted waters and new adventures . . . and I would like you to share the adventure with me. The pace will be slower and the facilities a little crowded, but you are all welcome.

____**PORTABLE SANDBOX:** Because you have helped me to discover a child inside that I didn't know was there, and the party is just beginning.

____**TRAVELING CIRCUS TRAIN:** Because you have said it was okay to laugh in the midst of pain, rejoice when times were tough, and celebrate life in all its fullness.

How do you say "goodbye"?

MY LAST WILL AND TESTAMENT

If you could give away some of your childhood possessions to the people in your small group, what would you want each person to have? Think of the others in your group right now as you read over the list below and jot down their names next to the item that you would like to share with each person . . . as a memento of your time together in this group.

Then explain your gifts and tell why you would like each one to have that particular "gift" from you. Let each person share in this way.

_____ **My U-2 concert T-shirt (slightly used)**
_____ **My first razor (still works)**
_____ **My class ring (returned by first love)**
_____ **My Heather Locklear life-size poster**
_____ **My old 50s record collection**
_____ **My movie star album**
_____ **My teddy bear**
_____ **My Chanel # 5 perfume (sexy)**
_____ **My set of weights (beginner)**
_____ **My letter jacket**
_____ **My backpacking pack**
_____ **My first love letter**
_____ **My own Linus blanket**
_____ **My little league ball glove**
_____ **My bug collection**
_____ **My baseball cards**
_____ **My Nancy Drew mysteries**

KEEPSAKES

Here is your chance to give the others in your group a memento of your time together to keep with them on the next leg of their spiritual journey.

Jot down the names of the others in your group next to the memento you would like for them to have *from* you as they travel.

_____ **My security blanket**—to clutch when you are scared and lonely

_____ **Snoopy doghouse bank**—to get away from it all when you need to

_____ **Superbowl ring**—you have already made it with me

_____ **Music box**—just wind and it plays "Climb Every Mountain"

_____ **Bloodbank card**—good for one pint of my blood at any time

_____ **Sweetheart locket**—you're extra special to me

_____ **Warm fuzzy**—to take out and feel when you're down

_____ **Ball and chain bracelet**—to remind you of the oneness we share

_____ **Bromoseltzer**—for quick, gentle relief when you need it

_____ **Party hat**—to remind you of the party. Everything's ready

_____ **St. Christopher's medal**—my special prayers will be with you

_____ **Monogrammed sweatshirt**—to keep in shape

_____ **Lucky silver dollar**—to remind you of the fortune you have inside of you

Group Building

STRUCTURED QUESTIONNAIRES

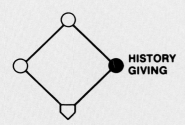

**HISTORY
GIVING**

Objective: To start the process of building support groups.

PROCEDURE:
The instructions are given in the words you can use in leading the group.

Silent Preparation / 5 min.
fill out the questionnaire.

Warm-up / 2's / 10 min.
Get together in 2's (find the person you know least) and share your answers to the Warm-up— and explain. (*Share how you would answer the Warm-up and Going Deeper, setting an example for openness and honesty by the way you explain your answers. Then ask the group to pair off in 2's and do the same. After 10 minutes, call time and move on.*)

Going Deeper/4's/15 min.
With your partner join another

How's it going?

WARM-UP

I prefer (circle your choice in each category):

1. drive-in . . . . fancy restaurant
2. going steady . . . . . playing the field
3. staying up late . . . getting up early
4. to be a big frog   to be a little frog
   in a little pond . . . . in a big pond
5. a blind date . . . . a second choice
6. getting a B in   getting an A in
   a tough course . . . . an easy course
7. playing touch . . . . watching pro
   football . . . . football
8. total honesty . . . . . insincere praise
9. to be second-   to be first-string
   string varsity . . . . junior varsity
10. playing it safe . . . .   going for broke

GOING DEEPER

1. For me, the toughest thing about school is (circle two):
   a. getting up in the morning
   b. studying
   c. monotony
   d. homework
   e. getting along with teachers
   f. staying awake in class
   g. grades
   h. tests
   i. English
   j. making friends
   k. hassles from parents
   l. becoming popular
   m. feeling lonely

2. After a tough day at school, I like to relax by (circle two):
   a. napping
   b. watching TV
   c. goofing off
   d. snacking
   e. changing my clothes
   f. playing ball
   g. talking on the phone
   h. reading
   i. taking a walk
   j. going somewhere with a friend

3. Before a big test, I (circle three):
   a. am nervous and shaky
   b. talk a lot
   c. get very quiet
   d. munch constantly
   e. forget about it   i. can't sleep
   f. do crazy things   j. get worried
   g. cram   k. pray a lot
   h. get a headache   l. can't eat

4. I look upon school as (choose three and rank 1, 2, 3):
   _____ prison
   _____ good times
   _____ getting me ready for life
   _____ wasted time
   _____ a chance to make friends
   _____ a refuge from home
   _____ mind-building
   _____ a chance to prove myself
   _____ part of growing up
   _____ unnecessary
   _____ something I have to do
   _____ the best days of my life

OVERTIME CHALLENGE

(Choose the five goals that are most important to you and rank them 1, 2, 3, etc.)
During this program I want to:
   _____ have a ball
   _____ discipline myself
   _____ learn more about the Bible
   _____ meet some new friends
   _____ discover myself
   _____ get my feet on the ground
   _____ improve my personal habits
   _____ learn to love
   _____ belong to a group of people who
         are really serious about God
   _____ develop some deep friendships
   _____ learn about God's will for my life
   _____ settle down in school
   _____ deal with my boredom

twosome (people you know the least) and make a foursome. Then share your answers to the first question in Going Deeper, explaining the whys. Then go around a second time with the second question, etc. (Share your answer to the first question and set the pace for openness and honesty. Call time after 15 minutes and move on.)

Overtime Challenge / 4's or 8's / 15 min.

(You will have to decide if there is time to share the Overtime Challenge and, if so, whether to use groups of 4 or 8. If you are limited for time, stay with the 4's. If you have plenty of time, ask the groups of 4 to double up to make groups of 8.)

Go around your group and let each person share his first, second and third choice and why. (Share your own top three choices and set the pace for openness and honesty.)

Close-out

Stack your hands together in the center of your group (Now offer a brief prayer, saying something like: "Thank you, God, for each other. Amen." Before dismissing the group, ask everyone to write his name on his book. Then collect the books so they are available for the next session.)

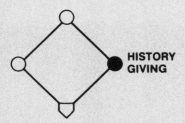

HISTORY GIVING

Objective: To start the process of building support groups.

PROCEDURE

The instructions are given in the words you can use in leading the group.

Silent Preparation / 5 min.
fill out the questionnaire.

Warm-up / 2's / 10 min.
Get together in twos (find the person you know least) and give your answers to the Warm-up in the questionnaire—and explain. *(Share how you would answer the first couple of things and set an example for openness and honesty by the way you explain your answers. After 10 minutes call time and move on.)*

Going Deeper / 4's / 15 min.
With your partner join another twosome (people you know least) to make a foursome. Share your answers to the first question in Going Deeper in the questionnaire and why. Then go around on the

What do you look for?

WARM-UP

I am more like a...than a...*(circle one in each category)*:

1. trapeze artist......... circus clown
2. sprinter.......... distance runner
3. television............... CB radio
4. magnifying glass........ telescope
5. first and 10.............. goal to go
6. Johnny Cash....... Johnny Carson
7. picture.................... puzzle
8. candle.................. light bulb
9. amusement park.......... library
10. quarterback........ blocking back
11. dill pickle............. sugar plum
12. dictionary........... encyclopedia
13. in the game.......... on the side
14. golf ball................ mush ball
15. hotel................. hospital
16. bear..................... tiger
17. spark plug............... battery
18. New York City.......... Arkansas
19. bridge.................... tower
20. oak tree................ evergreen
21. ballet dancer......... two left feet

GOING DEEPER

1. Around people I don't know, I am usually *(circle two)*:
   a. Mr. Super Cool
   b. nervous   g. clumsy
   c. quiet   h. a little uptight
   d. out-going   i. the liberated woman
   e. goosey   j. the life of the party
   f. confident   k. all thumbs
        l.

3. The qualities I look for in a friend are *(choose three and rank 1, 2, 3)*:
   ___ honesty   ___ easygoingness
   ___ openness   ___ brown eyes
   ___ understanding   ___ spiritual depth
   ___ loyalty   ___ good looks
   ___ warmth   ___ compatibility
   ___ compassion   ___ sharp dresser
   ___ fun   ___ moral guts
   ___ muscles   ___ social prestige
   ___ personality   ___ popularity

OVERTIME

If your friends were to describe you with some of the modern-day advertising slogans, which ones would they pick for you? *(choose 3 and rank 1, 2, 3, on the left. On the right rank the top three to describe your group—if there is time.)*

YOURSELF   **YOUR GROUP**

____ Reach out and touch someone (Bell Telephone) ____
____ Things Go better with (Coke) ____
____ Gentle but effective (EX-Lax) ____
____ Everything you want and a little bit more (Safeway) ____
____ Oh what a feeling (Toyota) ____
____ When you care enough to send the very best (Hallmark) ____
____ You've come a long way, baby (Virginia Slims) ____
____ The friendly skies (United Airlines) ____
____ Just one look. That's all it took (Mazda) ____

____ When _____ talks, people listen (E. F. Hutton) ____
____ Don't leave home without it (American Express) ____
____ Let the good times roll (Kawasaki) ____
____ Takes a lickin' and keeps on tickin' (Timex) ____
____ Leave the driving to us (Greyhound) ____
____ Has a better idea (Ford) ____
____ You've got a lot to live (Pepsi) ____
____ Put a tiger in your tank (Exxon) ____
____ We try harder (Avis) ____
____ I can't believe I ate the whole thing (Alka Seltzer) ____
____ You're in good hands (Allstate) ____
____ Think small (Volkswagen) ____
____ Put the snap, crackle, pop into your life (Kelloggs) ____
____ Life is too short not to go first class (Mercedes-Benz) ____
____ We do it all for you (McDonalds) ____
____ What the big boys eat (Wheaties) ____
____ We treat you right (Dairy Queen) ____
____ Because time goes by (Kodak) ____

second question, etc. *(Explain your answer to the first question with the whole group and set the pace for openness and honesty. Call time after 15 minutes and move on.)*

Overtime Challenge / 4's or 8's / 15 min.

(You will have to decide if there is time to share the Overtime Challenge and, if so, whether to use groups of 4 or 8. If time is limited, stay with the 4's. If there is plenty of time, ask two groups of 4 to get together to make groups of 8.)

Go around your group and let each person share the top three slogans his friends would choose for him and explain why. If there is time, go around a second time and let everyone explain the top three slogans he chose for his group. *(Share your top three choices for yourself and set the pace for honesty.)*

Close-out

In each group, stack your hands together in the center. *(While everyone's hands are stacked, say something like: "Thank you, God, for each other. Amen." Ask everyone to write his name on his book. Then collect the books to have them available for the next session.)*

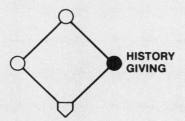

HISTORY GIVING

What's up?

Objective: To start the process of building support groups.

PROCEDURE
The instructions are given in the words you can use in leading the group.

Silent Preparation / 5 min.
fill out the questionnaire.

Warm-up / 2's / 10 min.
Get together in twos (find the person you know least) and give your answers to the Warm-up in the questionnaire—and explain

WARM-UP

I am someone who would *(circle Y for yes, N for no, M for maybe)*:

Y N M   1. holler at the umpire

Y N M   2. kiss on the first date

Y N M   3. gamble on fourth down

Y N M   4. rather walk than ride

Y N M   5. blush at the mention of sex

Y N M   6. stand up for the underdog

Y N M   7. go to the bathroom when the movie got scary

Y N M   8. leave if the game got dull

Y N M   9. slurp for the last drop

Y N M 10. go on a blind date

Y N M 11. rather play ball than eat

Y N M 12. tell a friend he has bad breath

Y N M 13. stay in shape year around

Y N M 14. get to a game early to watch the practice

GOING DEEPER

1. The most exciting thing that is happening in my life at the moment is *(circle one)*:
   a. being in love
   b. getting to know God personally
   c. discovering who I am
   d. belonging to a real Christian fellowship
   e. being on the team at school
   f. making it with my family
   g. discovering my independence
   h. starting a new venture
   i. studying the Bible for myself
   j. running around with friends

2. **In new situations, I usually feel**
   (circle two):
   a. frightened
   b. comfortable
   c. funny/awkward
   d. outgoing
   e. painfully shy
   f. relaxed—easy going
   g. uptight
   h. tongue-tied

3. **The way I feel about this group is**
   (circle two):
   a. OK, but...
   b. warm   e. serene
   c. uneasy   f. excited
   d. a little   g. mixed
        threatened   h. huh?

OVERTIME CHALLENGE

A variety of things are necessary for a healthy, balanced life. Rank the following from 1 to 10, where you need to improve. For instance, you might rank number one "regular physical exercise" because you are getting flabby.

____ regular physical exercise
____ healthy self-image
____ consistent devotional habits
____ well-organized study/work habits
____ clearly defined life goals
____ good family relationships
____ strong personal convictions/values
____ peace of mind about being in God's will
____ steady growth in assuming responsibility
____ good, solid friendships

them. *(Share how you would answer a couple of items and set an example for openness and honesty. Then ask the group to pair off and do the same. After 10 minutes call time and move on.)*

Going Deeper / 4's / 15 min.

With your partner join another twosome (a pair you know the least). Share your choices in the first part of Going Deeper and explain why. Then go around on the second question, etc. *(Explain your answer to the first question and set the pace for openness and honesty. Call time after 15 minutes and move on.)*

Overtime Challenge / 4's or 8's / 15 min.

(You will have to decide if there is time to share the Overtime Challenge and, if so, whether to use groups of 4 or 8. If the time is limited, stay with the 4's. If there is plenty of time, ask two 4's to get together to make groups of 8.)

Go around your group and let each person share the things he ranked 1, 2 and 3 on the list and why. *(Share your own top three and set the pace for openness and honesty.)*

Close-out

Stack your hands together in the center of your group. *(While hands are stacked, say something like: "Thank you, God, for each other. Amen." Ask everyone to write his name on his book. Then collect the books so they are available for the next session.)*

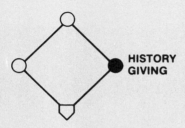

HISTORY GIVING

Objective: To continue the process of building the *same* groups that were started in the previous session/s.

PROCEDURE
The instructions are given in the words you can use in leading the group.

Silent Preparation / 5 min.
fill out the questionnaire.

Warm-up / 2's / 10 min.
Get together with someone from your group of 8 in the last session and explain your answers to the questionnaire Warm-up. *(If you have new people at the meeting, it would be better to start a new group—unless one of the old groups is short. When everyone is paired off, share how you would answer the first two items on the list, setting an example for openness and honesty by the way you explain your answers. After 10 minutes, call time and move on.)*

Going Deeper/4's/15 min.
With your partner join another twosome (from your group of 8 in the last session). Then share your

What's major in your life?

WARM-UP

(Circle the words that best describe the way you see yourself.) I see myself more like a _____ than a _____.
1. quiet lake . . . . rushing stream
2. newsstand . . . . library
3. cultured pearl . . . diamond in rough
4. glossy photo . . . . . . original painting
5. sunrise . . . . sunset
6. clinging vine . . . . touch-me-not
7. country road . . . . . . super highway
8. short story . . . . heavy novel
9. mountain . . . . seashore
10. yesterday . . . . tomorrow
11. morning . . . . evening
12. 100-yd. dash . . . cross-country run
13. Cadillac . . . . jalopy
14. Burt Reynolds . . . . John Wayne
15. rock music . . . . country western

GOING DEEPER

1. When I was a youngster, I really looked forward to *(circle two)*:
   a. summer vacations
   b. family picnics
   c. Little League
   d. Christmastime
   e. state fairs
   f. visits from my grandparents
   g. the day school was out
   h. getting my braces off

2. When school was out, my favorite thing in the summer was *(circle two)*:
   a. camping out
   b. staying up late
   c. sleeping over
   d. goofing off
   e. going to camp
   f. playing ball
   g. hanging around
   h. reading a lot

3. The best adult friend I ever had outside my family was my *(circle one)*:
   a. boss
   b. next door neighbor
   c. scoutmaster
   d. church youth leader
   e. coach
   f. teacher
   g. friend's parents
   h. Sunday School teacher
   i. uncle/aunt

4. The best way for my parents to
   bring out the best in me is to
   (choose three and rank 1, 2, 3):
   ——trust me
   ——leave me alone
   ——lay it on me

——encourage me
——ask my opinion about something
——let me know I'm important
——try to understand me
——love me
——work out expectations with me
——tell me they are proud of me

OVERTIME CHALLENGE

How would you describe yourself with
a recognition plaque? *(Fill in the open
areas according to your own self-
understanding. Start at the bottom
and work up.)*

My Creed. I want my life to stand for *(list three qualities)*:

MY RECOGNITION PLAQUE

Two things I am good at (like singing and swimming):	**Two things that turn me on** (like a sunset and country music):
Two words that describe how I see myself (like timid and caring):	**Two words that describe how I think my friends see me** (like friendly and fun-loving):

answers to the first question in
Going Deeper and explain why. Then
go around a second time on the
second question, etc. *(Share your
own answer to the first question
to help everyone get started. After
15 minutes call time and move on.)*

**Overtime Challenge / 4's or
8's / 15 min.**

*(You will have to decide if there is
time to share the Overtime Challenge and, if so, whether to use
groups of 4 or 8. If you are limited
for time, stay with the 4's. If you
have plenty of time, use the groups
of 8 from the last session.)*

Go around the group, each person sharing what he put down in
the upper left box: *Two things I am
good at.* Then go around with: *Two
things that turn me on.* Cover all
four areas, going around four
times. Finally, go around for the
fifth time with the three things you
put across the top. *(Share what
you put down in a couple boxes
and set the pace for openness
and honesty.)*

Close-out

Stack your hands together in the
center of your group. *(Now give a
few words of prayer, saying something like: "Thank you, God, for
giving us life. Amen." Be sure
everyone has written his name on
his book. Then collect the books
so they are available for the
next session.)*

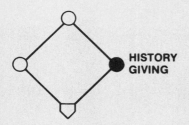

HISTORY GIVING

Where are you coming from?

Objective: To continue the process of building the same teams or support groups that were started in the previous session/s.

PROCEDURE

The instructions are given in the words you can use in leading the group.

Silent Preparation / 5 min.
fill out the questionnaire.

Warm-up / 2's / 10 min.
Get together in twos (with someone from your group of 8 in the last session) and share your answers to the Warm-up in the questionnaire —and why. *(If you have new people at the meeting, start a new group—unless one of the old groups is short. When everyone is paired off, share how you would answer the first three or four things in the Warm-up. Be candid. Be honest. Your explanation will set the pace for sharing. After 10 minutes call time and move on.)*

94

WARM-UP

Down deep inside I am a...*(put a dot on each line someplace between the two words to indicate where you are):*

1. listener _____ talker
2. spender _____ saver
3. driver _____ rider
4. optimist _____ pessimist
5. loner _____ grouper
6. leader _____ follower
7. doer _____ thinker
8. pitcher _____ catcher
9. rabbit _____ turtle
10. fighter _____ peacemaker
11. giver _____ receiver
12. player _____ spectator
13. pioneer _____ settler
14. right now _____ later
15. easy going _____ hyper

GOING DEEPER

1. When I was a kid, the high point of my summer vacation was *(circle one)*:
   a. playing ball
   b. family trips
   c. reading lots of books
   d. camp
   e. goofing off
   f. visiting my grandparents
   g. biking
   h. swimming
   i. going fishing
   j.

2. The event I remember most in my childhood was *(circle one)*:
   a. the assassination of
   _____
   b. the death of my pet
   c. winning the _____
   d. my first holy communion
   e. the first time I played hooky
   f. my own brush with death
   g. my biggest licking
   h.

3. Outside my parents, the people who had the greatest influence upon my life were my *(rank top three 1, 2, 3)*:
   _____ teachers
   _____ grandparents
   _____ pastor
   _____ scoutmaster
   _____ coach
   _____ uncle/aunt
   _____ youth leader
   _____ brother/sister
   _____ sports heroes
   _____ friends

OVERTIME CHALLENGE

If you were to compile a scrapbook of what you liked best as a child, what pictures would you collect? *(For each photo jot down a word or sketch.)*

MY CHILDHOOD SCRAPBOOK

> At age 6, my favorite TV show

> At age 10, my favorite sport *(like soccer or horseback riding)*

> The biggest disappointment I ever had

> At age 8, my favorite pet *(like my pony or turtle)*

> At age 12, the hero in my life *(like O.J. Simpson or Robert Redford)*

> The time in my life when God became more than a name to me *(like at summer camp or first communion)*

Going Deeper / 4's / 15 min.

With your partner join another twosome (from your group of 8 in the last session) to make a foursome. Take the first question and let everyone give his answer and explain why. Then go around on the second question, etc. *(Share your own answer to the first question. Be honest. Call time after 15 minutes and move on.)*

Overtime Challenge / 4's or 8's / 15 min.

(You will have to decide if there is time to share the Overtime Challenge and, if so, whether to use groups of 4 or 8. If time is limited, stay with the 4's. If there is plenty of time, use the groups of 8 from the last session.)

Go around your group and let each person share what he put in the top left box. Then go around on another box, etc.

Close-out

In each group stack your hands together in the center. *(While everyone's hands are stacked, say something like: "Thank you, God, for this time together. Amen." Ask newcomers to write their names in their books. Then collect all of the books.)*

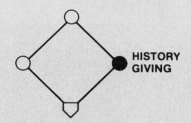

HISTORY GIVING

Objective: To continue the process of building the same teams or groups that were started in the previous session/s.

PROCEDURE

The instructions are given in the words you can use in leading the group.

Silent Preparation / 5 min.

fill out the questionnaire.

Warm-Up / 2's / 10 min.

Get together in twos (find someone from your previous group of 8) and explain your answers to the Warm-up in the questionnaire. *(Take a moment and explain your answer for the first question...Set the pace for good-natured fun. After 10 minutes call time and move on.)*

Going Deeper / 4's / 15 min.

With your partner join another pair (from your previous group of 8). Share your answers to the first question in Going Deeper and explain why. Then go around on the second question, etc. *(Share your own answer to the first question and set the pace for*

What are your values?

WARM-UP

1. When it comes to making a tough decision, I generally *(circle one)*:
   a. struggle for days
   b. make a snap decision
   c. wait to see what someone else will do
   d. ask for advice
   e. never ask for advice
   f. hope it will go away
   h. take myself on a long walk

2. The hardest decisions for me are usually when *(rank top three)*:
   _____ money is involved
   _____ friendship is involved
   _____ my reputation is on the line
   _____ my popularity is at stake
   _____ my moral values are involved

3. The biggest fear I have to deal with in standing up for what I believe is *(circle one)*:
   a. being laughed at
   b. standing alone
   c. getting someone else in trouble
   d. being wrong
   e. losing my friends
   f. _____

4. In my home, my parents stressed that morality is *(circle one)*:
   a. a very individual thing
   b. a matter of black and white
   c. the mark of a gentleman/lady
   d. relative
   e. dependent upon the circumstances
   f. _____

GOING DEEPER

There are many touchy situations in life that call for decisions. You may take one of a variety of actions or do nothing. *(Choose one for each situation below.)*

1. You don't agree with the behavior of a friend. What do you do?
   a. ignore it
   b. confront him about it
   c. stop running around with him
   d. talk to someone else about it

2. You are the friend of someone who has been deliberately omitted from a party. What do you do?
   a. ignore the affront and go
   b. refuse to go
   c. call and ask why

3. Your friends are going out for a beer bust and you're invited. What do you do?
   a. tell them you don't drink
   b. make some excuse
   c. go along but don't drink
   d. join the party
   e. tell their parents

4. Your best friend never studies. It's exam time and he wants to cheat off your paper. He'll flunk if you don't let him. What do you do?
   a. let him copy
   b. tell the teacher
   c. cover your paper
   d. quietly explain your feelings about cheating
   e. refuse him but offer to help him study for the next exam

OVERTIME CHALLENGE

When it comes to making the major decisions in your life, whom are the people you consult—or unconsciously listen to? *(Write the names in the proper categories around the table. You may use two names for one position or the same name twice if the person serves in both capacities. Then go back and write the appropriate symbols next to the names.)*

1. *Head Coach:* makes the final decision, the overall strategy, the game plan.
2. *Assistant Coach:* back-up person; carries out coach's instructions; go-between for coach with players.
3. *Offensive Coach:* mainly works on forward movement for players.
4. *Defensive Coach:* mainly works on holding the line, neutralizing the opposition.
5. *Trainer:* helps with conditioning; soothes players after workouts.

✗   if you would like to remove the person from your staff

↑   if the person gives you a lot of encouragement and uplift

↓   if the person tends to drag you down or exert negative influence

✓   if the person were freely chosen by you to serve on your staff

☆   if the person is likely to remain on your staff a long time

Head Coach

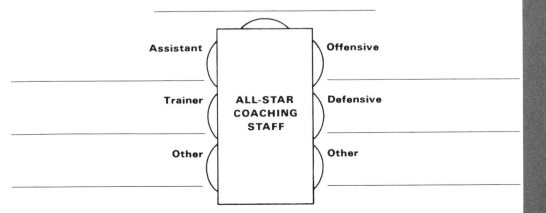

Assistant   Offensive

Trainer   **ALL-STAR COACHING STAFF**   Defensive

Other   Other

honesty. Call time after 15 minutes and move on.)

Overtime Challenge / 4's or 8's / 15 min.

(You will have to decide if there is time to share the Overtime Challenge and, if so, whether to use groups of 4 or 8. If you are limited for time, stay with the 4's. If you have plenty of time, have the groups of 8 from the last session get together.)

Go around your group and let each person explain his All-Star Coaching Staff. In particular, tell why you chose the person you did as Head Coach. *(Explain whom you put down for your Coaching Staff and set the pace for openness and honesty with your explanation.)*

For instance:
Head Coach—my group of friends
Assistant Coach—myself
Offensive Coach—my teacher
Defensive Coach—my father
Trainer—my mother
Other—my coach
Other—my girlfriend/boyfriend

Close-out

Stack your hands together in the center of the group. *(While everyone's hands are stacked, say something like: "Thank you, God, for giving us life. Amen." Be sure everyone has his name on his book. Then collect the books so they are available for the next session.)*

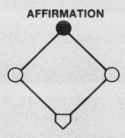

Objective: To have fun as a sharing group, affirming the good things you see in each other.

PROCEDURE

The instructions are given in the words you can use in leading the group.

Silent Preparation / 5 min.

(Ask the groups of 8 who have been together up to now in the program to sit together so they can see each other while filling out the questionnaire. If you have newcomers, ask them to join the group where they know most of the people.)
fill out the questionnaire.

Warm-up / 8's / 10 min.

In your group of 8, ask one person to sit in silence while the others explain the handles they picked to describe him and why. When everyone has finished, let this person explain the handle he picked for himself.

Then ask the next person to stay quiet while the others explain

98

How do I look?

WARM-UP

If you had to describe the others in your group with a comic strip character, what would you choose for each person? Below is a list of some comic strip characters . . . and you can add others if you wish. Jot down the initials of the people in your group next to the characters in the comic you associate with their personalities.

_____Charlie Brown
_____Snoopy
_____Schroeder
_____Garfield
_____Miss Piggy
_____Animal
_____Winnie the Pooh
_____Yogi Bear
_____Paddington
_____Scooby Doo
_____Big Bird
_____Kermit
_____E.T.
_____Red Baron
_____Superman
_____Pink Panther
_____Cookie Monster
_____Dino
_____Other _____
_____Other _____

GOING DEEPER

If you were asked to give an award to each person in your group, based on the contribution each has made to your life and the life of the group, what would you give them? *(Jot the name of each person next to the award you feel he deserves.)*

_____ **SPARK PLUG: for the person who ignited the group experience.**
_____ **MEGAPHONE: for the person who cheered us on with his encouragement.**
_____ **DEAR ABBY AWARD: for the person who cared enough to listen whenever someone had a problem to unload.**
_____ **ROYAL GIRDLE: for the person who drew us together into a real team.**
_____ **WATER BALLOON: for the person who came through at the right moment with a little humor to keep us laughing.**
_____ **ROCK OF GIBRALTER: for the person who stood strong in the tough times when we needed a rock.**
_____ **RHINESTONE COWBOY: for the person who went out of his way to accept me and make me feel good.**
_____ **GLASS SLIPPER: for the person who came to the party and showed the rest of us how exciting the Christian lifestyle really is.**
_____ **KING ARTHUR'S SWORD: for the one who found a new mission in life and caused the rest of us to stop and think.**
_____ **SERENDIPITY CROWN: for the person who as far as I am concerned has shown the greatest growth during this program.**

OVERTIME CHALLENGE

To describe how you feel about the crazy group of guys and gals in this program, how about comparing your involvement to a football stadium! *(Put three marks on the diagram to symbolize your feelings. For instance you might put the 0 in the grandstand because you felt like a spectator at the beginning of the program. And you might put the X on the bench because right now you are on the team but not really in the game.)*

○   where you were at the beginning of this program

✗   where you are right now

☆   where you would like to be soon

```
┌─────────────────────────────┐
│      GRANDSTAND             │
│      (for spectators)       │
└─────────────────────────────┘

      ┌───────────────┐
      │ BENCH (team)  │
      └───────────────┘

┌──────────────────────┐  ┌──────┐
│                      │  │ THE  │
│   PLAYING FIELD      │  │SHOW- │
│  (where the action   │  │ ERS  │
│       is)            │  │      │
└──────────────────────┘  └──────┘
```

Also:

1. What is the score right now in the game?

2. Is your team ahead or behind?

3. What is the next play you would call?

their choices of handles for him, etc., until everyone has been covered. *(Pick somebody in a group near you and explain the handle you would pick for him. Set the pace for good-natured fun with your explanation. Give the groups 10 minutes, then call time and move on.)*

Going Deeper/8's/15 min.

Stay with your group and move on to Going Deeper. Ask one individual to sit in silence while the others explain the awards they picked for him and why. Then, move on to the next person and go around again, etc., until everyone has been the subject. *(Pick out one person and explain the award you would give him and why. By your example set the pace for genuine, sincere affirmation.)*

Overtime Challenge / 8's / 15 min.

Go around in your group and let each person show where he put the three marks on his stadium diagram and explain why. *(Describe your feelings by explaining to the group where you put your marks.)*

Close-out

Stack your hands together in the center of your group. *(Offer a brief prayer, saying something like: "Thank you, God, for giving us one another. Amen." Ask newcomers to write their names in their books. Then pick up all the books.)*

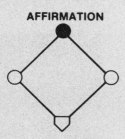

AFFIRMATION

What's my thing?

Objective: To have fun affirming the good things you see in each other as a support group.

PROCEDURE

The instructions are given in the words you can use in leading the group.

Silent Preparation / 5 min.

(Ask the groups of 8 who have been together up to now in the program to sit together so that they can see each other while filling out the questionnaire. If you have newcomers, ask them to join a group in which they know most of the people.)
fill out the questionnaire.

Warm-up / 8's / 10 min.

In your group of 8, ask one person to sit in silence while everyone else explains the car he picked for this person and why. When everyone has finished, let this person name the car he would pick for himself and explain why.

Then move on to the next person. Ask him to remain quiet while the others explain the cars they have chosen for him and why, etc., until everyone has been covered. *(Name someone in a group near you and explain which*

WARM-UP

If you were to choose cars for the members of your group, what kinds would you get? *(Jot the name of each group member next to the car you feel best fits him.)*

_____ fire-red Corvett with telephone (used)

_____ Dune Buggy with a roll bar

_____ rebuilt 62 Chevy convertible with lots of class

_____ pink T-Bird with fur steering wheel and leopard skin interior

_____ customized van with hand painted exterior and built-in hi-fi

_____ Volkswagen with Rolls Royce front

_____ 4-wheel-drive Jeep—built for wilderness driving

_____ 1929 Model T Ford with rumble seat

_____ pick-up truck with high-jacks for all the girls

_____ Lincoln Continental, with built-in "refreshment" bar

_____ good used car with low mileage, dependable transportation

GOING DEEPER

If you were to compare the various members in your group to essential car parts, based on the contributions they have made to the group, what would you choose for each one? *(Jot each person's name next to the part you feel fits him.)*

_____ tire—carries weight of group, takes bumps, keeps us going

_____ accelerator—sets the pace for the group

_____ headlights—gives us a clear view of where we're going

_____ springs/shocks—willing to cushion the hard knocks

_____ radio: music—keeps us inspired all along the way

_____ air conditioner—helps us to keep our cool

_____ transmission—good at shifting into deeper things

_____ steering wheel—outspoken decision maker

_____ roll bar—comes through in times of crisis

_____ road map—keeps us heading in the right direction

_____ spark plug—gets things started with lots of energy

_____ brakes—avoids the collisions that hurt

OVERTIME CHALLENGE

Explain how you feel about this program and the group you are in by comparing your feelings to a basketball game! Here is a basketball court with the various positions where you might be. *(Put three marks on the diagram. For instance, you might put an O in the bleachers because you felt like a spectator at the beginning of the program. And you might put an X on the player's bench because you are on the team now but not yet really in the game.)*

○ **where you were at the beginning of the program**

✕ **where you are right now**

☆ **where you want to be**

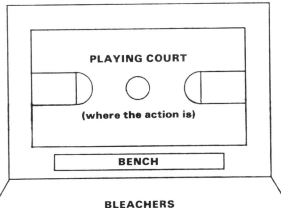

```
┌──────────────────────────────────┐
│   SHOWERS                        │
└──────────────────────────────────┘
```

Also:

What is the score right now?

What is the game plan for the next quarter?

```
        PLAYING COURT

      (where the action is)

         BENCH

        BLEACHERS
      (for spectators)
```

car you would choose for him and why. Set the pace for good-natured fun and honest affirmation. After 10 minutes call time and move on.)

Going Deeper / 8's / 15 min.

Stay with your group but move on to Going Deeper in the questionnaire. Ask one person to remain silent while the others explain why they chose the particular car parts they did for him. Move on to the next person and go around again, etc., until everyone has been covered. *(Pick out one person and explain the parts you would choose for him. Set the pace for genuine, honest affirmation.)*

Overtime Challenge / 8's / 15 min.

Go around in your group and let each person explain where he put the marks in his basketball diagram and why. *(Start this off with your own explanation.)*

Close-out

In each group, stack your hands together in the center of your group. *(While everyone's hands are stacked, say something like: "Thank you, God, for what we have experienced together as a support team. Amen." Ask newcomers to write their names in their books. Collect all the books.)*

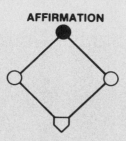

What's my style?

Objective: To have fun affirming the good things you see in each other as a support group.

PROCEDURE

The instructions are given in the words you can use in leading the group.

Silent Preparation / 5 min.

(Ask the groups of 8 who have been together up to now in this program to sit together so they can see each other while filling out the questionnaire. If there are newcomers, ask them to join the groups in which they know the most people.)

fill out the questionnaire.

Warm-up / 8's / 10 min.

In your group of 8, ask one person to sit in silence while the others explain which special jeans they picked for him and why.

When everyone has finished, let the person explain which ones he picked for himself. Then move on to the next person. He remains quiet while the others explain their choices of jeans.

WARM-UP

If you had to get a pair of jeans for everybody in your group, what kind would you get to fit each one's personality? *(Jot down the names of the people in your group beside the jeans you feel they would be most comfortable in.)*

_____ green jeans
_____ new jeans
_____ cut-offs
_____ holey jeans
_____ patched jeans
_____ lots of pockets
_____ fringed jeans
_____ embroidered jeans
_____ straight-legged
_____ faded
_____ tie-dyed
_____ tight
_____ flares
_____ boot-cut
_____ zipper loaded
_____ designer jeans

GOING DEEPER

If you had to pick one person from your sharing group for each of the following situations, who would you pick? *(Write one name beside each situation.)*

_____ you are in trouble and need someone to talk to at 3a.m.
_____ you need someone to be the godparent of your child
_____ you need a best man or maid of honor for your wedding
_____ you need someone to accompany you around the world
_____ you need someone in charge of your estate after you die
_____ you need a business partner
_____ you need someone to go shopping with
_____ you need someone to entrust your kids to in the event of your death
_____ you need someone to go backpacking with you in the wilderness for seven days
_____ you need someone from whom you can get a quick loan
_____ you need someone to stand by you when the whole world is against you—no matter what the consequences are

OVERTIME CHALLENGE

If you had to describe how you felt about your support group by comparing your involvement to a baseball game, how would you do it? *(Put three marks someplace on the diagram. For instance, you might put an O in the grandstand because you felt like a spectator at the beginning of the program; you might put an X on the player's bench because now you feel that you are really on the team but not yet in the game.)*

O where you were at the beginning of this program

X where you are right now

☆ where you would like to be soon

Infield

Outfield (feelin' out of it)

Bench (for non-players)

Grandstand (for spectators)

Shower

Also:
1. What is the score right now in the game? _____
2. What strategy would you suggest for the next inning? _____

(Choose someone in a group near you and explain the product you would pick for him. Set the pace for good-natured fun with your explanation. After 10 minutes call time and move on.)

Going Deeper / 8's / 15 min.

Stay with your group and move on to Going Deeper in the questionnaire. Ask one person to sit silently while the others explain the occasion they picked for him and why. Then move on to the next person and go around again, etc., until everyone has been covered. *(Choose a person and explain the occasion you would like to share with him and why. Set the pace for genuine, sincere affirmation by what you say.)*

Overtime Challenge / 8's / 15 min.

Go around in your group and let each person explain where he put the three marks on the baseball diagram and why. *(Model this by explaining to the group where you see yourself.)*

Close-out

In each group, stack your hands together in the center of your group. *(While everyone's hands are stacked, say something like: "Thank you, God, for giving us one another. Amen." Ask newcomers to write their names in their books. Then pick up all the books.)*

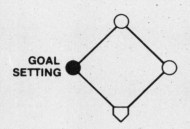

GOAL
SETTING

Objective: To evaluate the program up to this point.

PROCEDURE

The instructions are given in the words you can use in leading the group.

Silent Preparation / 5 min.
fill out the questionnaire.

Warm-up / 4's / 10 min.
Get together with 3 other people from your group of 8 and share your answers to the Warm-up in the questionnaire—one question at

What's the score?

WARM-UP

1. The time I do my best thinking is *(circle one)*:
   a. in the shower
   b. late at night
   c. when I'm alone
   d. at camp
   e. listening to music
   f. at church
   g. when I'm challenged

2. The thing that causes me to stop and think about my life is *(circle two)*:
   a. sickness
   b. death in the family
   c. loss of a close friend
   d. failure
   e. a big disappointment
   f. being alone
   g. coming to a crossroads

3. When I die, I would like it to be said of me *(circle one)*:
   a. I followed the quest
   b. I had a ball
   c. I gave it all I had
   d. I was true to my convictions
   e. I lived life to the fullest
   f. I was a loyal friend
   g. _____

4. If I could give three things to my children, I would want them to have *(rank your top three choices 1, 2, 3)*:
   ____ good health
   ____ happy marriage
   ____ secure job
   ____ a lot of money
   ____ an opportunity to make something of themselves
   ____ moral courage
   ____ success in their fields
   ____ leaders in the community

GOING DEEPER

1. The thing I appreciate most about this program is *(circle one)*:
   a. the good time together
   b. the deep friendships
   c. the time away from home
   d. the chance to talk about our problems
   e. our spiritual growth

2. The two greatest things I have learned during our times together are *(circle two)*:
   a. it's not "sissy" to be a Christian
   b. it's OK to have problems
   c. I have some great gifts
   d. I need to work on my spiritual priorities
   e. living a Christian life isn't easy
   f. I am an important member of God's team

3. If I had the chance to do this program again, I think I would *(circle one)*:
   a. get more involved at the beginning
   b. open up more
   c. get others involved
   d. take it more seriously
   e. have to think about it
   f. not join the next time

OVERTIME CHALLENGE

The three playing fields represent three areas of your life. Where do you see yourself? *(Place three marks on each field.)*

◯ where you were at the beginning of this program

✕ where you are right now

☆ where you want to be a year from now

A. IN MY RELATIONSHIP WITH MYSELF: believing in myself—that I am important, that I have unique ability, that I am a valuable person.

SAFETY grim — TOUCH-DOWN wow!

B. IN MY RELATIONSHIP WITH MY FAMILY: believing in my family—that I am a valuable and important member of my family.

SAFETY grim — TOUCH-DOWN wow!

C. IN MY RELATIONSHIP WITH OTHERS: believing in my friendships—that I am a valuable and important person to my friends.

SAFETY grim — TOUCH-DOWN wow!

a time. Go around on the first question; then go around a second time on the second question, etc. *(Share your answer to the first question and set the pace for openness and honesty. Give the group 10 minutes, then call time and move on.)*

Going Deeper/8's/15 min.

Regather your group of 8 and give everyone a chance to share his answers to Going Deeper— one question at a time. *(Share your answer first and set the pace for honesty.)*

Overtime Challenge / 2's / 15 min.

Pair off with someone from your group of 8 and give each other a chance to describe the three relationships in your life and how you marked yourself. Explain in detail the reasons for marking yourself as you did. *(Set the pace here for openness and honesty by taking one of the three areas and explaining how and why you marked yourself as you did.)*

Close-out

Stack your hands together in the center of your group. *(Offer a few words of prayer, saying something like: "Thank you, God, for the chance to be together and to discover what you want in our lives. Amen." Collect the books.)*

How did it go?

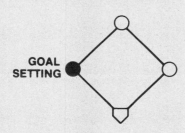

GOAL SETTING

Objective: To evaluate the program up to this point and make plans for the days ahead.

PROCEDURE

The instructions are given in the words you can use in leading the group.

WARM-UP

1. The place I retreat to when I need to "get myself together" is *(circle one)*:
   a. the park
   b. a lake
   c. fishing spot
   d. the bathtub
   e. TV
   f. the woods
   g. a quiet chapel
   h. a ball game
   k. the movies
   l. the beach
   m. the mountains
   n. an easy chair
   o. my room
   p. out of the house
   q. anywhere

2. The person I admire most is *(choose three and rank 1, 2, 3)*:
   ____ Ralph Nader
   ____ Billy Graham
   ____ Mother Theresa
   ____ John Denver
   ____ Chris Evert
   ____ Olivia Newton John
   ____ Aleksandr Solzhenitsyn
   ____ Helen Keller
   ____ Martin Luther King, Jr.
   ____ Albert Einstein
   ____ Pope John
   ____ Albert Schweitzer
   ____ Edmund Hillary
   ____ Marie Curie
   ____ Vince Lombardi
   ____ Cesar Chavez

3. My philosophy of life might be summarized by the phrase *(circle first and last choice)*:
   a. if it feels good, do it
   b. what the "heck"
   c. grab all the "gusto" you can
   d. love and be happy
   e. do unto others as you want them to do unto you
   f. look out for number one
   g. roll with the punches
   h. I don't want to grow up
   i. if you want something bad enough you'll get it

4. If I had a million dollars, I would *(circle one)*:
   a. quit school/work right now
   b. buy a yacht
   c. start my own business
   d. run for president
   e. take my friends around the world
   f. feed everybody
   g. invest it all
   h. get my parents to retire and enjoy life
   i. give it all away and stay as I am
   j. have one great, big, continuous party

GOING DEEPER

1. As I think back, the reason why I started coming to this group was (circle one):
   a. someone made me
   b. everyone else was coming
   c. someone special invited me
   d. I wanted to find out what this was all about
   e. I didn't have anything else to do
   f. I was searching for something and I thought this might help
   g. don't know

2. The experience of opening up and sharing my ideas and problems with this support group has been (circle two):
   a. scary
   b. invaluable
   c. very difficult
   d. OK, but
   e. exciting
   f. just what I needed
   g. a life-changing experience
   h. a beautiful breakthrough

3. The high point for me in this program has been the (circle two):
   a. fun
   b. times of prayer
   c. feeling of belonging to others who really care
   d. being with people who are committed to Christ

(continued)

   e. knowing you are not alone in your problems
   f. finding myself again
   g. Bible study
   h. learning to deal with my hangups

OVERTIME CHALLENGE

How about a strategy program for helping you to think through your personal goals?

a. *First column. (Jot down three concerns in your life right now, such as: to increase my grades, to work on my relationships at home, to save some money for college.)*

b. *Second column. (Take the most important concern and jot down three "wishes" you would like to make about that area of concern. For instance if working on your relationships at home was number 1, then your wishes might be: I wish I could talk to my dad alone, I wish I could explain to him how I feel, etc.)*

c. *Third column. (With your wishes in mind, list three specific projects for this next week—to start solving your most important concern. For instance: I will write my dad a note telling him how I feel and asking him to give me an hour next week, I will invite him out for a hamburger where we can talk alone, etc.)*

MY MAJOR CONCERNS	I WISH I COULD	I WILL

Silent Preparation / 5 min.
fill out the questionnaire.

Warm-up / 4's / 10 min.
Get together with four people from your group of 8 and share your answers to the Warm-up— one question at a time. That is, go around on the first question; then go around on the second question, etc. *(Share your answer to the first question and set the pace for openness and honesty. After 10 minutes call time and move on.)*

Going Deeper / 8's / 15 min.
Regather your group of 8 and give everyone a chance to share his answers to Going Deeper in the questionnaire—one question at a time. *(Share your answer to the first question and set the pace for honesty.)*

Overtime Challenge / 2's / 15 min.
Pair off with one other person from your group of 8 and give each other a chance to explain his goal-setting exercise. Go into detail on the second and third columns —"I wish I could" and "I will." Nail down the plan of action you intend to take in the next seven days. *(Set the pace here for openness and honesty by explaining your own wishes and your plan of action.)*

Close-out
In each group, stack your hands together in the center. *(While everyone's hands are stacked, say something like: "Thank you, God, for this chance to think through the next steps in our lives. Amen." Collect the books.*

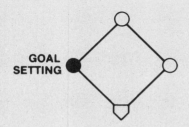

GOAL SETTING

Where are you going?

Objective: To evaluate the program up to this point.

PROCEDURE

Instructions are given in the words you can use in leading the group.

Silent Preparation / 5 min.
fill out the questionnaire.

Warm-up / 4's / 10 min.

Get together with four people from your group of 8 and share your answers to the Warm-up — one question at a time. That is, go around on the first question; then go around on the second question, etc. *(Share your answer to the first question and set the pace for openness and honesty. After 10 minutes call time and move on.)*

WARM-UP

1. I put the most effort into doing a good job when *(circle two)*:
   a. I get near my goal
   b. others are watching me
   c. I am challenged
   d. everything is new
   e. there is a lot of competition
   f. someone needs my help
   g. the pressure is intense
   h. everything is great at home
   i. there is no one else to do it
   j. no one thinks I can do it
   k. everyone thinks I can do it
   l. the pay is right

2. When I lose out on something I want, I usually *(circle two)*:
   a. get down on myself
   b. blame somebody else
   c. hide from people
   d. throw a tantrum
   e. stay calm and cool
   f. shake it off easily
   g. am deeply hurt
   h. take it out on someone at home
   i. expected the worst
   j. am terribly angry
   k. cry and get over it

GOING DEEPER

1. Since being in this support group, I feel that I have made real progress in *(rank top three 1, 2, 3)*:
   ____ sorting out my priorities
   ____ settling down at school or at work
   ____ developing my self-confidence
   ____ developing my spiritual life
   ____ letting others know me
   ____ dealing with my family hassles
   ____ dealing with my relationships at school/on the job

2. I still have a long way to go in *(rank top three)*:
   ____ working on my temper
   ____ cleaning up my thought-life
   ____ risking deeper relationships
   ____ my spiritual consistency
   ____ my quality of work
   ____ my self-confidence

3. If I am going to go any further, I will need a little more *(circle one)*:
   a. guts
   b. group support
   c. spiritual commitment
   d. help from God
   e. determination
   f. time alone
   g. self-confidence

OVERTIME CHALLENGE

Below are three baseball diamonds to represent three relationships of your life. *(On each baseball diamond, put two marks.)*

○ **where you were at the beginning of this program**

✗ **where you are right now**

A. MY RELATIONSHIP WITH MYSELF:
I am feeling good about myself; believing I have real abilities, a lot of things going for me; able to love myself.

B. MY RELATIONSHIP WITH OTHERS:
I am feeling good about sharing myself with others without fear of being put down or laughed at. I am able to reach out, care about others, share my deep feelings—even some of my needs and problems.

C. MY RELATIONSHIP WITH GOD: I am feeling good about knowing God personally through Jesus Christ. I am getting my spiritual life together, putting God first in my life.

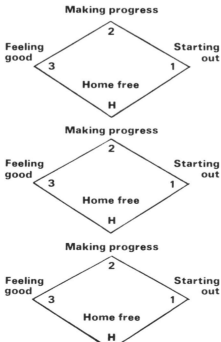

Making progress

Feeling good — 2 — Starting out

3 — 1

Home free

H

Making progress

Feeling good — 2 — Starting out

3 — 1

Home free

H

Making progress

Feeling good — 2 — Starting out

3 — 1

Home free

H

Going Deeper / 8's / 15 min.
Regather your group of 8 and give everyone a chance to share answers to Going Deeper —one question around at a time. *(Share your answer to the first question and set the pace for honesty.)*

Overtime Challenge / 2's / 15 min.
Pair off with one other person from your group of 8 and explain to each other why you marked the three relationships in your life as you did. Go into detail. *(Set the pace here for real honesty by taking one of the areas and explaining how and why you marked yourself as you did.)*

Close-out
In each group, stack your hands together in the center of your group. *(While everyone's hands are stacked, say something like: "Thank you, God, for the chance to be together this way, supporting one another. Amen." Collect the books.)*

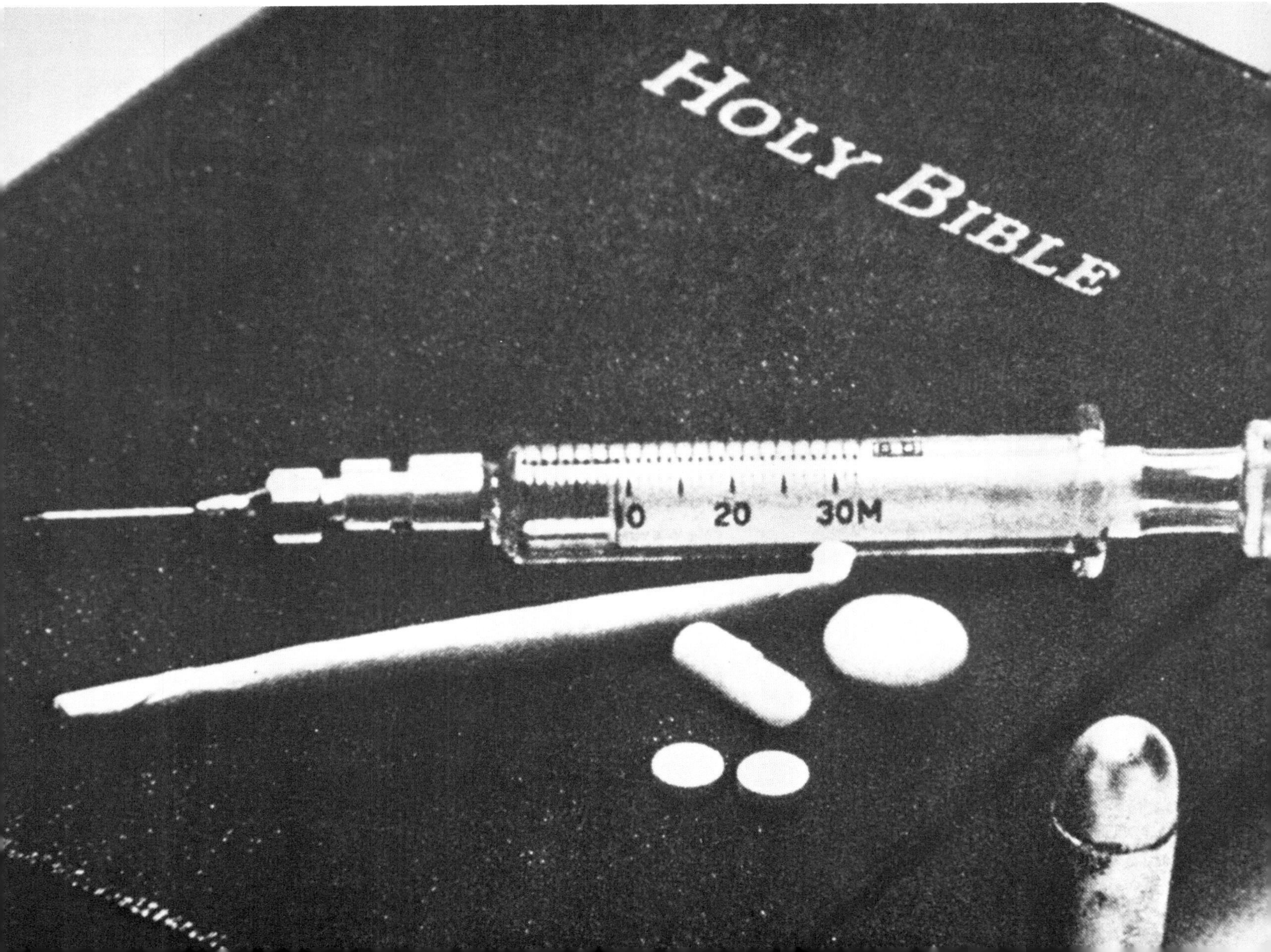
HOLY BIBLE
10 20 30M

Values Clarification

STRUCTURED QUESTIONNAIRES ON THE PARABLES

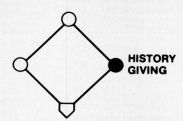

**HISTORY
GIVING**

Objective: To examine your possessions in the light of the parables of the Hidden Treasure and the Pearl of Great Price, and to use your results as the basis for a sharing experience.

PROCEDURE

The instructions are given in the words you can use in leading the group.

Silent Preparation / 5 min.
fill out the questionnaire.

Warm-up / 4's / 5 min.
Get together with 3 other people from your group of 8 and share the items you would grab in the event of fire. *(Take a moment and share your list with the entire group. Set the pace for honesty and openness. Then ask each group of 4 to proceed. After 5 minutes call time and move on.)*

Going Deeper / 4's / 15 min.
Stay in your group of 4 and, starting with the first symbol, let everyone explain where he placed

THE PARABLE OF THE HIDDEN TREASURE

Jesus said, "The Kingdom of heaven is like a treasure hidden in a field. A man happens to find it, so he covers it up again. He is so happy that he goes and sells everything he has, and then goes back and buys the field."

THE PARABLE OF THE PEARL

"Also, the Kingdom of heaven is like a buyer looking for fine pearls. When he finds one that is unusually fine, he goes and sells everything he has, and buys the pearl."

MATTHEW 13:44-46

What's your main thing?

WARM-UP

Assume for a moment that your house is on fire. The people and pets in the house are safe. You have two minutes to run through the house and snatch the the most important possessions in your life. In your imagination run through every room, including the garage. *(Jot down the specific items that you would grab—because of their personal value to you. For instance: letter jacket, hi-fi, checkbook, Honda, etc. Don't put down just "clothes"; put down which clothes. The more specific the better! And consider size and weight no problem!)*

_____

_____

_____

_____

_____

_____

_____

_____

GOING DEEPER

Read over the Scripture passage and consider the "treasures" you just listed. How would you describe them? *(Place the following symbols beside the appropriate items. You may use a symbol twice and you may apply two or three symbols to the same item.)*

○ has just recently become of value to me

↓ will likely go down in value *to me* in five years

↑ will likely go up in value *to me* in five years

△ to get this item I would risk returning to the house while it's in flames

✕ its loss would seriously affect my life and lifestyle

☆ would come the closest to being the "pearl of great price" in my life right now

P would probably be on my parents' list too

F would probably be on my friends' list too

OVERTIME CHALLENGE

1. From this exercise, it seems to me that my values, as far as my possessions are concerned, are *(circle one in each category):*
   a. really changing . . fairly constant
   b. fuzzy . . . . clear
   c. centered around   centered around
      people . . . . things
   d. closer to my   closer to my
      parents'. . . . . friends'
   e. close to the   far from the
      meaning of the   meaning of the
      Pearl of Great   Pearl of Great
      Price . . . . Price

2. Right now, the "pearl of great price" in my life is probably *(circle two):*
   a. girls
   b. sports   h. Christ
   c. fun   i. me
   d. grades   j. don't know
   e. popularity   k. money
   f. a college degree l. success
   g. kicks   m. the church

3. In comparison to the things on my list, I value the Kingdom of heaven *(circle one):*
   a. to the same degree
   b. the same, but
   c. but...but...
   d. ouch
   e. more all the time

it and why. Then go around on the next symbol, etc., until you have covered all of them. *(Take a moment and tell where you placed the circle and explain why. Be honest. Your example will set the pace for the groups. After 15 minutes call time and move on.)*

Overtime Challenge / 2's or 8's / 15 min.

Decide if there is time to share the Overtime Challenge and, if so, whether to use groups of 2 or 8. If you are limited for time, have the groups divide into 2's. If there is plenty of time, ask that the previous groups of 8 get together again—or the groups of 4's to double up.)

Take the first question and go around your group, letting each person explain his choices. Then go around on the second question, etc. *(Take a moment and share your choices on the first question. Be painfully honest!!! Your example will set the pace for the groups to follow.)*

Close-out

In each group, stand together in a close circle—with your arms over each other's shoulders. *(Pray briefly, saying something like: "Thank you, God, for giving us something of great value to live for. Amen." Ask everyone to write his name in his book. Collect the books.)*

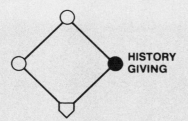

HISTORY GIVING

Who can you count on?

Objective: To examine your friendships in the light of the parable of the Good Samaritan, and to use your results as the basis for a sharing experience.

PROCEDURE

The instructions are given in the words you can use in leading the group.

Silent Preparation / 5 min.
fill out the questionnaire.

Warm-up / 4's / 5 min.
Get together with 3 other people from your group of 8 in the previous session and explain the phone numbers you use most often. *(Take a moment and explain your list to the entire group. Set the pace for openness and honesty. Then ask each group of 4 to proceed. After 5 minutes call time and move on.)*

Going Deeper / 4's / 15 min.
Stay with your group of 4 and explain to each other where and why you placed the symbols as you did. Start with the first symbol

WARM-UP

What phone numbers do you use the most right now? (*List the numbers you call most frequently. If you cannot remember a number, jot down the person or location. Include your home and church phone numbers.*)

_____
_____
_____
_____
_____
_____
_____
_____
_____
_____
_____

THE PARABLE OF THE GOOD SAMARITAN

Jesus answered, "There was a man who was going down from Jerusalem to Jericho, when robbers attacked him, stripped him, and beat him up, leaving him half dead. It so happened that a priest was going down that road; when he saw the man he walked on by, on the other side. In the same way a Levite also came there, went over and looked at the man, and then walked on by, on the other side.

"But a certain Samaritan who was traveling that way came upon him, and when he saw the man his heart was filled with pity. He went over to him, poured oil and wine on his wounds and bandaged them; then he put the man on his own animal and took him to an inn, where he took care of him.

"The next day he took out two silver coins and gave them to the innkeeper. 'Take care of him,' he told the innkeeper, 'and when I come back this way I will pay you back whatever you spend on him.'"

And Jesus concluded, "In your opinion, which one of these three acted like a fellow-man toward the man attacked by the robbers?"

The teacher of the Law answered, "The one who was kind to him."

Jesus replied, "You go, then, and do the same."

LUKE 10:30-37 GNFMM

GOING DEEPER

Who would you call when? *(Read the Scripture passage and then think about the phone numbers you listed. Place the following symbols next to the numbers you would call for the various situations. You may use a symbol more than once and more than one symbol next to a number if it is appropriate.)*

$ if you needed money but could not explain why

⚡   if you were at a crossroads in your life and needed some good counsel

P   if you had a serious personal problem and needed someone to talk to—one who would keep his mouth shut

†   if you had a spiritual problem and needed someone to listen and understand

☺   if you were really down and needed a good laugh and a good time

S   if you received a "Dear John" letter and needed a shoulder to cry on

OVERTIME CHALLENGE

1. When it comes to friends, I tend to *(circle one in each category)*:
   a. make friends
      quickly . . . . slowly
   b. change friends
      constantly . . . . never
   c. break off
      friendships easily . with great pain
   e. when I'm in trouble
      call on my friends . keep to myself

2. In times of trouble, I tend to rely on *(rank top three)*:
   ___ my partner
   ___ my friends
   ___ my family
   ___ my teachers/coach
   ___ myself alone
   ___ one friend
   ___ God

3. When one of my friends is in trouble, I am best at *(circle two)*:
   a. listening
   b. going to bat for him
   c. praying
   d. cheering him up
   e. sticking by him
   f. bringing him home
   g. getting others to help
   h. keeping my mouth shut
   i. sharing my struggles with him

and let everyone explain where he placed this symbol and why. Then go around on the next symbol, etc., until you have gone through all of the symbols. *(Take a moment and explain where you placed the first symbol and why. Be honest. Your example will set the pace for the groups. After 15 minutes call time and move on.)*

Overtime Challenge / 2's or 8's / 15 min.

(You will have to decide if there is time to share the Overtime Challenge and, if so, whether to use groups of 2 or 8. If time is limited, use 2's. If there is plenty of time, ask the 4's to double up to make the same groups of 8 as in previous sessions.)

Take the first question and go around your group, letting each person explain his choices. Then go around in your group on the second question, etc. *(Take a moment and share your choices on the first question. Be painfully honest! Your example will set the pace for the others.)*

Close-out

In each group, gather together in a football huddle—with your arms around each other's shoulders. *(While everyone is in a huddle, say something like: "Thank you, God, for giving us friends who love and support us in times of trouble. Amen." Ask everyone to write his name in his book. Then collect all of the books.)*

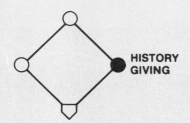

**HISTORY
GIVING**

Objective: To examine your own major concerns in the light of the parables of Salt and Light, and to use your results as the basis for a sharing experience.

PROCEDURE

The instructions are given in the words you can use in leading the group.

Silent Preparation / 5 min.
fill out the questionnaire.

Warm-up / 4's / 15 min.
Get together with 3 other people from your group of 8 in the previous session and share what you put down in the Warm-up phase in the questionnaire—the top five issues in which you would get involved. *(Take a moment and share what you listed as the top five issues. Be honest. Then turn the groups of 4 loose. After 15 minutes call time and move on.)*

Where can you make a difference?

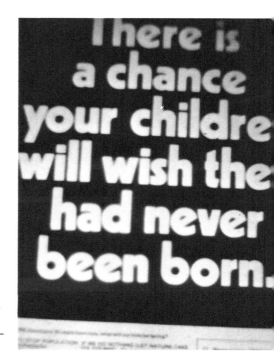

WARM-UP

In what current issues are you willing to be involved? *(Here is a list of issues or concerns that are demanding attention today, needing action by those who are interested in a better world tomorrow. Choose five of the following situations and rank 1 to 5 according to your own desire to do something about it.)*

_____ *Ecology:* your neighborhood is being polluted by smoke stacks from an industry that employs many townspeople. To close the plants would throw them out of work.

_____ *Abortion:* you know that a clinic in your community is performing illegal abortions.

_____ *Motorcycle helmets and seat belts:* you are forced to take safety measures for your own protection— you feel it is an infringement on

---

SALT AND LIGHT

"You are like salt for all mankind. But if salt loses its taste, there is no way to make it salty again. It has become worthless, so it is thrown away and people walk on it.

"You are like light for the whole world. A city built on a hill cannot be hid. No one lights a lamp to put it under a bowl; instead he puts it on the lampstand, where it gives light for everyone in the house. In the same way your light must shine before people, so that they will see the good things you do and give praise to your Father in heaven."

MATTHEW 5:13-16 GNFMM

your own personal freedom.

_____ *Firearms:* in your community the deaths caused from gun wounds have doubled in the last five years because of the unrestricted sale of firearms.

_____ *Smoking:* many public places are crowded with people smoking. The Surgeon General has claimed that smoke inhaled through any means is harmful to a person's health.

_____ *Equality:* a firm in your community has a history of not hiring blacks. You are asked to join a picket line protesting their discriminatory tactics.

_____ *Women's lib:* you have been turned down by an employer in your community because you are a woman.

_____ *Pornography:* the local drive-in is showing hard-core pornography and you have learned that minors are being admitted—illegally.

_____ *Hospital aids:* the local hospital has appealed for volunteers to "empty bedpans" and "serve in the recovery room."

_____ *Conservation:* you have learned that ranchers in your state have killed some eagles by placing poison in sheep carcasses.

_____ *Evangelism:* Billy Graham is holding a crusade in your town and you have the chance to take your friends.

_____ *World hunger:* the Council of Churches is sponsoring a 25-mile walk for UNICEF and you are asked to participate—and get your neighbors to sponsor you.

_____ *Public prayers:* you are asked to say the opening prayer at the Thanksgiving Day football game in front of the whole community.

GOING DEEPER

How would you describe today's issues? *(Read the Scripture passage. Then go back to the list of issues and jot the following symbols beside the appropriate items.)*

↑ issues that have become more important to you since joining this program

↓ issues that have become less important to you since joining this program

⟲ issues that primarily effect your own health, freedom and welfare

♂ issues that primarily effect others' health, freedom and welfare

✗ issues in which you feel a Christian should not get involved

℞ issues in which you feel your parents would get involved

OVERTIME CHALLENGE

1. The issues that seem to get me stirred up are ones that *(circle one in each category):*
   a. threaten my own life or interests.................. threaten the lives or interests of others
   b. involve physical health and well-being............ involve spiritual health and well-being
   c. my friends are concerned about. my family is concerned about

2. I am more likely to get involved in an issue if *(circle two):*
   a. everybody is
   b. it doesn't hurt my popularity
   c. there is a personal principle involved
   d. there is one close friend to support me
   e. I feel I can personally make a difference
   f. I feel this is what Christ would do
   g.

3. As far as being the "salt for all mankind" and "the light for the whole world" that Jesus talked about, I feel I am right now *(circle one):*
   a. still suiting up
   b. waiting for the game to start
   c. playing defense only
   d. in the game, but
   e. needing someone to run interference for me
   f. giving it everything I've got

Going Deeper / 4's / 15 min.

Stay with your group of 4 and share Going Deeper in the questionnaire. Start with the first symbol and let everyone explain where he placed this symbol and why. Then go around on the next symbol, etc. *(Take a moment and explain where you placed the first symbol and why. Set the pace for openness and honesty.)*

Overtime Challenge / 2's or 8's / 15 min.

(You will have to decide if there is time to share the Overtime Challenge and, if so, whether to use groups of 2 or 8. If time is limited, use 2's. If there is plenty of time, have the foursomes double up— to make the same groups of 8 as in previous sessions.)

Take the first question and go around your group, letting each person explain his choice. Then go around on the second question, etc. *(Take a moment and share your choices on the first question. Be painfully honest! Your example will set the pace.)*

Close-out

In each group, gather together in a football huddle—with your arms over each other's shoulders. *(While everyone is in a huddle, say something like: "Thank you, God, for giving us your light, and for the challenge of passing this light to our world. Amen." Ask everyone to write his name in his book. Then collect the books.)*

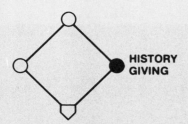

**HISTORY
GIVING**

Where are you going?

Objective: To examine the major turning points in your life in the light of the parable of the Prodigal Son, and to use your results as the basis for a sharing experience.

PROCEDURE

The instructions are given in the words you can use in leading the group.

Silent Preparation / 5 min.
fill out the questionnaire.

Warm-up / 2's / 10 min.
Get together with one other person from your group of 8 and explain the three turning points in your life. *(Show your book to the entire group and explain the three turning points in your life. Go into detail about the reason why you selected one particular experience. Your example will set the pace for everyone. Ask the groups to proceed. After 10 minutes call time and move on.)*

THE PARABLE OF THE PRODIGAL SON

Jesus went on to say, "There was a man who had two sons. The younger one said to him, 'Father, give me now my share of the property.' So the man divided the property between his two sons. After a few days the younger son sold his part of the property and left home with the money.

He went to a country far away, where he wasted his money in reckless living. He spent everything he had. Then a severe famine spread over that country, and he was left without a thing. So he went to work for one of the citizens of that country, who sent him out to his farm to take care of the pigs. He wished he could fill himself with the bean pods the pigs ate, but no one gave him anything to eat.

At last he came to his senses and said, 'All my father's hired workers have more than they can eat, and here I am, about to starve! I will get up and go to my father and say, "Father, I have sinned against God and against you. I am no longer fit to be called your son; treat me as one of your hired workers."' So he got up and started back to his father.

"He was still a long way from home when his father saw him; his heart was filled with pity and he ran, threw his arms around his son, and kissed

him. 'Father,' the son said, 'I have sinned against God and against you. I am no longer fit to be called your son.'

But the father called his servants: 'Hurry!' he said. 'Bring the best robe and put it on him. Put a ring on his finger and shoes on his feet. Then go get the prize calf and kill it, and let us celebrate with a feast! Because this son of mine was dead, but now he is alive; he was lost, but now he has been found.' And so the feasting began."

LUKE 15:11-24 GNFMM

WARM-UP

Thinking over your life, what three times did an event or experience cause a major change in your life, lifestyle or values? *(Assume for a moment that the line below represents your life—from birth to now. Working backward from Right Now, put three dots on the line to represent the three major turning* points in your life. Jot a word or two above each dot to describe the experience. For instance: (1) at age 16, divorce of my parents; (2) at age 13, my confirmation; (3) at age 11, death of my little brother. A turning point can be anything that radically affected your life and/or values—for good or bad.)

BIRTH   RIGHT NOW

GOING DEEPER

Read over the Scripture passage and consider the turning points in the younger son's life. *(Put three symbols on the line below to indicate three kinds of changes in the life of the Prodigal Son.)*

V for the time or times when his values changed

E for the time or times when his emotions (inner feelings) changed

R for the time or times when his relations with his father changed

AT HOME	IN FAR COUNTRY			BACK HOME	
Asks father for his inheritance.	Wastes his money in reckless living.	Broke, lives with pigs.	Starving, decides to go home.	Father runs to meet him.	Party for son.

OVERTIME CHALLENGE

1. If I could compare my life to the parable of the Prodigal Son, I would be *(circle one in each category):*
   a. rebelling against the values of my home .... / living in harmony with the values of my home
   b. wasting the inheritance of my family ...... / appreciating the inheritance of my family
   c. living with low values .... / living up to the highest values I know
   d. in relationship with my parents .... / out of relationship with my parents
   e. mostly in a far country spiritually ...... / mostly back at home spiritually
   f. feeling that I've blown it .... / feeling that I've found it

2. Up to this point, my life has been *(circle two):*
   a. purposeful
   b. goofing off
   c. like a yo-yo
   d. steady
   e. meaningless
   f. disappointing
   g. waiting for the game to start
   h. beautiful
   i. OK, but...

Going Deeper / 4's / 10 min.

With your partner get together with two others from your group of 8 and explain where you put the V's, E's and R's for the Prodigal Son. *(Explain to everyone where you placed the V's. Be specific about your reasons. Call time after 10 minutes and move on.)*

Overtime Challenge / 4's or 8's / 15 min.

(Decide if there is time to share the Overtime Challenge and, if so, whether to use groups of 4 or 8. If the time is limited, use the same 4's. If there is plenty of time, use the groups of 8 that have been together before.)

Take the first question and go around your group, letting each person explain his choices. Then go around on the second question. *(Take a moment and share your choices on the first question. Be painfully honest. Your example will set the pace for the groups to follow.)*

Close-out

In each group, stand together in a close circle—with your arms over each other's shoulders. *(Pray briefly, saying something like: "Thank you, God, for the Prodigal Son and for the hope he gives to every one of us when we blow it. Amen." Be sure everyone has his name on his book. Collect all the books.)*

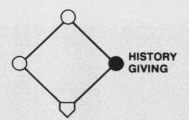

**HISTORY
GIVING**

Objective: To examine your responses in conflict situations in the light of the parable of the Unforgiving Servant, and to use your results as the basis for a sharing experience.

PROCEDURE
The instructions are given in the words you can use in leading the group.

Silent Preparation / 5 min.
fill out the questionnaire.

Warm-up / 2's / 10 min.
Get together with one other person from your group of 8 and share the Warm-up—one situation at a time. *(Explain your choice for the first situation and set the pace for candor and honesty. Remember, your example will set the tone for the whole session. After 10 minutes call time and move on.)*

What's the next move?

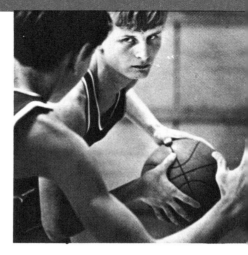

WARM-UP

Here are a series of true-to-life situations that ask for a moral decision on your part. *(Read over each situation and indicate what you would do.)*

1. The guy next to you in class never studies. It's exam time and he wants to cheat off your paper. He'll flunk if you don't let him. What do you do?
   a. let him copy
   b. tell the teacher
   c. cover your paper
   d. quietly tell him your feelings about cheating
   e. refuse him but offer to help him study for the next exam

2. You want to break up with the person you have been going with for

---

THE PARABLE OF THE UNFORGIVING SERVANT

Then Peter came to Jesus and asked, "Lord, how many times can my brother sin against me and I have to forgive him? Seven times?"

"No, not seven times," answered Jesus, "but seventy times seven. Because the Kingdom of heaven is like a king who decided to check on his servants' accounts. He had just begun to do so when one of them was brought in who owed him millions of dollars. The servant did not have enough to pay his debt, so his master ordered him to be sold as a slave, with his wife and his children and all that he had, in order to pay the debt.

"The servant fell on his knees before his master. 'Be patient with me,' he begged, 'and I will pay you everything!' The master felt sorry for him, so he forgave him the debt and let him go.

"The man went out and met one of his fellow servants who owed him a few dollars. He grabbed him and started choking him. 'Pay back what you owe me!' he said. His fellow servant fell down and begged him, 'Be patient with me and I will pay you back!' But he would not; instead, he had him thrown into jail until he should pay the debt. ...The master was very angry, and he sent the servant to jail to be punished until he should pay back the whole amount."

And Jesus concluded, "That is how my Father in heaven will treat you if you do not forgive your brother, every one of you, from your heart."

MATTHEW 18:21-35 GNFMM

two years. What would you do?
a. write a letter
b. call the person on the phone
c. speak to the person face to face
d. put off doing anything
e. wait for the person to ask what's wrong

3. Your black friend is conspicuously omitted from a social given by the popular crowd you want to get in with. What would you do?
a. call and ask why
b. refuse to go and explain why
c. refuse but make some other excuse
d. ignore the problem and go
e. call your friend and ask advice
f. crash the party with your friend

4. You are the coach of a team that is tied for the championship. Before the final and deciding game, you learn that one of the "stars" has broken training rules. What would you do?
a. suspend the kid immediately
b. wait until after the game and suspend the kid
c. make an exception for the sake of the team
d. play as though you never heard about it
e. ask the team to decide for you
f. ask the kid to set his own punishment

5. You are the parents of a daughter who was just expelled from school for cutting class. What would you do?
a. give her a stern lecture
b. persuade the principal to accept her back in school
c. complain to the school board that the rules are too strict
d. threaten her with juvenile court
e. find out why she was cutting class
f. get her away from friends who influence her
g. offer her some incentive for attending class
h. don't do anything for her; let her work it out
i. try to deepen your relationship with her and hope for the best

6. While your parents are each drinking a stiff highball, they tell you to stay away from drugs. What do you do?
a. tell them to practice what they preach
b. remain silent but angry
c. refuse to let it bother you
d. figure it is legal for them to drink and illegal for you to take drugs
e. discuss the situation rationally
f. blow up and leave the room
g. laugh at them
h. accept the fact that there are many contradictions in life
i. listen with respect, but say nothing either way

GOING DEEPER

Who or what strongly influenced your decisions in the Warm-up? *(Read over the Scripture passage and then go back to the choices that you marked and add a symbol to indicate who or what influenced you.)*

✝ my commitment to Jesus Christ
⌂ my training at home
F my outside friends
O my participation in this support group

OVERTIME CHALLENGE

1. I find it easier to *(circle one in each category)*:
a. forgive . . . . ask for forgiveness
b. forgive my   forgive my
   friends . . . . family
c. forgive   forgive
   myself . . . . someone else

2. In making moral decisions I tend to *(put a dot someplace between the words)*:
a. follow   rely on my
   the crowd _____ own judgment
b. listen to   listen to
   my parents _____ my friends
c. stick to my   waver back
   convictions _____ and forth

3. Since being in this program my moral principles have changed *(circle one)*:
a. a lot   c. very little
b. some   d. not at all

4. In making moral decisions my commitment to Jesus Christ seems to have *(circle one)*:
a. a great deal of influence
b. some influence
c. very little influence
d. not as much as I would like

Going Deeper/4's/10 min.

With your partner get together with two others from your group of 8 and explain where you put the symbols indicating who or what influenced your choices. *(Take the first symbol and explain where you placed it and why. Be painfully honest! Call time after 10 minutes and move on.)*

Overtime Challenge / 4's or 8's / 15 min.

(You will have to decide if there is time to share the Overtime Challenge and, if so, whether to use groups of 4 or 8. If time is limited, use the same 4's. If there is plenty of time, ask the groups of 8 that have been together before to regather.)

Take the first question and go around your group, letting each person explain his choices. Then go around on the second question, etc. *(Take a moment and share your choices for the first question.)*

Close-out

In each group, gather together in a football huddle—with your arms over each other's shoulders. *(While in the huddles, say something like: "Thank you, God, for the chance to be on your team. Amen." Collect the books.)*

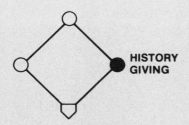

HISTORY GIVING

Objective: To examine your time and priorities in the light of the Parable of the Four Soils, and to use your results as the basis for a sharing experience.

PROCEDURE

The instructions are given in the words you can use in leading the group.

Silent Preparation / 5 min.
fill out the questionnaire.

Warm-up / 2's / 5 min.
Get together with one other person from your group of 8 and share the Warm-up—how you spend your spare time. *(Explain how your spare time is spent. Be painfully honest. Your example will set the pace for the others. After 5 minutes call time and move on.)*

Going Deeper / 4's / 15 min.
With your partner get together with 2 others to form a group of 4. Explain the Going Deeper part of the questionnaire—your life at the beginning of the program and your life now. *(Explain the soils in your*

How are you making it?

WARM-UP

How much of your spare time is spent in the following areas? *(Jot down a percentage for each item on the list below, making a total of 100%. For instance, reading for pleasure 5%; TV 34%; dating 20%, etc.)*

MY SPARE TIME

_____ reading for pleasure
_____ TV
_____ dating/social life
_____ physical conditioning/sports
_____ family
_____ goofing off with friends
_____ spiritual development
_____ studying/homework
_____ service/helping others
100%

THE PARABLE OF THE SOWER

"Listen! There was a man who went out to sow. As he scattered the seed in the field, some of it fell along the path, and the birds came and ate it up. Some of it fell on rocky ground, where there was little soil. The seeds soon sprouted, because the soil wasn't deep. Then when the sun came up it burned the young plants, and because the roots had not grown deep enough the plants soon dried up. Some of the seed fell among thorns, which grew up and choked the plants, and they didn't bear grain. But some seeds fell in good soil, and the plants sprouted, grew, and bore grain: some had thirty grains, others sixty, and others one hundred."

MARK 4:3-8 GNFMM

GOING DEEPER

To represent the kinds of people who are given the "seed," here are four types:
(1) On-the-go Goofus, (2) Shallow Sam, (3) Choke Charlie and (4) Clutch Clarence.
(Read the Scripture and the descriptions of the four lifestyles. Under each character, put two marks on the percentage line to indicate how much of your time you are like him. For instance, for On-the-go Goofus, you might put an X in the middle to represent 50% of your time when you started this program; and an O nearer 0% to represent 30% of your time right now.)

X you at the beginning of this
    program
O you right now

"On-the-go Goofus" *(seed along the path). His lifestyle:* hectic, always running; into everything; everybody's friend; travels with the "in" crowd on the popular, crowded asphalt paths where nothing has time to take root and grow. *Result:* the good seed is quickly destroyed.

0% _____ 100%

"Shallow Sam" *(seed on rocky ground). His lifestyle:* on and off, up and down like a yo-yo; great promise; on everybody's pre-season list but loses interest when the going gets tough; Mr. Good Intentions who never lives up to expectations. *Result:* the good seed withers as the heat increases.

0% _____ 100%

"Choke Charlie" *(seed among thorns). His lifestyle:* overcrowded, caught in a thicket of conflicting priorities that sap the time and energy; no time to weed out the unimportant. *Result:* the weeds overtake the good seed and strangle the life out of the plant.

0% _____ 100%

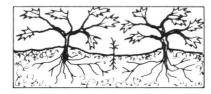

"Clutch Clarence" *(seed in good soil). His lifestyle:* purposeful; uncluttered; he knows what he wants to do and makes time for it; the unimportant is weeded out of the schedule. *Result:* the good seed has time to take root and mature and bear fruit to the fullest.

0% _____ 100%

OVERTIME CHALLENGE

What percentage of time do you spend each day doing things that are the following? *(Fill in the percentages.)*
_____ % unnecessary (wasted)
_____ % necessary but unexciting (boring)
_____ % exciting but not lasting (unproductive)
_____ % exciting and productive (lasting)

life before and now. Again, be honest. Be honest. Then turn the groups of 4 loose. After 10 minutes call time and move on.)*

Overtime Challenge / 4's or 8's / 15 min.

(You will have to decide if there is time to share the Overtime Challenge and, if so, whether to use groups of 4 or 8. If time is limited, use groups of 4. If there is plenty of time, ask the groups of 4 to double up to make the same groups of 8 that have been together before.)

Go around and let everyone explain the Overtime Challenge—how he would describe the largest percentage of his time—and how he feels about it. If there is time, go around again and share one thing this exercise has taught you about your time and your life. *(Take a moment and explain what you have discovered in this exercise about yourself—and what you plan to do about it.)*

Close-out

In each group, gather together in a football huddle—with your arms over each other's shoulders. *(While everyone is in a huddle, say something like: "Thank you, God, for the challenge to live every day to the fullest—for your glory. Amen." Collect the books.)*

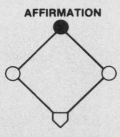

AFFIRMATION

Objective: To examine your growth areas in the light of the parable of the Mustard Seed, and to use your results as a basis for a sharing experience.

PROCEDURE

The instructions are given in the words you can use in leading the group.

Silent Preparation / 5 min.

(Ask the groups of 8 who have been together up to now in the program to sit together in silence while filling out the questionnaire. This will help them when they start working on the Overtime Challenge.)
fill out the questionnaire.

Warm-up / 2's / 5 min.

Get together with one other person from your group of 8 and share how you feel about the various areas of your life. *(Explain to the group the mark you put on the first line concerning your*

Where are you?

WARM-UP

How do you feel about the various areas of your life? Here are a series of lines to represent your feelings. *(Put two marks on each line. For instance, on the first line you might put the O close to "kinda blah" because you were really feeling down when you joined this* group. *And you might put the X in the middle because right now you are sort of in between "blah" and "great.")*

○ **where you were at the beginning of this program.**

✕ **where you are right now.**

ABOUT MYSELF, I'M FEELING

kinda blah ——————————————great

ABOUT MY FUTURE

scared ——————————————excited

ABOUT MY SCHOOL OR WORK

bummer ——————————————super

ABOUT MY CHURCH

indifference ——————————————involvement

ABOUT MY GROUP

I could tell ——————————————I could tell
them nothing   them anything

THE PARABLE OF THE MUSTARD SEED

"What shall we say the Kingdom of God is like?" asked Jesus. "What parable shall we use to explain it? It is like a mustard seed, the smallest seed in the world. A man takes it and plants it in the ground; after a while it grows up and becomes the biggest of all plants. It puts out such large branches that the birds come and make their nests in its shade."

MARK 4:30-32 GNFMM

GOING DEEPER

Read over the Scripture passage and consider how you would describe your spiritual growth. *(On the line put an O* to indicate where you were at the be-ginning of this program, an X to indicate where you are right now.)*

IN MY RELATIONSHIP WITH JESUS CHRIST

very cold _____ very warm

IN MY UNDERSTANDING OF GOD'S WILL FOR MY LIFE

huh? _____ right on

IN MY PRIVATE STUDY OF SCRIPTURE AND PRAYER

ouch _____ whoopee

IN DEALING WITH MY HANGUPS

woe is me _____ oh, yes!

OVERTIME CHALLENGE

What improvement or growth have you noticed in the members of your group? The series of circles are to represent them. *(Jot a name in each circle. Beside each name write down one thing or area in which you have recognized changes for the positive. For instance, beside Tom's name you might jot down "patience," because he has had more patience getting out the school paper than ever before. For Debbie you might put "consistency," because she has shown a lot of improvement in matching her actions to her words.)*

feelings about yourself. Be honest. Your example will set the pace for their sharing. Then turn them loose for 5 minutes.)

Going Deeper / 4's / 10 min.

With your partner get together with two others from your group of 8, making a group of 4. Then give everyone a chance to explain the Going Deeper part of the quest-tionnaire. *(Be the first to share and let your openness and honesty be an example for everyone to follow.)*

Overtime Challenge

Regather your group of 8. Ask one person to remain silent while the others, one at a time, explain the areas where they have ob-served the greatest growth or improvement in this person. Go around the group until everyone has been covered. *(Pick out some-one in a group near you and ex-plain an area in his life where you have observed real growth. It may be in an attitude, a skill or a change in behavior. Be genuine in your affirmation. Your example will set the pace for the group.)*

Close-out

In each group, stand together in a close circle—with your arms over each other's shoulders. *(Pray something like: "Thank you, God, for the growth we have experienced in each of our lives and together as a group. Amen." Collect all the books.)*

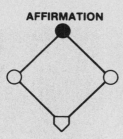

AFFIRMATION

Objective: To affirm the qualities you have observed in one another in the light of the parable of the Final Judgment, and to use your results as a basis for a beautiful affirmation experience.

PROCEDURE

The instructions are given in the words you can use in leading the group.

Silent Preparation / 5 min.

(Ask the groups of 8 who have been together up to now in the program to sit together while filling out the questionnaire.) fill out the questionnaire.

Warm-up / 8's / 10 min.

Ask one person in your group of 8 to remain quiet while the others

Who's there when you need it?

WARM-UP

How would you describe the members of your group? *(In the circles write the names of the members of your sharing group. Then beside each name, jot down two words that describe him. For instance, for Tom you might put "loyal" and "dependable." You may use the same description for two people if it applies and you may add ones that are not on the list of suggestions.)*

THE FINAL JUDGMENT OF SHEEP AND GOATS

"When the Son of Man comes as King, and all the angels with him, he will sit on his royal throne, and all the earth's people will be gathered before him. Then he will divide them into two groups, just as a shepherd separates the sheep from the goats: he will put the sheep at his right and the goats at his left.

"Then the King will say to the people on his right, 'You that are blessed by my Father: come! Come and receive the kingdom which has been prepared for you ever since the creation of the world. I was hungry and you fed me, thirsty and you gave me drink; I was a stranger and you received me in your homes, naked and you clothed me; I was sick and you took care of me, in prison and you visited me.'

"The righteous will then answer him, 'When, Lord, did we ever see you hungry and feed you, or thirsty and give you drink? When did we ever see you a stranger and welcome you in our homes, or naked and clothe you? When did we ever see you sick or in prison, and visit you?'

"The King will answer back, 'I tell you, indeed, whenever you did this for one of the least important of these brothers of mine, you did it for me!'"

MATTHEW 25:31-40 GNFMM

loyal (sticks up for friends)
open-minded (open to new ideas)
enterprising (adventurous)
decisive (initiates action)
conscientious (industrious)
cheerful (happy and contented)
sensitive (aware of others)
gentle (tender and kind)
self-confident (self-assured)
self-controlled (stable)
persevering (strong)
caring (warm)
friendly (smiles easily)
forgiving (no grudges)
well-organized (plans sufficiently)
disciplined (consistent)
imaginative (visionary)
patient (serene)
fun-loving (sense of humor)

GOING DEEPER

How have the members of the group contributed to your life in these sessions? *(Read the Scripture passage. Then read the following "caring" list and jot down the names of each one in your sharing group next to the particular item he has contributed to your life. For instance, you might put Cindy's name next to: "I was a stranger and you received me," because it was Cindy who went out of her way to make you feel welcome in this group.)*

_____ I WAS HUNGRY AND YOU FED ME: Your sharing of yourself in this group has caused me to grow.

_____ I WAS THIRSTY AND YOU GAVE ME DRINK: Your spiritual life and devotion to God has helped me find spiritual refreshment.

_____ I WAS A STRANGER AND YOU RECEIVED ME: Your welcome when I came made me feel at home.

_____ I WAS NAKED AND YOU CLOTHED ME: Your own caring when I felt naked and alone made me feel that somebody understands me.

_____ I WAS SICK AND YOU TOOK CARE OF ME: Your reaching out to me when I was really down caused me to feel better and whole again.

_____ I WAS IN PRISON AND YOU VISITED ME: Your ministry to me when I shared some of my hangups released me from the bondage.

OVERTIME CHALLENGE

1. It is harder for me to *(circle one in each category)*:
   a. give a   receive a
      compliment..........compliment
   b. see the good   see the good
      in others.............in myself
   c. believe I   believe you
      am OK..................are OK

2. When I get a compliment, I *(circle two)*:
   a. don't know what to do
   b. wonder what is coming next
   c. try to pass it off
   d. blush
   e. am deeply touched
   f. try harder than ever
   g. feel awkward and embarrassed
   h. believe in myself more
   i. accept it with no problem

3. My support group in this program has helped me to: *(choose three and rank 1, 2, 3)*:
   ____ believe in myself more
   ____ feel it is OK to have problems
   ____ accept God's love and forgiveness
   ____ show my feelings
   ____ respond when someone else has a need
   ____ say I'm sorry
   ____ compliment others more
   ____ discover what love is all about

go around and explain the two qualities they have observed in his life. Then ask another person to sit in silence while the others explain the qualities they chose for this person, etc., until you have covered everyone in your group. *(Name one person and explain two special qualities you have observed in his life. Be genuine in your praise. Your example will set the pace for the groups to follow. Then turn the groups loose. After 10 to 15 minutes call time and move on.)*

Going Deeper/8's/10 min.

Stay with your group of 8 and repeat the same procedure with the Going Deeper part of the questionnaire. Ask one person to sit in silence while the others explain the "caring" he has given them. Then go on to another person and repeat the process, until everyone in your group has been covered. *(Choose one person and explain the phrase you would use to explain his contribution to your life and group.)*

Overtime Challenge / 2's / 15 min.

(You will have to decide if there is time to cover the Overtime Challenge.)

Divide into pairs and go over the Overtime Challenge with your partner—one question at a time. *(Explain how you would answer the first question.)*

Close-out

Regather your group of 8 and form a football huddle. *(While everyone is in a huddle, say something like: "Thank you, God, for the wonderful presence of your love. Amen." Pick up all of the books.)*

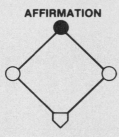

AFFIRMATION

Objective: To affirm the strengths you see in each other, and to let each person explain two areas that need work, based on the parable of the Tree and its Fruit.

PROCEDURE

The instructions are given in the words you can use in leading the group.

Silent Preparation / 5 min.
(Ask each group of 8 who has been together up to now in the program to sit together while filling out the questionnaire.) fill out the questionnaire.

Warm-up / 2's / 5 min.
Get together with one other person from your group of 8 and share the Warm-up part of your questionnaire—two qualities in which you feel you excel from each category. *(Share the two qualities you checked. Be honest. Your*

What are you good at?

WARM-UP

Here is a list of qualities or strengths. There are three categories. *(In each category check your two best points.)*

MENTAL *(check two)*
- ___ intelligence
- ___ creativity
- ___ sense of humor
- ___ discernment
- ___ reasonableness
- ___ good memory
- ___ alertness
- ___ understanding
- ___ perceptivity
- ___ comprehension

EMOTIONAL *(check two)*
- ___ warmth
- ___ self-confidence
- ___ stick-ability
- ___ consistency
- ___ endurance
- ___ inspiration
- ___ stability
- ___ dependability
- ___ sensitivity
- ___ cheerfulness
- ___ patience
- ___ enthusiasm
- ___ supportive
- ___ coolness

SPIRITUAL *(check two)*
- ___ dedication
- ___ discipline
- ___ leadership
- ___ purity
- ___ humility
- ___ compassion
- ___ openness
- ___ honesty
- ___ hopefulness
- ___ Bible info
- ___ self-control
- ___ hope

GOING DEEPER

In what qualities do you feel the members of your group are particularly strong? *(Read the Scripture passage. Then write in the circles the names of the other members of your group. Beside each name write three qualities —one from each category—in which you feel this person excels. You may use the same quality for more than one person if it fits.)*

A TREE AND ITS FRUIT

"A healthy tree does not bear bad fruit, nor does a poor tree bear good fruit. Every tree is known by the fruit it bears; you do not pick figs from thorn bushes, or gather grapes from bramble bushes. A good man brings good out of the treasure of good things in his heart; a bad man brings bad out of his treasure of bad things. For a man's mouth speaks what his heart is full of."

LUKE 6:43-45 GNFMM

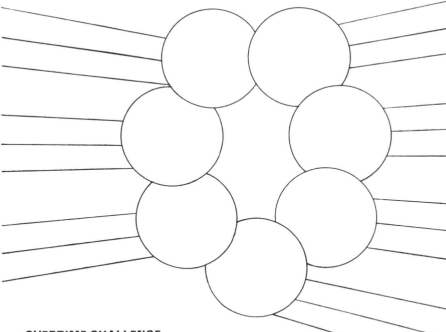

OVERTIME CHALLENGE

Where is the fruit "bad" in your life?
(Check two areas that need to change for the good.)

___ bad temper
___ bad habits
___ bad sportsmanship
___ bad attitude at home

___ bad self-image
___ bad language
___ bad thoughts
___ bad study habits
___ bad training habits
___ bad attitude on the job
___ bad attitude at school

example will set the pace for sharing. After 5 minutes call time and move on.)

Going Deeper / 8's / 15 min.

Get together with your group of 8 and share the Going Deeper part of your questionnaire. Ask one person in your group to remain quiet while the others go around and explain the three qualities they selected for him. Then ask another person to sit in silence while the other seven explain their qualities for him, etc., until you have covered everyone. *(Choose one person and explain the three qualities you would select for this person. Be genuine as well as honest. Then have the groups proceed. After 15 minutes call time and move on.)*

Overtime Challenge / 4's / 15 min.

Divide into groups of 4 and give everyone a chance to explain the two areas in his life where he needs to change. *(Explain your two areas. Again, set the pace for honesty.)*

Close-out

Get together and form a football huddle. *(While everyone is in a huddle, say something like: "Thank you, God, for the help you give us through each other—to live your kind of life. Amen." Collect the books.)*

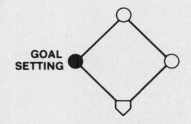

GOAL SETTING

Your turn!

Objective: To examine your philosophy of life in the light of the parable of the Talents, and to use your results as a basis for a sharing experience.

PROCEDURE

The instructions are given in the words you can use in leading the group.

Silent Preparation / 5 min.
fill out the questionnaire.

WARM-UP

Think back in your life to the all-day Monopoly games and see what your strategy for winning at Monopoly will tell you about your lifestyle.

1. When I play Monopoly, I usually *(circle two)*:
   a. get in a fight
   b. give up before the game is over
   c. forget all about being kind and generous
   d. feel sorry for the ones who are losing and help them out
   e. hang in until the bitter end
   f. cheat
   g. get bored and quit

2. My advice for anyone who wants to win at Monopoly is *(choose one)*:
   a. Go for broke! Buy everything you land on. Mortgage and swap and sacrifice to get a monopoly. Then risk everything on that monopoly and hang on for the long-run payoff.
   b. Hang loose! Buy the best properties you land on, but hedge your bets with a little caution. Hold back until you see which way the game is going. Then make your move.
   c. Play it safe! Buy only the quick return properties like the utilities and railroads. Put the rest into savings for a rainy day. You don't want to get caught without enough money to pay your obligations.

3. If I could compare my own philosophy of life to Monopoly, I would say a successful player is one who *(circle one)*:
   a. wins the game, period!
   b. plays to win, whether he wins or not
   c. has a good time whether he wins or not
   d. learns how to adapt to losing

GOING DEEPER

Read over the Scripture passage and complete the following questions.

1. If the man who was given one bag of gold were playing soccer, he would probably *(circle one)*:
   a. immediately charge the man with the ball
   b. wait for the right chance, then charge the man with the ball
   c. wait for the man with the ball to come to him

2. I feel the man with one bag of gold dug a hole in the ground and hid the money because *(circle one)*:
   a. he lacked ambition
   b. he was afraid of making a mistake
   c. he was hurt because he was not given as much as the others
   d. he felt insecure and inadequate
   e. he had a defeatist attitude

3. For the man with one bag of gold, I feel a little *(circle one)*:
   a. pity   d. identity
   b. sympathy   e. patience
   c. regret   f. remorse

OVERTIME CHALLENGE

How do you deal with the various twists and turns of your life? *(Put a dot on each line somewhere between the two extremes.)*

IN TAKING RISKS, I
never take a risk _____ try anything once

IN LEADING INTO UNCHARTED WATERS, I
am the last to volunteer _____ jump at the chance

IN TOUGH SITUATIONS, I
collapse under pressure _____ hang in all the way

IN LONG-RANGE ENDURANCE, I
tire easily _____ rise to the occasion

THE PARABLE OF THE THREE TALENTS

"It will be like a man who was about to leave home on a trip; he called his servants and put them in charge of his property. He gave to each one according to his ability: to one he gave five thousand dollars, to the other two thousand dollars, and to the other one thousand dollars. Then he left on his trip.

"The servant who had received five thousand dollars went at once and invested his money and earned another five thousand dollars. In the same way the servant who received two thousand dollars earned another two thousand dollars. But the servant who received one thousand dollars went off, dug a hole in the ground, and hid his master's money.

"After a long time the master of those servants came back and settled accounts with them. The servant who had received five thousand dollars came in and handed over the other five thousand dollars...

"Then the servant who had been given two thousand dollars came in and said, 'You gave me two thousand dollars, sir. Look! Here are another two thousand dollars that I have earned.'...

"Then the servant who had received one thousand dollars came in and said. 'Sir, I know you are a hard man; you reap harvests where you did not plant, and gather crops where you did not scatter seed. I was afraid, so I went off and hid your money in the ground. Look! Here is what belongs to you.'

"'You bad and lazy servant!' his master said. 'You knew, did you, that I reap harvests where I did not plant, and gather crops where I did not scatter seed? Well, then, you should have deposited my money in the bank, and I would have received it all back with interest when I returned. Now, take the money away from him and give it to the one who has ten thousand dollars. For to everyone who has, even more will be given, and he will have more than enough; but the one who has nothing, even the little he has will be taken away from him. As for this useless servant—throw him outside in the darkness; there he will cry and gnash his teeth.'"

MATTHEW 25:14-30 GNFMM

Warm-up / 4's / 10 min.
Get together with three others from your group of 8 to form a group of 4. Share your answers to the Monopoly exercise—one point at a time around your group. *(Explain your two choices for the first point. Set the tone for good-natured fun. Then turn the group loose. After 10 minutes call time and move on.)*

Going Deeper / 4's / 10 min.
Stay with your group of 4 and share your answers to Going Deeper in the questionnaire—one point at a time around your group. *(Explain to everyone how you would complete the first sentence.)*

Overtime Challenge / 2's or 8's / 15 min.
(If time is limited, have the groups divide into twos so all can have an opportunity to participate and share. If there is plenty of time, have the groups of 8 regather.) Share your answers to the Overtime Challenge with one another. *(Show where you would put a dot on the first line—and explain why. Then turn them loose.)*

Close-out
In each group, stand together in a close circle—with your arms over each other's shoulders *(Pray briefly, including something like: "Thank you, God, for giving us life and the chance to go all the way with you. Amen." Collect the books.)*

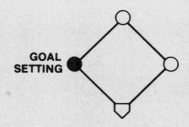

GOAL SETTING

What do you want to do?

Objective: To examine your life goals in light of the parable of the Rich Fool.

PROCEDURE

The instructions are given in the words you can use in leading the group.

Silent Preparation / 5 min.
fill out the questionnaire.

Warm-up / 4's / 10 min.
Get together with 3 others from your group of 8 and form a group of 4. Share your Warm-up in the questionnaire—the goals you have accomplished and the future goals for your life. *(Take a moment and explain your number 1 accomplishment up to now and several things on your list of future goals. Be painfully honest. Your example will set the pace for the groups to follow.)*

WARM-UP

1. **What are your life goals? Here is a line to show your life span.** *(At the left end, jot down the year of your*

BIRTH ———————————————— **DEATH**

birth. On the right end write down the year and age you will be at the end of your life. Then put an X for now, along with today's date and your age.

2. **Thinking about the time represented by my lifeline up to this point in my life, I feel I have already accomplished the following** *(rank top three 1, 2, 3):*
   ____ a lot of friends
   ____ good grades
   ____ good mental attitude
   ____ settled down in life
   ____ a lot of fun
   ____ thought through my values
   ____ developed my physical body
   ____ developed my spiritual life
   ____ made some money
   ____ practically nothing

3. **As I think about my future, my most important priorities are** *(rank 1 to 14):*
   ____ pleasure/fun
   ____ contentment/inner peace
   ____ recognition/achievement
   ____ freedom/opportunity
   ____ sexual fulfillment
   ____ self-respect/integrity
   ____ excitement/adventure
   ____ happiness/feeling good
   ____ spiritual fulfillment
   ____ personal satisfaction
   ____ money/all the comforts of life
   ____ deep relationships
   ____ good health
   ____ security/guaranteed income

GOING DEEPER

How would you describe your goals for the future? *(Read over the Scripture passage. Then go back to your list of future goals and put symbols in the margin where they apply.)*

P   probably number 1 on my parent's list

F   probably number 1 on most of my friends' lists

†   was number 1 on my list five years ago

↓   has gone down in value to me most recently

↑   has gone up in value to me most recently

C   is the thing I would like to be number 1 on my children's lists

OVERTIME CHALLENGE

1. **When it comes to my life goals, I am** *(circle one in each category):*
   a. pretty definite . . . . pretty confused
   b. closer to my friends' goals . . . . closer to my parents'
   c. rather content . . . . rather disturbed

2. **Since I joined this support group, my life goals have** *(circle one):*
   a. come into focus
   b. changed
   c. blurred
   d. stayed about the same

3. **My commitment to Jesus Christ has influenced my life goals** *(circle one):*
   a. a lot
   b. a little
   c. not as much as I would like
   d. not at all

THE PARABLE OF THE RICH FOOL

A man in the crowd said to him, "Teacher, tell my brother to divide with me the property our father left us."

Jesus answered him, "Man, who gave me the right to judge, or to divide the property between you two?" And he went on to say to them all, "Watch out, and guard yourselves from all kinds of greed; because a man's true life is not made up of the things he owns, no matter how rich he may be."

Then Jesus told them this parable, "A rich man had land which bore good crops. He began to think to himself, 'I don't have a place to keep all my crops. What can I do? This is what I will do,' he told himself; 'I will tear my barns down and build bigger ones, where I will store the grain and all my other goods. Then I will say to myself: Lucky man! You have all the good things you need for many years. Take life easy, eat, drink, and enjoy yourself!'

"But God said to him, 'You fool! This very night you will have to give up your life; then who will get all these things you have kept for yourself?'"

And Jesus concluded, "This is how it is with those who pile up riches for themselves but are not rich in God's sight."

LUKE 12:13-21 GNFMM

Going Deeper/4's/10 min.

Stay with your group of 4 and share your answers to Going Deeper. Take the first symbol and let everyone explain where he put the P on his list. Then go around a second time on the F, etc., until you have covered all the symbols. *(Explain to everyone where you put the P on your list. Set the pace for fairness and honesty.)*

Overtime Challenge / 2's or 8's / 15 min.

(If time is limited, divide the foursomes so the participation can be greater and the sharing deeper. If there is plenty of time, have the foursomes double up—into the same groups of 8 as in previous sessions.)

Share your answers to the Overtime Challenge with one another. *(Explain your answers to the first question. Then turn them loose.)*

Close-out

Regather your group of 8 and form a football huddle—with your arms over the shoulders of each other. *(While the groups are in huddles, say something like: "Thank you, God, for the chance to build our lives around you. Amen." Pick up the books.)*

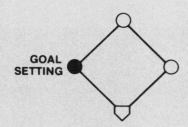

GOAL SETTING

Objective: To examine the ultimate values in your life in light of the Parable of Two House Builders, and to use the results as the basis for sharing.

PROCEDURE

The instructions are given in the words you can use in leading the group.

Silent Preparation / 5 min.
fill out the questionnaire.

Warm-up / 4's / 10 min.
Get together with 3 others from your group of 8. Share the Warm-up in the questionnaire—the three things that would be the easiest for you to give up and the three that would be the hardest, and why. *(Take a moment and share how you would rank your losses. Be painfully honest. Your example will set the tone for sharing.)*

What's gonna last?

WARM-UP

If a situation beyond your control came upon your life causing losses, what could you give up and still continue as a person? *(Rank the following 1 to 10, starting with the easiest to give up.)*

___ **my health** *(physical stamina)*

___ **my savings** *(my money, stocks and bonds)*

___ **my home** *(my house, clothes, material possessions)*

___ **my country** *(my homeland, political freedom)*

___ **my religious freedom** *(the right to worship God as I please)*

___ **my career** *(my job and the future job opportunities in my field)*

___ **my reputation** *(outside recognition, popularity)*

___ **my friends** *(close relationships)*

___ **my family** *(parents, brothers, sisters)*

___ **my self-esteem** *(sense of worth, importance)*

___ **my faith in God** *(my trust in an all-powerful, all-knowing, personal God who knows me)*

THE TWO HOUSE BUILDERS

"So then, everyone who hears these words of mine and obeys them will be like a wise man who built his house on the rock. The rain poured down, the rivers flooded over, and the winds blew hard against that house. But it did not fall, because it had been built on the rock.

"But everyone who hears these words of mine and does not obey them will be like a foolish man who built his house on the sand. The rain poured down, the rivers flooded over, the winds blew hard against that house, and it fell. What a terrible fall that was!"

MATTHEW 7:24-27 GNFMM

GOING DEEPER

How would you describe the above areas of your life? Read the Scripture passage. *Then go back to your "losses" and put the following symbols next to them.)*

↑ has increased in value since joining this sharing group

↓ has decreased in value since joining this sharing group

M F C will probably mean more to me in 10 years

I would fight to keep this at all cost

what I want most for my children

OVERTIME CHALLENGE

Are you ready for bad weather? Imagine that the house in the parable is *your* life and that this house has many rooms. *(Read over the list of rooms and give yourself a building inspector's rating on each room—1 being very shakey and 10 being very strong.)*

LIVING ROOM: I have my life in order; I know what I want to do; my values are well-defined; my moral principles are clear; I am feeling good about myself and my lifestyle right now.

1 2 3 4 5 6 7 8 9 10

RECREATION ROOM: I have a healthy balance in my schedule for leisure; I use my spare time purposefully—to restore my mind and spirit as well as my body. I am feeling good about my priorities and the way I use my time.

1 2 3 4 5 6 7 8 9 10

FAMILY ROOM: I have a good relationship with my family. We have learned to talk about our differences; we deal with our conflicts; we "build up" one another when "outside weather" is a problem; I am feeling good about my family and enjoy being with them.

1 2 3 4 5 6 7 8 9 10

LIBRARY ROOM: I have a balanced diet in my reading habits—for mental and spiritual stimulation as well as pleasure. I try to think for myself, to make my own decisions based on definite values and moral principles, and don't just "cave in" to the pressure of my friends.

1 2 3 4 5 6 7 8 9 10

PHYSICAL FITNESS ROOM: I try to keep in shape; to deal with flabbiness. I feel good about my manhood/womanhood and sexuality, but I do not let my sexual desires get the best of me. I can sleep nights and weather the "storms" without getting fatigued and depressed.

1 2 3 4 5 6 7 8 9 10

GUEST ROOM: I have a good relationship with my friends and schoolmates. I enjoy being with people without feeling dependent upon them. I can belong to the crowd without accepting or bowing to their values. I can stand against social pressure to conform, yet am sensitive to open the door when someone needs a little warmth.

1 2 3 4 5 6 7 8 9 10

Going Deeper / 4's / 10 min.
Stay with your group of 4 and share your answers to Going Deeper. Take the first symbol and let everyone explain where he put an up arrow on your list. Then go around with the down arrow, etc., until you have covered all the symbols. *(Explain to everyone where you put the down arrow on your list and why. Set the pace for fairness and honesty.)*

Overtime Challenge / 2's or 8's / 15 min.
(If time is limited, split into groups of 2, so everyone can share. If there is plenty of time, move back into the original groups of 8.)
Go around your group and let each person explain where he marked himself on the Living Room and why. Then go around on the Recreation Room and why, etc., until the list is covered. *(Explain your markings on the first two and set the pace for sharing.)*

Close-out
Gather together in a football huddle—with your arms over each other's shoulders. *(While everyone is in a huddle, say something like: "Thank you, God, for the strength of belonging to a team of guys who are committed to your things in the world. Amen." Collect the books to have them ready for the next session.)*

135

Scripture Happenings

STRUCTURED QUESTIONNAIRES ON LIFE OF CHRIST

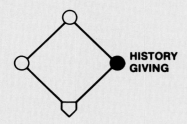

HISTORY GIVING

Objective: To discover how your spiritual pilgrimage and the pilgrimage of Simon Peter have points in common, and to use your insights as the basis for a sharing experience with your support group.

PROCEDURE

The instructions are given in the words you can use in leading the group.

Silent Preparation / 5 min.

fill out the questionnaire.

Warm-up / 2's / 5 min.

Get together with someone from your group of 8 and share what you put down in your Warm-up—one question at a time. *(Take a moment and share your answer to the first question. Then ask each twosome to share their answers to the first question with each other, etc...until they have finished all three questions or run out of time. Call time after 5 minutes and move on.)*

Going Deeper / 4's / 15 min.

With your partner get together with 2 others from your group of 8 to form a group of 4. Share your answers to Going Deeper in the questionnaire—one question at a time around your group. Take this

What motivated you?

WARM-UP

1. I think Jesus told Simon Peter, *"Push the boat out further to the deep water and...let your nets down for a catch,"* in order to *(circle one):*
   a. get away from the crowd
   b. get to know Peter personally
   c. get his hook into Peter
   d. help Peter in his work in return for Peter's help
   e. demonstrate a larger principle about risk-taking
   f. show that he knew a little about fishing
   g. embarrass Peter

2. If I had been Peter, I would have responded by *(circle one):*
   a. humoring Jesus, but that's all
   b. suggesting that we try it the next morning
   c. telling Jesus how much I knew about fishing
   d. thinking to myself, "who does he think he is to tell me how to fish?"
   e. taking him up on the invitation

3. When Peter said, *"Go away from me, Lord, for I am a sinful man!"* he was really saying *(circle one):*
   a. "Stop bugging me"
   b. "I feel guilty being with you"
   c. "You embarrass me because you know more about fishing than I do"
   d. "I know you are more than a teacher but I am not ready to risk the consequences of following you"
   e. "I don't know how to say 'yes' and 'no' at the same time, but this is how I feel"
   f. "Why do you waste your time helping me?"

JESUS CALLS THE FIRST DISCIPLES

One time Jesus was standing on the shore of Lake Gennesaret while the people pushed their way up to him to listen to the word of God. He saw two boats pulled up on the beach; the fishermen had left them and were washing the nets. Jesus got into one of the boats—it belonged to Simon—and asked him to push off a little from the shore. Jesus sat in the boat and taught the crowd.

When he finished speaking, he said to Simon, "Push the boat out further to the deep water, and you and your partners let your nets down for a catch."

"Master," Simon answered, "we worked hard all night long and caught nothing. But if you say so, I will let down the nets." They let the nets down and caught such a large number of fish that the nets were about to break. So they motioned to their partners in the other boat to come and help them. They came and filled both boats so full of fish that they were about to sink. When Simon Peter saw what had happened, he fell on his knees before Jesus and said, "Go away from me, Lord! I am a sinful man!"

He and the others with him were all amazed at the large number of fish they had caught. The same was true of Simon's partners, James and John, the sons of Zebedee. Jesus said to Simon, "Don't be afraid; from now on you will be catching men."

They pulled the boats on the beach, left everything, and followed Jesus.

LUKE 5:1-11 GNFMM

GOING DEEPER

1. In comparison to Simon Peter's experience, my own "meetings" with God have been *(circle one)*:
   a. tame
   b. more intellectual
   c. just as confusing
   d. about the same
   e. even more crazy
   f. huh
   g. fuzzy
   h. scary
   i. sporadic
   j. mystical
   k. right on

2. The first time I can recall feeling God's call on my life was when I was *(circle one)*:
   a. a child
   b. in trouble— a crisis
   c. away on retreat
   d. all alone
   e. facing death
   f. just recently
   g. all my life
   h. never

3. My relationship with Christ right now might be described by the words *(circle two)*:
   a. grim
   b. confused
   c. blah
   d. growing
   e. struggling
   f. slipping
   g. great
   h. up and down
   i. a new beginning
   j. exciting
   k. don't know

OVERTIME CHALLENGE

1. The idea of "pushing out into the deeper water" with Jesus sounds *(circle two)*:
   a. risky
   b. crazy
   c. exciting
   d. OK, but
   e. corny
   f. difficult
   g. fine, if someone will join me
   h. just the challenge I've been looking for

2. The whole idea of belonging to a group that is committed to helping each other grow spiritually sounds *(circle one)*:
   a. ridiculous
   b. frightening
   c. valuable
   d. just what I need
   e. wonderful
   f. childish
   g. demanding
   h. OK, if everybody else is willing
   i. threatening

3. Before I can honestly join in this venture, I need to *(circle one)*:
   a. get myself together
   b. think it over
   c. consider what this is going to cost
   d. straighten out a few things
   e. get some help
   f. get my relationship with Christ squared away
   g. forget my fear of failure
   h. clean up my life

opportunity to really explain your own spiritual pilgrimage—from the earliest beginnings to this moment. *(Explain something of your own early spiritual "meetings." Set the pace for real openness. After 15 minutes call time and move on.)*

Overtime Challenge / 4's or 8's / 15 min.

(You will have to decide if there is time to share the Overtime Challenge and if so, whether to use groups of 4 or 8. If time is limited, stay with the 4's. If there is plenty of time, use groups of 8 —the same 8's that have been together before.)

Take the first question and go around your group, letting each person explain his answer and why. Then go around on the second question, etc. *(Explain your answer to the first question and set the pace for honesty.)*

Close-out

Stand together in a close circle— with your arms over each other's shoulders. If anyone in your group wants to say a short prayer—a word of thanks or a request for help about something in his life—he can do so while we pause. Then I will close with prayer. *(Wait about 60 seconds then break in with a few words of prayer. Pick up the books so they are available for the next session.)*

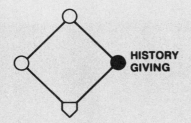

HISTORY GIVING

Who cared enough?

Objective: To discover the people who have contributed most to your spiritual life, and to use your insights as the basis for a sharing experience.

PROCEDURE

The instructions are given in the words you can use in leading the group.

Silent Preparation / 5 min.
fill out the questionnaire.

Warm-up / 2's / 5 min.
Get together with someone from your group of 8 and share what you put down in the Warm-up— one question at a time. *(Take a moment and explain your answer to the first question. Call time after 5 minutes and move on.)*

JESUS HEALS A PARALYZED MAN

A few days later Jesus came back to Capernaum, and the news spread that he was at home. So many people came together that there wasn't any room left, not even out in front of the door. Jesus was preaching the message to them, when a paralyzed man, carried by four men, was brought to him.

Because of the crowd, however, they could not get the man to Jesus. So they made a hole in the roof right above the place where Jesus was. When they had made an opening, they let the man down, lying on his mat. Jesus saw how much faith they had, and said to the paralyzed man, "My son, your sins are forgiven."

Some teachers of the Law who were sitting there thought to themselves,

WARM-UP

1. This story about four men removing the roof to get their friend to Jesus sounds *(circle one)*:
   a. incredible
   b. beautiful
   c. wild
   d. phony
   e. thrilling

2. If I had been in the room when those four people started to tear away the roof, I probably would have *(circle one)*:
   a. joined in
   b. objected
   c. suspected something
   d. tried to ignore it
   e. cleared out
   f. hung around to see what would happen

3. If something like this ever happened today in my church, I would be *(circle one)*:
   a. overjoyed
   b. furious
   c. curious
   d. concerned about the cost
   e. happy to see anything happen

4. The thing that impresses me about the four friends is their *(circle one)*:
   a. faith
   b. friendship
   c. ingenuity
   d. determination/persistence
   e. total dedication
   f. concern about their friend's life

GOING DEEPER

1. The people in my life who have cared enough to bring me to Christ are my *(rank top three 1, 2, 3)*:
   _____ parents
   _____ friends
   _____ relatives
   _____ Sunday School teachers
   _____ neighbors
   _____ pastors
   _____ support group

2. The time in my life when I felt closest to God was *(circle one)*:
   a. in my childhood   d. right now
   b. in my teens   e. always
   c. recently   f. never have

OVERTIME CHALLENGE

1. If I am going to move on in my spiritual life, I need a little more *(circle two)*:
   a. commitment   e. discipline
   b. support   f. understanding
   c. love   g. self-confidence
   d. guts   h. courage

2. My support group can help me best by *(circle two)*:
   a. holding me to my commitment
   b. listening
   c. being open about their struggles
   d. praying for me
   e. really being my friends
   f. joining me in this commitment
   g. giving me a good kick in the pants when I need it
   h. doing exactly what they're doing

"How does he dare talk against God like this? No man can forgive sins; only God can!"

At once Jesus knew their secret thoughts, so he said to them, "Why do you think such things? Is it easier to say to this paralyzed man, 'Your sins are forgiven,' or to say, 'Get up, pick up your mat, and walk'? I will prove to you, then, that the Son of Man has authority on earth to forgive sins." So he said to the paralyzed man, "I tell you, get up, pick up your mat, and go home!"

While they all watched, the man got up, picked up his mat, and hurried away. They were all completely amazed and praised God, saying, "We have never seen anything like this!"

MARK 2:1-12 GNFMM

Going Deeper/4's/15 min.

With your partner get together with two others from your group. Share your answers to Going Deeper, going around the group. *(Describe how you ranked your spiritual enablers and why. Set the pace for real openness. After 15 minutes call time and move on.)*

Overtime Challenge / 4's or 8's/ 15 min.

(You will have to decide if there is time to share the Overtime Challenge and, if so, whether to use groups of 4 or 8. If you are limited for time, stay with the 4's. If you have plenty of time, have the groups double up to form the same 8's as before.)

Take the first question and go around your group, letting each person explain his answer and the why. Then go around on the second question, etc. *(Explain your answer to the first question and set the pace for honesty.)*

Close-out

In each group, gather together in a football huddle—with your arms over each other's shoulders. If anyone wants to say a short prayer—a word of thanks or a request for help about something in his life—he can do so while we pause. Then I will close with a final prayer. *(Wait about 60 seconds for the groups to pray among themselves. Then break in with a prayer and Amen for all the groups. Pick up the books.)*

**HISTORY
GIVING**

Objective: To discover where the storms are in your life at the moment and what you can do about them.

PROCEDURE

The instructions are given in the words you can use in leading the group.

Silent Preparation / 5 min.

fill out the questionnaire.

Warm-up / 2's / 5 min.

Get together with someone from your group of 8 and share what you put down in the Warm-up— one question at a time. *(Take a moment and explain your answer to the first question. Call time after 5 minutes and move on.)*

Going Deeper / 4's / 15 min.

With your partner get together with two others from your group. Share your answers to Going Deeper, going around the group.

What's wrong?

WARM-UP

1. If I had been one of the disciples when the boat was about to sink in the storm, I probably would have: *(circle one):*
   a. jumped overboard
   b. screamed for help
   c. frozen
   d. started bailing water
   e. taken command of the whole situation
   f. drop out and come back fighting
   g. act like nothing is wrong

JESUS CALMS A STORM

On the evening of that same day Jesus said to his disciples, "Let us go across to the other side of the lake." So they left the crowd; the disciples got into the boat that Jesus was already in, and took him with them. Other boats were there too.

A very strong wind blew up and the waves began to spill over into the boat, so that it was about to fill with water. Jesus was in the back of the boat, sleeping with his head on a pillow. The disciples woke him up and said,

2. I think the disciples awakened Jesus because they (circle one):
   a. resented anyone sleeping in a time of crisis
   b. were afraid for his life
   c. were afraid for their own lives
   d. wanted a little help from him
   e. expected a miracle

3. Jesus calmed the wind because he wanted to (circle one):
   a. impress the disciples
   b. relieve their anxiety
   c. demonstrate his power
   d. teach them a lesson in faith
   e. show them how to deal with future storms in their lives

GOING DEEPER

1. When I am going through a storm in my life, I usually (circle two):
   a. turn to someone I can trust
   b. withdraw into myself
   c. turn to God
   d. get very touchy and irritable
   e. stay pretty calm and collected
   f. play like nothing is wrong
   g. don't know

2. If I told my family about some of the struggles I am going through right now, they would probably (circle one):
   a. die on the spot
   b. kick me out of the house
   c. reach out to me
   d. try to understand
   e. pour out their love as never before
   f. share some of their struggles with me

3. Somehow I have gotten the feeling that (circle one):
   a. it is not OK to have a problem
   b. it is OK for me to have a problem, but not for some others
   c. it is OK for others to have a problem, but not for me
   d. it is OK to have a problem but not to talk about it
   e. it is OK to have a problem and to talk about it

OVERTIME CHALLENGE

1. If I could compare my own life right now to a storm, I would be (circle one):
   a. floating on smooth waters
   b. feeling just a few ripples
   c. sensing a storm is brewing
   d. going through a storm, bailing water like mad to keep afloat
   e. calling for help
   f. seeing the storm winds subside and the calm return
   g. checking weather reports

2. "Be quiet!"..."Be still!" If Jesus were to speak these words to me today, I would take it to mean (circle one):
   a. settle down
   b. shut up and listen
   c. hang in there
   d. expect a miracle
   e. relax and let God handle this
   f. keep the faith, baby
   g. learn the secret of relying on God's energy
   h. commit your life to God and let him run it
   i. let go and let God

"Teacher, don't you care that we are about to die?"

Jesus got up and commanded the wind, "Be quiet!" and said to the waves, "Be still!" The wind died down, and there was a great calm. Then Jesus said to his disciples, "Why are you frightened? Are you still without faith?"

But they were terribly afraid, and began to say to each other, "Who is this man? Even the wind and the waves obey him!"

MARK 4:35-41 GNFMM

(Share how you would answer the first couple of things and set a pace for real openness. After 15 minutes call time and move on.)

Overtime Challenge / 4's or 8's/ 15 min.

(You will have to decide if there is time to share the Overtime Challenge and, if so, whether to use groups of 4 or 8. If you are limited for time, stay with the 4's. If you have plenty of time, have the groups double up to form the same 8's as before.)

Take the first question and go around your group, letting each person explain his answer and the why. Then go around on the second question, etc. *(Explain your answer to the first question and set the pace for honesty.)*

Close-out

In each group, gather together in a football huddle—with your arms over each other's shoulders. If anyone wants to say a short prayer—a word of thanks or a request for help about something in his life—he can do so while we pause. Then I will close with a final prayer. *(Wait about 60 seconds for the groups to pray among themselves. Then break in with a prayer and Amen for all the groups. Pick up the books.)*

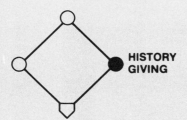

HISTORY GIVING

Where's your head?

(continued)

WARM-UP

1. If I had been one of the disciples of Jesus right after his death, I probably would have been *(circle one)*:
   a. hiding too
   b. brokenhearted
   c. terrified
   d. totally disillusioned
   e. skeptical about everything
   f. cynical

2. When Thomas said, *"If I do not see the scars of the nails in his hands, and put my finger on those scars...I will not believe,"* he meant *(circle one)*:
   a. "Prove it"
   b. "Show me"
   c. "I don't believe it"
   d. "You're crazy"

Objective: To discover how your own quest for spiritual truth and certainty and the story of "doubting" Thomas in Scripture are parallel, and to use the insight as the basis for a sharing experience in your support group.

PROCEDURE

The instructions are given in the words you can use in leading the group.

Silent Preparation / 5 min.
fill out the questionnaire.

Warm-up / 4's / 10 min.
Get together with 3 others from your group of 8 and share the Warm-up in the questionnaire with each other. Go around on the first question. Then go around on the second question, etc. *(Take a moment and explain your answer to the first question. Set the pace for gut honesty—especially in this*

e. "I want to believe, but..."

f. "Don't break my heart a second time"

3. Thomas reminds me of a *(circle two)*:
   a. research scientist
   b. politician
   c. spoiled child
   d. honest doubter
   e. college student
   f. myself
   g. know-it-all teacher

GOING DEEPER

1. This whole idea of being open and honest about one's religious doubts strikes me as *(circle one)*:
   a. dangerous
   b. healthy
   c. disrespectful
   d. helpful
   e. part of growing up spiritually
   f. really encouraging to me
   g. childish

2. If I could ask one question of Jesus about my own faith, it would be *(circle one)*:
   a. how do you know when you have "touched" God?
   b. what happens when you don't feel like a Christian?
   c. how do you deal with feelings of doubt and failure?
   d. what about the guys who say that Christianity is a bunch of superstitions?
   e. how can I know for sure that I am in God's will?

OVERTIME CHALLENGE

1. The times in my life when Jesus Christ has made himself especially known to me are *(circle two)*:
   a. Easter
   b. seeing a sunset
   c. during pain and sorrow
   d. meditating on Scripture
   e. at communion
   f. hearing a great piece of music
   g. at the death of a close friend
   h. right now
   i. when I found wonderful fellowship with another Christian
   j. _____

2. In my own quest for religious certainty, I am the kind who relies on *(circle two)*:
   a. a bolt of lightning
   b. scientific verification
   c. emotional peace
   d. simple faith
   e. what others say
   f. the Scripture
   g. feeling good
   h. logic
   i. don't know
   j. Christian friends
   k. pastor/priest

3. The thing that helps me to believe in the resurrection is *(circle two)*:
   a. the fact that the Bible says it
   b. the evidence of daily miracles
   c. the faith of my parents
   d. the historical endurance of the church
   e. experiencing his presence in this support group
   f. my own life-change

JESUS AND THOMAS

One of the twelve disciples, Thomas (called the Twin), was not with them when Jesus came. So the other disciples told him, "We saw the Lord!"

Thomas said to them, "If I do not see the scars of the nails in his hands, and put my finger on those scars, and my hand in his side, I will not believe."

A week later the disciples were together indoors again, and Thomas was with them. The doors were locked, but Jesus came and stood among them and said, "Peace be with you." Then he said to Thomas, "Put your finger here, and look at my hands; then stretch out your hand and put it in my side. Stop your doubting, and believe!"

Thomas answered him, "My Lord and my God!"

Jesus said to him, "Do you believe because you see me? How happy are those who believe without seeing me!"

JOHN 20:24-29 GNFMM

Scripture passage about honesty. After 10 minutes call time and move on.)

Going Deeper / 2's / 10 min.

Split into 2's and share your answers to Going Deeper in the questionnaire. *(Share your thoughts about the first question. Let your answer permit other's to feel it is OK to have spiritual doubts. After 10 minutes call time and move on.)*

Overtime Challenge / 4's or 8's / 15 min.

(You will have to decide if there is time to share the Overtime Challenge and if so, whether to use groups of 4 or 8. If time is limited, go back to 4's. If you have plenty of time, use 8's—the same 8's that have been together before.)

Take the first question and go around your group, letting each person explain his answer. Then go around on the second question, etc. *(Explain your answer to the first question. Then turn the groups loose.)*

Close-out

Stand together in a close circle— with your arms over each other's shoulders and spend a time in prayer. Anyone who wants to pray may do so, and I will close. *(Wait just a few moments then break in and pray for all the groups. Collect the books.)*

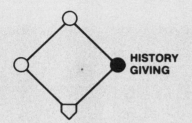

**HISTORY
GIVING**

Objective: To discover how the people in your group have enabled you to come forth as a new person in Christ, and to use the insight as the basis for a sharing experience.

PROCEDURE
The instructions are given in the words you can use in leading the group.

Silent Preparation/5 min.
fill out the questionnaire.

Warm-up / 4's / 10 min.
Get together in 4's—with others from your group of 8—and share the Warm-up. Go around on the first question. Then go around on the second question, etc. *(Take a moment and explain your answer to the first question. Set the pace for candor and honesty. Remember, your example will set the tone. After 10 minutes call time and move on.)*

Why get excited?

WARM-UP

1. Personally, I find the whole idea of death *(circle one)*:
   a. upsetting
   b. far off
   c. something I don't like to think about
   d. mysterious
   e. part of life
   f. something I need to deal with
   g. haven't thought about it

2. The closest I have come to seeing a person brought back from the dead is *(circle one)*:
   a. a drowning person
   b. a heart attack victim
   c. an attempted suicide
   d. my own mental attitude about life
   e. my spiritual life

3. The thing that amazes me about this story is *(circle one)*:
   a. the faith that Mary had in Jesus: *"Lord, if you had been here, my brother would not have died."*
   b. the love of Jesus for his friends: *"his heart was touched, and he was deeply moved...Jesus wept."*
   c. the willingness of the friends to do the outrageous: *"They took the stone away."*
   d. the power of Jesus to command a dead person to come back: *"Lazarus, come out."*
   e. the way Jesus called on the friends to help in the healing process: *"Untie him...and let him go."*

THE DEATH OF LAZARUS

A man named Lazarus, who lived in Bethany, became sick....His sisters (Mary and Martha) sent Jesus a message....When Jesus arrived, he found that Lazarus had been buried four days before....Mary fell at Jesus' feet. "Lord," she said, "if you had been here, my brother would not have died!"
Jesus saw her weeping, and the Jews who had come with her weeping also; his heart was touched, and he was deeply moved. "Where have you buried him?" he asked them.
"Come and see, Lord," they answered.
Jesus wept. So the Jews said, "See how much he loved him!"...

LAZARUS BROUGHT TO LIFE

Deeply moved once more, Jesus went to the tomb, which was a cave with a stone placed at the entrance. "Take the stone away!" Jesus ordered.
Martha, the dead man's sister, answered, "There will be a bad smell, Lord. He has been buried four days!"
Jesus said to her, "Didn't I tell you that you would see God's glory if you believed?" They took the stone away. Jesus looked up and said, "I thank you, Father, that you listen to me. I know that you always listen to me, but I say this because of the people here, so they will believe that you sent me." After he had said this he called out in a loud voice, "Lazarus, come out!" The dead man came out, his hands and feet wrapped in grave cloths, and a cloth around his face. "Untie him," Jesus told them, "and let him go."

JOHN 11:1-44 GNFMM

GOING DEEPER

1. If I could compare my own feeling of spiritual freedom to Lazarus' experience, I am right now *(circle one)*:
   a. in the tomb—lifeless
   b. hearing the words of Jesus, *"Come out!"* but that's all
   c. out of the tomb, but tied up in the graveclothes so that I cannot move
   d. feeling a new freedom as the graveclothes are untied
   e. alive and free
   f. someplace inbetween

2. The people in my support group have helped "untie some of the old graveclothes" by *(circle one)*:
   a. letting me share some of my hangups
   b. sharing some of their hangups
   c. accepting me with all of my hangups
   d. telling me it is OK to have hangups
   e. affirming my good points
   f. not letting me dwell on my hangups

OVERTIME CHALLENGE

1. When I feel down, I usually *(circle two)*:
   a. get away from it all
   b. seek out a friend
   c. turn to God
   d. just sit and watch TV
   e. don't want to talk to anybody
   f. take a long walk
   g. cry
   h. never cry
   i. take it out on everybody else
   j. seek out my pastor

2. The idea of opening up and sharing some of my struggles with my support group sounds *(circle one)*:
   a. risky
   b. difficult
   c. dangerous
   d. valuable, but
   e. OK, if everybody else will
   f. just what I'm looking for
   g. like what we're already doing
   h. immature

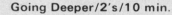

Going Deeper/2's/10 min.
Divide into 2's and share your answers to Going Deeper. *(Give your thoughts about the first question. Let your answer be the permission to feel OK about spiritual doubts. After 10 minutes call time and move on.)*

Overtime Challenge / 4's or 8's / 15 min.
(You will have to decide if there is time to share the Overtime Challenge and if so, whether to use groups of 4 or 8. If you are limited for time, go back to 4's. If you have plenty of time, move into 8's—the same 8's that have been together before.)
   Take the first question and go around your group, letting each person explain his answer. Then go around on the second question, etc. *(Take a moment and explain your answer to the first question. Then turn the groups loose.)*

Close-out
Get together in a football huddle and spend a time in prayer. Anyone that wants to say a prayer may do so while I pause. Then I will close in prayer for all of the groups. *(Wait 60 seconds while the groups pray. Then break in with a final prayer. Pick up all the books.)*

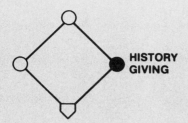

HISTORY GIVING

Objective: To discover how your own view of God and grace influences your desire to live a clean life, and to use your insight as the basis for a sharing experience.

PROCEDURE

The instructions are given in the words you can use in leading the group.

Silent Preparation/5 min.

fill out the questionnaire.

Warm-up / 4's / 10 min.

Get together in 4's—with others from your group of 8—and share the Warm-up. Go around on the first question. Then go around on the second question, etc. *(Take a moment and explain your answer to the first question. Set the pace for openness and honesty. After 10 minutes call time and move on.)*

Going Deeper / 2's / 10 min.

Divide into 2's and share your answers to Going Deeper. *(Give*

What's the good news?

WARM-UP

1. If I had been the girl who was caught in the act of sexual intercourse and dragged (naked) before Jesus, I would have been *(circle one)*:
   a. furious   d. bitter
   b. terrified   e. dazed
   c. ashamed   f. embarrassed

2. If I had been one of the crowd, I would have *(circle one)*:
   a. looked the other way
   b. blushed
   c. stood up for the girl
   d. joined in with the crowd
   e. probably done nothing

3. The beautiful thing about this story for me is the way Jesus *(circle one)*:
   a. was gentle with the girl
   b. exposed the double standards of the Pharisees
   c. doodled in the sand
   d. put down religious hypocrisy
   e. gave the girl a second chance

GOING DEEPER

1. If I could compare my idea of God to a football system, I would see God as a *(circle one)*:
   a. hard-nosed business manager
   b. rugged, demanding coach
   c. quarterback—calling the plays
   d. scout—checking out the opposition and recommending strategy
   e. owner—sitting in the stands
   f. water boy—ready with some instant energy for the game
   g. trainer—keeping the team in condition

2. In the last sentence Jesus was saying to the girl, "I will accept you..." *(circle one)*:
   a. if you change your ways
   b. whether you change your ways or not
   c. as you are, but I don't want you to stay this way

THE WOMAN CAUGHT IN ADULTERY

[*Then everyone went home, but Jesus went to the Mount of Olives. Early the next morning he went back to the temple. The whole crowd gathered around him, and he sat down and began to teach them. The teachers of the Law and the Pharisees brought in a woman who had been caught committing adultery, and made her stand before them all. "Teacher," they said to Jesus, "this woman was caught in the very act of committing adultery. In our Law Moses gave a commandment that such a woman must be stoned to death. Now, what do you say?" They said this to trap him, so they could accuse him. But Jesus bent over and wrote on the ground with his finger. As they stood there asking him questions, he straightened up and said to them, "Whichever one of you has committed no sin may throw the first stone at her." Then he bent over again and wrote on the ground. When they heard this they all left, one by one, the older ones first. Jesus was left alone, with the woman still standing there. He straightened up and said to her, "Where are they, woman? Is there no one left to condemn you?"*

"No one, sir," she answered.

"Well, then," Jesus said, "I do not condemn you either. Go, but do not sin again."]

JOHN 8:1-11 GNFMM

3. In my own life, the greatest motivation to lead a clean life is *(rank top three 1, 2, 3)*:
   __ my family—not to disappoint them
   __ my friends—not to let them down
   __ my own self-respect—to be true to myself
   __ my fear of God—not to incur his anger
   __ my love for God—to please him
   __ God's love for me—freely given

OVERTIME CHALLENGE

1. The people that accept me with the same unconditional love that Jesus offered to the girl are *(circle two)*:
   a. my family
   b. my friends
   c. my support group
   d. one special person
   e. my relatives
   f. no one that I know of

2. When I blow it in one way or another, I usually *(circle one)*:
   a. crawl into a hole
   b. see my priest
   c. talk to a friend who will listen
   d. try to forget it
   e. turn to God
   f. try to be extra good
   g. punish myself

3. Since being in this support group, I have learned that *(circle one)*:
   a. it is OK to have a problem
   b. everyone has problems
   c. we can help each other by sharing our problems
   d. we are supposed to confess our faults to each other
   e. everyone has blown it at one time or another
   f. there is forgiveness from God and acceptance from his people for anything we have done wrong

your thoughts about the first question. After 10 minutes call time and move on.)

Overtime Challenge / 4's or 8's / 15 min.

(You will have to decide if there is time to share the Overtime Challenge and if so, whether to use groups of 4 or 8. If you are limited for time, go back to 4's. If you have plenty of time, move into 8's—the same 8's that have been together before.)

Take the first question and go around your group, letting each person explain his answer. Then go around on the second question, etc. *(Take a moment and explain your answer to the first question. Then turn the groups loose.)*

Close-out

Get together in a football huddle and spend a time in prayer. Anyone that wants to say a prayer may do so while I pause. Then I will close in prayer for all of the groups. *(Wait 60 seconds while the groups pray. Then break in with a final prayer. Pick up all the books.)*

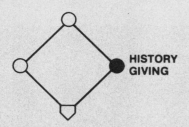

HISTORY GIVING

Why me?

Objective: To discover how your spiritual encounter with Jesus Christ and the encounter of Zacchaeus with Christ are similar, and to use the insight as the basis for a sharing experience with your support group.

PROCEDURE

The instructions are given in the words you can use in leading the group.

Silent Preparation / 5 min.
fill out the questionnaire.

Warm-up / 4's / 10 min.
Get together with 4 people from your group of 8 and share what you put down in the Warm-up—one question at a time. *(Take a moment and explain your answer for the first question. After 10 minutes call time and move on.)*

JESUS AND ZACCHAEUS

Jesus went on into Jericho and was passing through. There was a chief tax collector there, named Zacchaeus, who was rich. He was trying to see who Jesus was, but he was a little man and could not see Jesus because of the crowd. So he ran ahead of the crowd and climbed a sycamore tree to see Jesus, who would be going that way. When Jesus came to that place, he looked up and said to Zacchaeus, "Hurry down, Zacchaeus, because I must stay in your house today."

Zacchaeus hurried down and welcomed him with great joy. All the people who saw it started grumbling, "This man has gone as a guest to the home of a sinner!"

Zacchaeus stood up and said to the Lord, "Listen, sir! I will give half my belongings to the poor; and if I have cheated anyone, I will pay him back four times as much."

Jesus said to him, "Salvation has come to this house today; this man, also, is a descendant of Abraham. For the Son of Man came to seek and to save the lost."

LUKE 19:1-10 GNFMM

WARM-UP

1. If I had been Zacchaeus when Jesus stopped and told him, "Hurry down," I would have been *(circle one)*:
   a. flabbergasted
   b. scared spitless
   c. overwhelmed with joy
   d. apprehensive about his motives
   e. embarrassed
   f. excited and afraid at the same time

2. When Jesus called Zacchaeus by name and asked to stay at his house, he probably wanted to *(circle one)*:
   a. talk to him about his shady tax collecting
   b. touch him up for a loan
   c. demonstrate to everyone that even the most hated man in town was also worth saving
   d. remind Zacchaeus of his great heritage as a son of Abraham
   e. make a lonely little man feel OK
   f. stay in the nicest house in town

3. The amazing turn-around in Zacchaeus' life probably came about because Jesus *(circle one)*:
   a. made this a condition for acceptance
   b. accepted him as he was
   c. made Zacchaeus feel worthwhile
   d. threw down a challenge
   e. let him see what "greatness" looked like

GOING DEEPER

1. In my own life, God's call got through to me by *(circle one)*:
   a. showing me a better way
   b. convicting me of wrongdoing
   c. accepting me as I am
   d. lifting my own self-esteem
   e. giving me his own love
   f. coming to me through a caring friend

2. As I honestly consider my own life and purpose right now, I feel *(circle two)*:
   a. nervous
   b. frustrated
   c. empty
   d. excited
   e. uncertain
   f. satisfied
   g. contented
   h. fulfilled
   i. foreboding
   j. up-tight

3. The idea of opening up and talking about my life this way strikes me as *(circle two)*:
   a. awkward
   b. silly
   c. scary
   d. awful
   e. helpful
   f. easy
   g. dumb
   h. fine, but...
   i. difficult
   j. mature
   k. immature

OVERTIME CHALLENGE

1. If Jesus were to pass my way today, he would probably *(circle one)*:
   a. ask me, "Why are you always dodging me?"
   b. give me a bawling out
   c. put his arms around me and hug me
   d. give me a swift kick in the pants
   e. slap me on the shoulder and tell me I'm great
   f. make me whole

2. Down deep inside, I wish I could *(circle one)*:
   a. accept myself
   b. accept God
   c. relate more easily to others
   d. have a good friend
   e. have the strength to improve
   f. stand up for what I believe
   g. lead more people to God
   h. share my feelings
   i. get along with my parents

3. If I could give myself a gift right now, it would be a little more *(circle one)*:
   a. patience
   b. love
   c. joy
   d. peace
   e. talent
   f. ability
   g. kindness
   h. faith
   i. courage
   j. understanding
   k. trust

Going Deeper / 2's / 10 min.

Split into 2's and share your answers to Going Deeper with each other. *(Share your answer to the first question—how God's call got through to you. Set the pace for real openness. After 10 minutes call time and move on.)*

Overtime Challenge / 4's or 8's / 15 min.

(You will have to decide if there is time to share the Overtime Challenge and if so, whether to use groups of 4 or 8. If time is limited, go back to the 4's. If there is plenty of time, use 8's—the same 8's that have been together all along.)

Take the first question and go around your group, letting each person explain his answer. Then go around on the second question, etc. *(Explain what Jesus would likely do with you. Set the pace for understanding His nature and one's need.)*

Close-out

Stand together in a close circle—with your arms over each other's shoulders and let anyone who wants to volunteer a prayer do so. *(After a few moments offer a word of thanks for the lives the Lord turns around and the love he gives us. Collect the books.)*

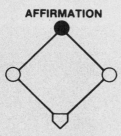

How's your serve?

Objective: To discover how the persons in your support group have ministered to your needs during this program, and to use the insight as the basis for a sharing experience.

PROCEDURE

The instructions are given in the words you can use in leading the group.

Silent Preparation / 5 min.

fill out the questionnaire.

Warm-up / 4's / 10 min.

Get together with four people from your group of 8 and share what you put down in the Warm-

JESUS WASHES HIS DISCIPLES' FEET

It was now the day before the Feast of Passover. Jesus knew that his hour had come for him to leave this world and go the Father. He had always loved those who were his own in the world, and he loved them to the very end.

Jesus and his disciples were at supper. The Devil had already decided that Judas, the son of Simon Iscariot, would betray Jesus. Jesus knew that the Father had given him complete power; he knew that he had come from God and was going to God. So Jesus rose from the table, took off his outer garment, and tied a towel around his waist. Then he poured some water into a washbasin and began to wash the disciples' feet and dry them with the towel around his waist....

After he had washed their feet, Jesus put his outer garment back on and returned to his place at the table. "Do you understand what I have just done to you?" he asked. "You call me Teacher and Lord, and it is right that you do so, because I am. I am your Lord and Teacher, and I have just washed your feet. You, then, should wash each other's feet. I have set an example for you, so that you will do just what I have done for you."

JOHN 13:1-15 GNFMM

WARM-UP

1. If I had been one of the disciples when Jesus came to wash their feet, I would have *(circle one)*:
   a. been humiliated
   b. refused
   c. felt like refusing
   d. insisted on washing his feet
   e. cried
   f. considered it a great honor

2. Frankly, I find the idea of washing another's feet *(circle one)*:
   a. degrading
   b. silly
   c. embarrassing
   d. childish
   e. the greatest kind of leadership
   f. what Christianity is all about
   g. what we need more of
   h. old-fashioned
   i. ridiculous

3. In my estimation, the reason why Jesus washed the feet of his disciples was to *(circle one)*:
   a. show his deep love for them
   b. teach them a lesson in servanthood
   c. shame them for being insensitive to each other's needs
   d. show them real leadership
   e. give them a new model for their lives together

GOING DEEPER

1. The reason why we do not see more genuine footwashing in Christian relationships today is because we *(circle one)*:
   a. don't need each other
   b. don't know we need each other
   c. don't know each other's needs
   d. don't want to know each others' needs
   e. don't want others to know our needs

2. If Jesus were to step into our support group to "wash our feet" in a meaningful way, I think he would probably *(circle one)*:
   a. give us a good pat on the back
   b. tell us he was proud of us
   c. put his arms around us and give each one of us a great big hug
   d. wash our feet just like he did for his disciples

3. If I were serious about "footwashing," I would have to start in my home *(fill in the blanks with the service you would perform for each)*:
   a. with my mom by _____
   b. with my dad by _____
   c. with my brother/sister by _____

OVERTIME CHALLENGE

How has each one in your group "washed your feet"? *(In the circles write the names of your support group and beside each name, jot down a service that each has performed for you.)*

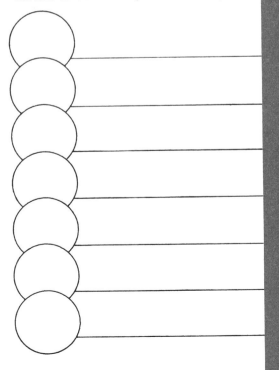

up—one question at a time. *(Take a moment and explain your answer for the first question. After 10 minutes call time and move on.)*

Going Deeper/2's/10 min.

Divide into 2's and share your answers to Going Deeper. *(Take a moment and explain your answer to the first question. Set the pace for real openness. After 10 minutes call time and move on.)*

Overtime Challenge / 4's or 8's / 15 min.

(You will have to decide if there is time to share the Overtime Challenge and, if so, whether to use groups of 4 or 8. If you are limited for time, go back to the 4's. If you have plenty of time, move into 8's —the same groups that have been together all along.)

Ask one person in your group to sit in silence while the others explain how he has ministered to their needs during the program. Then move to the next person and go around again, etc., until everyone has been covered. *(Choose one person you know well and share how he has ministered to you.)*

Close-out

In your group, join in a football huddle and let anyone who wants to volunteer a prayer do so while I pause. Then I will close with a prayer for the whole group. *(Wait about 60 seconds while the groups pray. Then break in with a final prayer. Pick up all the books.)*

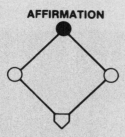

Objective: To discover how you respond to human need situations in view of the disciples' reactions when the 5,000 were fed, and to use your insight as the basis for a sharing experience.

PROCEDURE

The instructions are given in the words you can use in leading the group.

Silent Preparation / 5 min.
fill out the questionnaire.

Warm-up / 4's / 10 min.
Get together with four people from your group of 8 and share what you put down in the Warm-up—one question at a time. *(Take*

What is God wanting you to do?

WARM-UP

1. If I had been one of the disciples when Jesus suggested that they feed the crowd, I would have *(circle one)*:
   a. fainted on the spot
   b. quietly slipped away
   c. found some excuse to put off the problem
   d. passed the buck
   e. referred it to a committee
   f. reacted just as the disciples did

JESUS FEEDS THE FIVE THOUSAND

The apostles came back and told Jesus everything they had done. He took them with him and they went off by themselves to a town named Bethsaida. When the crowds heard about it they followed him. He welcomed them, spoke to them about the Kingdom of God, and healed those who needed it.

When the sun had begun to set, the twelve disciples came to him and said, "Send the people away so they can go to the villages and farms around here and find food and lodging, because this is a lonely place."

But Jesus said to them, "You yourselves give them something to eat."

They answered, "All we have is five loaves and two fish. Do you want us to go and buy food for this whole crowd?" (There were about five thousand men there.)

Jesus said to his disciples, "Make the people sit down in groups of about fifty each."

The disciples did so and made them all sit down. Jesus took the five loaves and two fish, looked up to heaven, thanked God for them, broke them, and gave them to the disciples to distribute to the people. They all ate and had enough; and the disciples took up twelve baskets of what the people left over.

LUKE 9:10-17 GNFMM

2. The thought of my having special gifts to contribute to the world's needs makes me feel *(circle two)*:
   a. sort of responsible
   b. kinda funny
   c. scared
   d. guilty
   e. like doing something
   f. never thought about it

3. My favorite way of avoiding my own responsibility is usually to *(circle one)*:
   a. say the problem is too large
   b. blame somebody else
   c. insist that someone else go first
   d. put off the decision
   e. confess how inadequate I am
   f. decide that nothing can be done about the situation, so why bother

OVERTIME CHALLENGE

1. If my support group had been the disciples of Jesus at the time of this crisis, we would probably *(circle one)*:
   a. still be trying to decide what to do
   b. have organized a committee among ourselves
   c. still be running (in the other direction)
   d. jumped at the chance to do something

2. If our support group had to come up with five loaves and two fishes among ourselves, I think we would be able to offer a lot of *(circle two)*:
   a. caring for people
   b. commitment to Christ
   c. loyalty to one another
   d. Bible knowledge
   e. strong spiritual leadership
   f. dedication to be God's men in our world

3. Our support group might be lacking a bit in *(circle one)*:
   a. enthusiasm
   b. commitment
   c. desire
   d. follow-through
   e. know-how
   f. clear-cut objectives
   g. courage
   h. confidence
   i. teamwork

2. I see this story primarily as a lesson in *(circle two)*:
   a. frustration
   b. ecology
   c. faith
   d. crowd psychology
   e. food conservation
   f. human resourcefulness
   g. spiritual power
   h. discipleship training
   i. compassion
   j. exhibitionism
   k. who Jesus is

GOING DEEPER

1. When faced with an overwhelming need like the one that the disciples of Jesus faced, I tend to *(circle two)*:
   a. panic
   b. rise to the occasion
   c. feel totally inadequate
   d. take charge
   e. shy away from responsibility
   f. get involved in any way I can
   g. cave in
   h. get interested in something else

a moment and explain your answer for the first question. After 10 minutes call time and move on.)

Going Deeper / 2's / 10 min.
Divide into 2's and share your answers to Going Deeper. *(Take a moment and explain your answer to the first question. Set the pace for real openness. After 10 minutes call time and move on.)*

Overtime Challenge / 4's or 8's / 15 min.
(You will have to decide if there is time to share the Overtime Challenge and, if so, whether to use groups of 4 or 8. If time is limited, stay with the 4's. If there is plenty of time, move into 8's.)
   Take the first question and go around your group, letting each person share his position. Then go around on the second question, etc. *(Share your position on the first question, but leave the door open for others to differ.)*

Close-out
In your group, join in a football huddle and let anyone who wants to volunteer a prayer do so while I pause. Then I will close with a prayer for the whole group. *(Wait 60 seconds while the groups pray among themselves. Then break in with a prayer and Amen for all the groups. Pick up the books.)*

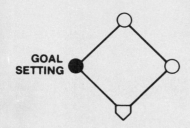

GOAL SETTING

What do you say?

Objective: To discover how your commitment to Jesus Christ and the challenge that Jesus put to his disciples coincide, and to use the insight as the basis for a sharing experience with your support group.

PROCEDURE

The instructions are given in the words you can use in leading the group.

Silent Preparation / 5 min.
fill out the questionnaire.

Warm-up / 2's / 5 min.
Get together with someone from your group of 8 and share your Warm-up with one another. *(Take a moment and explain your*

WARM-UP

1. When I compare my own life to the standard laid down in this passage for a "follower of Jesus," I feel like *(circle one)*:
   a. getting involved
   b. erasing my past
   c. rethinking where I am
   d. starting all over again
   e. going for broke
   f. ducking
   g. yawning

2. If Jesus were to ask the same question of me that he asked Peter, *"Who do you say I am?"* I would have to say he is *(circle two)*:
   a. my friend
   b. a great teacher
   c. an embarrassment
   d. the Son of God
   e. love
   f. Savior
   g. someone I want to know
   h. a mystery
   i. don't know

3. *"If anyone wants to come with me, he must forget himself, take up his cross every day, and follow me."* This sounds like *(circle two)*:
   a. a commercial
   b. a Sunday School lesson
   c. an appeal for help
   d. something worth giving my life to
   e. getting back to fundamentals
   f. a father-son or mother-daughter talk

PETER'S DECLARATION ABOUT JESUS

One time when Jesus was praying alone, the disciples came to him. "Who do the crowds say I am?" he asked them.

"Some say that you are John the Baptist," they answered. "Others say that you are Elijah, while others say that one of the prophets of long ago has come back to life."

"What about you?" he asked them. "Who do you say I am?"

Peter answered, "You are God's Messiah."

JESUS SPEAKS ABOUT HIS SUFFERING AND DEATH

Then Jesus gave them strict orders not to tell this to anyone, and added, "The Son of Man must suffer much, and be rejected by the elders, the chief priests, and the teachers of the Law. He will be put to death, and be raised to life on the third day."

And he said to all, "If anyone wants to come with me, he must forget himself, take up his cross every day, and follow me. For whoever wants to save his own life will lose it; but whoever loses his life for my sake will save it. Will a man gain anything if he wins the whole world but is himself lost or defeated? Of course not!

LUKE 9:18-25 GNFMM

GOING DEEPER

1. If I could compare my own Christian life to a football game, I would be right now *(circle one)*:
   a. suiting up
   b. waiting for the game to start
   c. sitting on the bench
   d. playing "catch up"
   e. at half time
   f. on the injured list
   g. worn out
   h. giving it all I've got

2. My favorite way of dodging the issue of Christian discipleship is by *(circle one)*:
   a. claiming I don't understand
   b. saying nobody else is serious
   c. just ignoring it
   d. putting it off until next week
   e. asking somebody else to go first

3. My biggest fear in going further in my Christian commitment is the fear of being *(circle one)*:
   a. laughed at by my friends
   b. considered anti-intellectual
   c. cramped in my lifestyle
   d. a failure
   e. "too" emotional
   f. called a sissy
   g. asked to give up something important

OVERTIME CHALLENGE

1. If God could deal with me right now like a principal, he would probably *(circle two)*:
   a. chew me out
   b. suspend me
   c. make me stay after school
   d. give me extra work
   e. be patient with my mistakes
   f. put his arm around me and say he is proud of me
   g. give me a swift kick in the pants
   h. put me in charge of something

2. An attitude I need to transfer from athletic training into my spiritual training is *(rank top three 1, 2, 3)*:
   ____ absolute dedication
   ____ knowledge of the game
   ____ team loyalty and support
   ____ day-to-day training
   ____ a good mental attitude
   ____ desire to win
   ____ ability to bounce back from a loss
   ____ long-range strategy
   ____ team spirit
   ____ concentration on the basics
   ____ _____
   ____ _____

answer to the first question. Then turn the groups of 2 loose. After 5 minutes call time and move on.)

Going Deeper / 4's / 10 min.
Take your partner and get together with 2 others from your group of 8 and share Going Deeper—one question at a time around the group. *(Explain your answer to the first question. Then turn the groups loose. After 10 minutes call time and move on.)*

Overtime Challenge / 8's / 15 min.
Regather your group of 8—the same that have been together before—and share the Overtime Challenge with one another. *(Explain your answer to the first question and set the pace for openness and honesty.)*

Close-out
Stand together in a close circle—with your arms over each other's shoulders. Anyone who wants to say a prayer—a few words of thanks or a request concerning a problem or need—can do so while we wait. Then I will close. *(After about 60 seconds break in with a brief prayer. Collect the books.)*

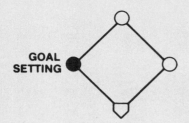

GOAL SETTING

Objective: To discover how you would respond to the question that Jesus asked Peter, "Do you really love me?" and to use the insight as the basis for a sharing experience.

PROCEDURE

The instructions are given in the words you can use in leading the group.

Silent Preparation / 5 min.
fill out the questionnaire.

Warm-up / 2's / 5 min.
Get together with someone from your group of 8 and share the Warm-up. *(Take a moment and explain your answer to the first*

What's your answer?

WARM-UP

1. If I had been Peter when Jesus asked three times: *"Do you love me?"* I think I would have *(circle one)*:
   a. burst out in tears
   b. blown my top
   c. refused to answer
   d. been deeply hurt
   e. gotten mad
   f. wondered what was wrong

2. I think Jesus put the question three times to Peter in order to *(circle one)*:
   a. get him to listen
   b. rub it in
   c. shame Peter with his past failure
   d. impress Peter with the importance of the answer
   e. _____

3. When Jesus said, *"Take care of my sheep,"* I think he was saying *(circle one)*:
   a. settle down to the job of spreading the Gospel
   b. cut out the Mickey-Mouse stuff
   c. people are more important than anything else
   d. watch your priorities
   e. quit fooling around
   f. _____

GOING DEEPER

1. If Jesus were to ask me, *"Do you love me more than all else?"* I would have to say *(circle one)*:
   a. yes—all of the time
   b. yes—most of the time
   c. yes—some of the time
   d. yes—when I am thinking of it
   e. huh?
   f. I wish you hadn't asked right now

2. Since being in this support group, my greatest growth has been in the area of my *(rank top three 1, 2, 3)*:
   ____ personal discipline
   ____ moral development
   ____ spiritual development
   ____ mental attitude
   ____ self-acceptance
   ____ Bible understanding
   ____ willingness to share myself
   ____ concern for others
   ____ attitude about school
   ____ family relationships

OVERTIME CHALLENGE

1. Right now, I feel that I am living up to *(circle one)*:
   a. all that I know is God's call for my life
   b. all that I am willing to know of God's call for my life
   c. less than what I know is God's call for my life
   d. just what's possible—I can't do anymore
   e. what I want to do. Please don't bother me with God's call

2. Frankly, if I were to take this matter of Christian commitment seriously, I would have to *(circle one)*:
   a. change a few things
   b. overhaul my priorities—decide what is really important
   c. give up some of my own desires
   d. clear up a few of my sour relationships
   e. start all over again

3. If I decided to do something about committing my whole life to God, I would need *(circle two)*:
   a. some support from my friends
   b. a good kick in the pants
   c. a little more self-confidence
   d. a greater spiritual commitment
   e. all of the love I can get
   f. an awareness of what God wants

JESUS AND PETER

After they had eaten, Jesus said to Simon Peter, "Simon, son of John, do you love me more than these?"

"Yes, Lord," he answered, "you know that I love you."

Jesus said to him, "Take care of my lambs." A second time Jesus said to him, "Simon, son of John, do you love me?"

"Yes, Lord," he answered, "you know that I love you."

Jesus said to him, "Take care of my sheep." A third time Jesus said, "Simon, son of John, do you love me?"

Peter became sad because Jesus asked him the third time, "Do you love me?" and said to him, "Lord, you know everything; you know that I love you!"

Jesus said to him, "Take care of my sheep."

JOHN 21:15-17 GNFMM

question. Then turn the groups loose. After 5 minutes call time and move on.)

Going Deeper/4's / 10 min.

With your partner get together with another pair from your group of 8 and share Going Deeper — one question at a time around the group. *(Explain your answer to the first question. After 10 minutes call time and move on.)*

Overtime Challenge / 8's / 15 min.

Regather your group of 8—the same group that has been together before—and share the Overtime Challenge with one another. *(Explain your answer to the first question and set the pace for openness and honesty.)*

Close-out

In your group join together in a football huddle and let anyone who wants to say a prayer—of thanksgiving or about a problem or need—do so while I wait. Then I will close in prayer for the entire group. *(Wait about 60 seconds. Then break in with a final prayer for all the groups. Collect all the books.)*

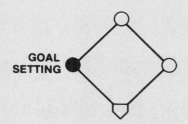

GOAL
SETTING

Objective: To discover how you respond to challenges that involve personal risk, and to use your insight as the basis for a sharing experience in your group.

PROCEDURE

The instructions are given in the words you can use in leading the group.

Silent Preparation / 5 min.

fill out the questionnaire.

160

What's your next step?

WARM-UP

1. If I had been Peter when Jesus invited him to step out of the boat and walk on the water, I probably would have *(circle one)*:

   a. shrunk back in horror
   b. made some excuse
   c. asked someone else to go first
   d. explained I was just kidding
   e. jumped at the chance

JESUS WALKS ON THE WATER

Then Jesus made the disciples get into the boat and go ahead of him to the other side of the lake, while he sent the people away. After sending the people away, he went up a hill by himself to pray. When evening came, Jesus was there alone; by this time the boat was far out in the lake, tossed about by the waves, because the wind was blowing against it. Between three and six o'clock in the morning Jesus came to them, walking on the water. When the disciples saw him walking on the water they were terrified. "It's a ghost!" they said, and screamed with fear.

Jesus spoke to them at once. "Courage!" he said. "It is I. Don't be afraid!"

2. When it comes to doing something new, I am (circle two):
   a. just plain scared
   b. very cautious
   c. daring
   d. afraid that someone will laugh
   e. willing to try anything once
   f. afraid of failing
   g. a follower, not a leader

GOING DEEPER

1. To me, the Christian life is like (circle one):
   a. a wild roller-coaster ride
   b. a smooth sailing ship
   c. a trapeze artist—letting go of one bar to reach for another
   d. fourth down and goal to go
   e. locked in by accident in a department store
   f. fire escape in a "towering inferno"
   g. swimming the English Channel after seeing "Jaws"
   h. _____

2. If I could count on the support of the others in my group, I would like to (circle one):
   a. make a new commitment of my life to Christ
   b. find out what God wants with my life
   c. go deeper with Christ
   d. stand up for what I believe
   e. get involved in some kind of action

3. Before I do anything, I must deal with my (circle one):
   a. fear of failure
   b. family relationships
   c. spiritual bankruptcy
   d. crippling thought-life
   e. sense of inadequacy
   f. inconsistency
   g. intellectual doubts
   h. fear of standing alone
   i. impulse to rush into things before counting the cost

OVERTIME CHALLENGE

1. The area in my life where I have experienced the greatest growth lately is my (rank 1, 2, 3):
   ___ spiritual life
   ___ relationships with people
   ___ self-acceptance
   ___ attitude toward the church
   ___ ability to take action
   ___ personal discipline

2. If God could deal with me right now as a teacher or boss, he would probably (circle one):
   a. chew me out
   b. be patient with my mistakes
   c. work me extra hours
   d. tell me to go home and rest
   e. give me a good kick in the pants
   f. put his arm around me and tell me that he was proud of me
   g. _____

Then Peter spoke up. "Lord," he said, "if it is really you, order me to come out on the water to you."

"Come!" answered Jesus. So Peter got out of the boat and started walking on the water to Jesus. When he noticed the wind, however, he was afraid, and started to sink down in the water. "Save me, Lord!" he cried.

At once Jesus reached out and grabbed him and said, "How little faith you have! Why did you doubt?"

They both got into the boat, and the wind died down. The disciples in the boat worshiped Jesus. "Truly you are the Son of God!" they exclaimed.

MATTHEW 14:22-33 GNFMM

Warm-up / 2's / 5 min.
Get together with someone from your group of 8 and share the Warm-up. *(Take a moment and explain your answer to the first question. Then turn the groups loose. After 5 minutes call time and move on.)*

Going Deeper / 4's / 10 min.
With your partner get together with another pair from your group of 8 and share Going Deeper— one question at a time around the group. *(Explain your answer to the first question. After 10 minutes call time and move on.)*

Overtime Challenge / 8's / 15 min.
Regather your group of 8—the same group that has been together before—and share the Overtime Challenge with one another. *(Explain your answer to the first question and set the pace for openness and honesty.)*

Close-out
In your group join together in a football huddle and let anyone who wants to say a prayer—of thanksgiving or about a problem or need—do so while I wait. Then I will close in prayer for the entire group. *(Wait about 60 seconds. Then break in with a final prayer for all the groups.)*

Scripture Heavies

STRUCTURED QUESTIONNAIRES ON CHARACTER

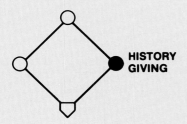

HISTORY GIVING

Shall I or shall I not?

WARM-UP
How do you see yourself in connection with the Ten Commandments? *(Read over the Scripture. Then rank your conduct on each commandment from 1 to 10—1 being very low and 10 being very*

Objective: To take inventory of your moral values in light of the Ten Commandments and to use your insight as the basis for a sharing experience.

PROCEDURE

The instructions are given in the words you can use in leading the group.

Silent Preparation / 5 min.
fill out the questionnaire.

Warm-up / 4's / 15 min.
Get together in groups of 4, with 3 others from your group of 8. Give each one in your group a chance to share how he ranked himself on two commandments: (a) the one on which he ranked himself the highest and (b) the one on which he ranked himself the lowest. *(Share the commandments on which you ranked yourself the*

THE TEN COMMANDMENTS

Then God spoke all these words. He said, "I am Yahweh your God who brought you out of the land of Egypt, out of the house of slavery.

"You shall have no gods except me.

"You shall not make yourself a carved image or any likeness of anything in heaven or on earth beneath or in the waters under the earth; you shall not bow down to them or serve them. For I, Yahweh your God, am a jealous God and I punish the father's fault in the sons, the grandsons, and the great-grandsons of those who hate me; but I show kindness to thousands of those who love me and keep my commandments.

"You shall not utter the name of Yahweh your God to misuse it, for Yahweh will not leave unpunished the man who utters his name to misuse it.

"Remember the sabbath day and keep it holy. For six days you shall labour and do all your work, but the seventh day is a sabbath for Yahweh your God. You shall do no work that day, neither you nor your son nor your daughter nor your servants, men or women, nor your animals nor the stranger who lives with you. For in six days Yahweh made the heavens and the earth and the sea and all that these hold, but on the seventh day he rested; that is why Yahweh has blessed the sabbath day and made it sacred.

"Honour your father and your mother so that you may have a long life in the land that Yahweh your God has given to you.

"You shall not kill.

"You shall not commit adultery.

"You shall not steal.

"You shall not bear false witness against your neighbour.

"You shall not covet your neighbour's house. You shall not covet your neighbour's wife, or his servant, man or woman, or his ox, or his donkey, or anything that is his." **EXODUS 20:1-17 NEB**

high. For instance, on the first commandment, you might circle "8" because you feel you have given first place to God in your life but you still need to give some areas of your lifestyle to God.)

You shall have no God except me

I have given God first place in my life. God is more important to me than popularity, money, friends, winning in sports, or any relationship that competes with God. Every part of my life has been surrendered to God—my time, my priorities, my values, my lifestyle.

1   2   3   4   5   6   7   8   9   10

You shall not misuse God's name

When I use the name of God or Christ, I use it with honor and respect, out of love and thanksgiving for what they mean to me. I cherish the name of God.

1   2   3   4   5   6   7   8   9   10

Remember the Lord's day

I set aside time in my schedule to be with God regularly; to slow down and let God speak to me; to share with God's people in worship and praise.

1   2   3   4   5   6   7   8   9   10

Honor your father and mother

I respect and cherish my parents and recognize their authority over me as from God. I try to make their responsibility easier for them. I tell them out loud how much I appreciate them.

1   2   3   4   5   6   7   8   9   10

You shall not kill

I have a reverence for life as from God. I share God's concern for the oppressed and unprotected peoples in the world.

1   2   3   4   5   6   7   8   9   10

You shall not commit adultery

I recognize that sexual relationship is the sacred heart of marriage—not to be engaged in with any other person after marriage. I am willing to discipline my sexual desires—to keep myself for the person God has for me.

1   2   3   4   5   6   7   8   9   10

You shall not steal

I do not take what does not belong to me. I work for what I get. I respect and protect the property of others. I refuse to go along with mischief that destroys the property of others.

1   2   3   4   5   6   7   8   9   10

You shall not bear false witness against your neighbor

I endeavor to tell the truth about my conduct and to reserve judgment about others until I know the facts. I refuse to engage in gossip. I try to stand up for someone who is falsely blamed, even at the risk of a few friends.

1   2   3   4   5   6   7   8   9   10

You shall not covet your neighbor's wife

I am not jealous for relationships that are already sealed with marriage. I will not engage in sexual competition, nor permit myself to be involved in something I know is wrong.

1   2   3   4   5   6   7   8   9   10

You shall not covet your neighbor's goods

I am content with what God has given me, both talents and possessions. I can honestly affirm my own unique gifts and opportunities and do not feel that someone else "got all the breaks."

1   2   3   4   5   6   7   8   9   10

GOING DEEPER

1. I found this check-up on my life in terms of the Ten Commandments to be (circle two):
   a. fascinating
   b. sobering
   c. challenging
   d. heavy
   e. confusing
   f. helpful
   g. awful
   h. valuable
   i. painful
   j. disturbing
   k. convicting

2. In the crowd that I associate with, living according to the Ten Commandments is (circle two):
   a. ridiculous
   b. out of date
   c. expected
   d. impossible today
   e. unnecessary
   f. just for religious people
   g. pooh-poohed
   h. OK, but...
   i. the Christian thing to do

3. Frankly, I find that my commitment to God influences my moral values (circle one):
   a. a lot
   b. a little
   c. not at all
   d. not as much as I would like
   e. huh?

highest and lowest. Set the pace for openness. After 10 minutes call time and move on.)

Going Deeper / 2's / 15 min.
Split into 2's and share with one another your answers to Going Deeper. (Explain your answer to the first point and set the pace for a deep discussion about influence upon moral values.

Close-out
Stand together in a close circle and pray for the person on your right either silently or out loud. This can be a prayer of thanks for what this person means to you, or a prayer about some need that this person has shared with your group. After a few moments I will pray. (Wait a bit, then break in and close with a prayer and "Amen" for all of the groups. Pick up all of the books.)

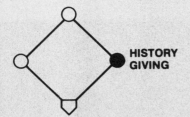

HISTORY GIVING

How's your love life?

Objective: To take inventory of your "love life" in light of the Love Chapter, and to use your insights as the basis for a sharing experience in your support group.

PROCEDURE

The instructions are given in the words you can use in leading the group.

Silent Preparation / 5 min.

fill out the questionnaire.

Warm-up / 4's / 10 min.

Get together in groups of 4, with others from your group of 8. Each of you share how you ranked your-

WARM-UP

How is your "love life" with your family, your neighbors and friends? *(Read the Scripture passage. Then in each aspect rank yourself from 1 to 10—1 being very weak and 10 being very strong. For instance, on "patience" you might circle 3 because you lose your temper a lot, but you are not as bad as you used to be! Be honest. Be very honest.)*

Love is patient: I keep my cool when people get on my back. I am slow to get angry with those I love. I rarely yell at people or lose my temper.
1   2   3   4   5   6   7   8   9   10

Love is kind: I really try to be thoughtful of those around me. I am willing to praise the success of others. I share my time and concern when it's needed, and I'm always on the lookout to "build up" others.
1   2   3   4   5   6   7   8   9   10

Love is not jealous: I'm not upset when others perform better than I do or get promoted ahead of me, even when it's undeserved. I am not threatened by other's talents. When I'm overlooked, I don't punish people with my moods.
1   2   3   4   5   6   7   8   9   10

Love is not conceited: I don't hog the spotlight in the group. I avoid focusing glory on myself. I strive to make others look good, and never

LOVE IS...

Love is patient and kind; love is not jealous, or conceited, or proud; love is not ill-mannered, or selfish, or irritable; love does not keep a record of wrongs; love is not happy with evil, but is happy with the truth. Love never gives up; its faith, hope, and patience never fail.

I CORINTHIANS 13: 4-7 GNFMM

tell exaggerated stories about my accomplishments.

1 2 3 4 5 6 7 8 9 10

Love is not proud: I know my limitations and work within them. I don't need special attention or favors to get me to cooperate. I don't go around putting people down.

1 2 3 4 5 6 7 8 9 10

Love is not ill-mannered: I avoid making any crude or sarcastic comments to others or about others. Instead, my conversation is polite and supportive and my approach to others is sincere and friendly.

1 2 3 4 5 6 7 8 9 10

Love is not selfish: I am not self-centered. I avoid making others fit my expectations. I am not possessive of my friends. I don't always insist on my way. I want to learn others' ways of doing things.

1 2 3 4 5 6 7 8 9 10

Love is not irritable: I am not touchy, cranky, defensive or super-sensitive. I don't lay my bad moods on others. I am approachable, warm, open and easy-to-get along with.

1 2 3 4 5 6 7 8 9 10

Love keeps no record of wrongs: I am quick to forgive those who have hurt me. I don't fight back or seek revenge when jumped on by someone. I forget mistakes others make and avoid holding grudges.

1 2 3 4 5 6 7 8 9 10

Love is not happy with evil: When someone is proven wrong, I avoid self-satisfaction. I never take delight in another's failure, even if it has made me look good. When anyone slips up, I am there with encouragement instead of an "I told you so."

1 2 3 4 5 6 7 8 9 10

Love is happy with the truth: I welcome honesty and justice, even when it shows my weaknesses. I am willing to give credit and praise wherever it is due. I live my commitment to God honestly, and am willing to admit my mistakes.

1 2 3 4 5 6 7 8 9 10

Love never gives up: When my relationship with someone is a struggle, I keep sharing. I never miss an opportunity to help someone. There is no rejection or failure that can make me give up my commitment to love.

1 2 3 4 5 6 7 8 9 10

GOING DEEPER

1. After taking this Inventory, I feel like *(circle one):*
   a. crawling into a hole
   b. giving up
   c. trying harder
   d. starting all over again
   e. crying for help
   f. shouting
   g. _____

2. For me, loving as Christ loved is *(circle two):*
   a. impossible
   b. beautiful
   c. hard, but worth trying
   d. a nice ideal, but
   e. something I'll need help on
   f. something I'm really committed to
   g. what it's all about

3. If I am going to do anything about this, I need a little more *(circle two):*
   a. guts
   b. faith in Christ
   c. support from those close to me
   d. confidence in myself
   e. grounding in the Scripture
   f. determination/commitment
   g. direction
   h. _____

self on two of the phrases: (a) the one on which you marked yourself the highest, (b) the one on which you marked yourself the lowest. *(Take a moment and share the two phrases—the ones you marked highest and lowest. Set the pace for openness. After 10 minutes call time and move on.)*

Going Deeper / 4's / 15 min.

Stay with your group of 4 and move on to Going Deeper in the questionnaire. Take the first question and go around your group, letting each person explain his answer. Then go around on the next question, etc. *(Explain your answer to the first question and set the pace for a deep sharing experience. After 15 minutes move on to the Close-out.)*

Close-out

In your groups of 4, spend a few moments in prayer for one another. Mention any needs that have been shared. After a couple minutes I will break in and close with prayer for the whole group. *(Pause for two or three minutes. Then offer a closing prayer. Pick up the books.)*

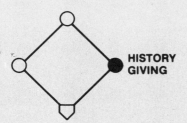

HISTORY
GIVING

Are you O.K.?

Objective: To take inventory of your life and lifestyle in light of the Beatitudes, and to use your insight as the basis for a sharing experience in your support group.

PROCEDURE

The instructions are given in the words you can use in leading the group.

Silent Preparation / 5 min.

fill out the questionnaire.

TRUE HAPPINESS

*"Happy are those who know they are spiritually poor;
the Kingdom of heaven belongs to them!*
"Happy are those who mourn; God will comfort them!
"Happy are the meek; they will receive what God has promised!
*"Happy are those who greatest desire is to do what God requires;
God will satisfy them fully!*
*"Happy are those who are merciful to others;
God will be merciful to them!*
"Happy are the pure in heart; they will see God!
*"Happy are those who work for peace among men;
God will call them his sons!*
*"Happy are those who are persecuted because they do what God requires;
the Kingdom of heaven belongs to them!"*

MATTHEW 5:3-10 GNFMM

WARM-UP

How do you stand in relation to the Beatitudes? *(Read over the Scripture passage. On each of the Beatitudes rank your life from 1 to 10—1 being very weak and 10 being very strong. For instance on the first Beatitude, you might circle number 8 because you know that you are far from perfect but that God accepts you anyway.)*

Happy are those who know they are spiritually poor: Are you ready to admit to yourself and others that you don't have all the answers? That you have needs? That you need God and others? Are you able to let others know where you are "spiritually poor" so they can help?
1   2   3   4   5   6   7   8   9   10

Happy are those who mourn: Are you sensitive enough to other people to help them when they are hurting? Are you able to show your feelings—and to let others show their feelings without your feeling like a sissy? Are you able to let others unload and to really enter into their pain?
1   2   3   4   5   6   7   8   9   10

Happy are the meek: Are you the kind of person who will let the other person carry the ball? Are you quiet enough inside yourself to hear what God and others are saying? Are you mellow enough to lead by listening, allowing others to have their say?
1   2   3   4   5   6   7   8   9   10

Happy are those whose greatest desire is to do what God requires: Is God number one in your life? Do you let him call the plays? Do you know the difference between his will and your will? In the tough choices of your personal life do you honestly seek to put God first?
1   2   3   4   5   6   7   8   9   10

Happy are those who show mercy to others: Are you a "caring" kind of person who warms up other people's lives? Are you quick to respond to need? Do you give without thought of getting something back? In short, are you a grace-giver—like Christ?
1   2   3   4   5   6   7   8   9   10

Happy are the pure in heart: Can you be your *real* self? Are you the same person in school that you are in church? Are you free to let others know you? Are you open and honest, letting God show through?
1   2   3   4   5   6   7   8   9   10

Happy are those who work for peace among men: Are you able to heal broken relationships through your caring and understanding? Are you a bridge builder—accepting others who differ with you—without giving up your own convictions? Do you bring harmony?
1   2   3   4   5   6   7   8   9   10

Happy are those who suffer persecution because they do what God requires: Are you able to take criticism from those near you without reacting defensively? Are you willing to let others know you are a Christian, even if it is unpopular? Can you "take the heat" and come back smiling?
1   2   3   4   5   6   7   8   9   10

GOING DEEPER

What Beatitudes are especially meaningful to you right now? *(Below are a series of statements adapted from the Beatitudes. Rank them 1, 2, 3, etc., in the order of their importance to you.)*

_____ God accepts me as I am. I don't have to have it all together.

_____ Jesus wept. Feelings are a part of life. It is OK to cry.

_____ Gentleness is a mark of strength. A person who is really strong does not have to prove it.

_____ God made us for his fellowship. The soul of man will be restless until it finds its rest in God.

_____ God showed his love for us by giving his life. We show our love for God by giving our lives for others.

_____ God made himself known through Christ. Christ makes himself known through us.

_____ Christ is the bridge over troubled waters for us. We are the bridge over troubled waters for the world.

_____ Obedience to God cost him his life. His followers were asked to follow in his steps.

Warm-up / 4's / 10 min.

Get together in 4's—with others from your regular group—and share two of the Beatitudes: (a) the one in which you ranked yourself the highest—closest to 10, (b) the one in which you ranked yourself the lowest—closest to 1. *(Take a moment and share the two Beatitudes in which you ranked yourself—the highest and the lowest. After 10 minutes call time and move on.)*

Going Deeper / 4's / 15 min.

Stay with your group 4 to share Going Deeper. Let each person explain the top three statements he checked on his list and explain why they are important to him at the moment. *(Share the top three statements you picked and explain why. Set the pace for real soul-searching by your own sharing. After 15 minutes call time and move on to the Close-out.)*

Close-out

In your groups of 4 spend a few moments in prayer for one another. Mention any particular needs that have been shared. After a couple minutes I will break in and close with prayer for the whole group. *(Pause for two or three minutes. Then break in with a closing prayer. Pick up the books.)*

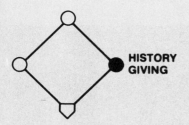

HISTORY GIVING

Are you going for it?

WARM-UP

How do you see your spiritual growth in relation to 2 Peter? *(Read over the Scripture. Then rank your growth in each of the qualities—after reading the description—by circling a number between 1 and 10. 1 is very weak and 10 is very strong. For instance, you might circle "7" under faith because you feel that your faith is pretty strong, but not as strong as it could be.)*

Faith

I am totally committed to Christ and his church. I am willing to go all the way with Christ—regardless of the cost. Christ is top priority in my life. I am ready for the risky, scary adventure of living with Christ.

1   2   3   4   5   6   7   8   9   10

Goodness

I am trying to live every day as Christ would live it; to clean up my life; to change the bad habits; to check out my priorities, values and lifestyle. I am willing to let God make me into the person he wants.

1   2   3   4   5   6   7   8   9   10

Objective: To take inventory of your spiritual development in light of the teaching in 2 Peter 1, and to use your insights as the basis for a sharing experience.

PROCEDURE

The instructions are given in the words you can use in leading the group.

Silent Preparation / 5 min.
fill out the questionnaire.

GOD'S CALL AND CHOICE

God's divine power has given us everything we need to live a godly life through our knowledge of the one who called us to share his own glory and goodness. In this way he has given us the very great and precious gifts he promised, so that by means of these gifts you may escape from the destructive lust that is in the world, and come to share the divine nature.

For this very reason do your best to add goodness to your faith; to your goodness add knowledge; to your knowledge add self-control; to your self-control add endurance; to your endurance add godliness; to your godliness add brotherly love; and to your brotherly love add love.

These are the qualities you need, and if you have them in abundance they will make you active and effective in your knowledge of our Lord Jesus Christ. But whoever does not have them is so shortsighted that he cannot see, and has forgotten that his past sins have been washed away.

2 PETER 1:3-9 GNFMM

Knowledge

I am giving priority to learning more about God and what he wants with my life. I spend time daily in prayer and in the study of Scripture. I am open to God's will for my life and willing to pay the price to follow it.

1   2   3   4   5   6   7   8   9   10

Self-control

I am taking seriously the lordship of Jesus Christ over my whole being, putting aside my own selfish interests and desires. I am willing to "get in shape" and "stay in shape" spiritually— whatever the cost.

1   2   3   4   5   6   7   8   9   10

Endurance

I am learning how to "hang in there" when the going gets tough. I can stand up under pressure; to take the heat; to stand up for what I believe and know is right, even if it means standing alone.

1   2   3   4   5   6   7   8   9   10

Godliness

I am as conscientious about my spiritual development as my physical and mental development, making my spiritual growth a daily discipline. I am not ashamed to let others know that I am a Christian. No matter where I am, I try to make my life count for God.

1   2   3   4   5   6   7   8   9   10

Brotherly love

I go out of my way to help my family, my friends. I am willing to take the initiative in clearing up misunderstanding; to go the second mile when there is a need; to build up others by affirming the good things; to always be on the lookout for ways to help.

1   2   3   4   5   6   7   8   9   10

Love

I am being an instrument of God's love, reaching out, touching, giving, sharing his grace in the same way that he gave up his life for me.

1   2   3   4   5   6   7   8   9   10

GOING DEEPER

1. After measuring my spiritual growth against this Scripture passage, I want to *(circle two)*:
   a. throw in the towel
   b. try harder
   c. start all over again
   d. cry for help
   e. get with it
   f. give up
   g. do something, but I don't know what

2. It would sure help if I had *(circle two)*:
   a. some support
   b. a better situation
   c. more time
   d. a great big kick in the pants
   e. an understanding friend
   f. love
   g. a little more peace of mind

Warm-up / 2's / 15 min.

Get together with someone from your support group and share how you ranked yourself on each of the qualities, one at a time. *(Explain how you ranked yourself on the first quality. Then turn the groups loose. After 15 minutes call time and move on.)*

Going Deeper / 4's / 15 min.

With your partner get together with 2 others from your group.

Take the first question and go around your group, letting each person share his position. Then go around on the second question, etc. *(Share your position on the first question, but leave the door open for others to differ.)*

Close-out

Stand together in a close circle and pray for the person on your right either silently or out loud. This can be a prayer of thanks for what this person means to you, or a prayer about some need that he has shared with your group. *(Wait about 2 minutes to give everyone an opportunity to pray. Then break in and close in prayer for all the groups. Collect the books.)*

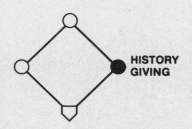

HISTORY GIVING

Are you feeling fit?

Objective: To take inventory of your spiritual equipment in light of the check list in Ephesians 6, and to use your insights as the basis for a sharing experience in your support group.

PROCEDURE
The instructions are given in the words you can use in leading the group.

Silent Preparation / 5 min.
fill out the questionnaire.

Warm-up / 2's / 15 min.
Get together in 2's—with someone from your support group—and share how you ranked yourself on each part of your spiritual equip-

THE WHOLE ARMOR OF GOD

Finally, build up your strength in union with the Lord, and by means of his mighty power. Put on all the armor that God gives you, so that you will stand up against the Devil's evil tricks. For we are not fighting against human beings, but against the wicked spiritual forces in the heavenly world, the rulers, authorities, and cosmic powers of this dark age. So take up God's armor now! Then when the evil day comes, you will be able to resist the enemy's attacks, and after fighting to the end, you will still hold your ground.

So stand ready: have truth for a belt tight around your waist: put on righteousness for your breast-plate, and the readiness to announce the Good News of peace as shoes for your feet. At all times carry faith as a shield; with it you will be able to put out all the burning arrows shot by the Evil One. And accept salvation for a helmet, and the word of God as the sword that the Spirit gives you. Do all this in prayer, asking for God's help. Pray on every occasion, as the Spirit leads. For this reason keep alert and never give up; pray always for all God's people.

EPHESIANS 6:1-18 GNFMM

WARM-UP

How are you spiritually equipped right now? *(Read over the Scripture passage. Then on each point below rank yourself from 1 to 10—1 being very weak and 10 being very strong. For instance, for "truth" you might circle 8, because you are pretty firm in your Christian convictions but you could improve.)*

Truth
I am prepared to stake my life on the fact that Jesus Christ is the Son of God. I have thought through what I believe, and I am willing to take a stand.

1　2　3　4　5　6　7　8　9　10

Righteousness
I am prepared to put my life where my mouth is—in clean and right living—with genuine integrity—as Christ did. I am serious about being God's man/woman.

1　2　3　4　5　6　7　8　9　10

Readiness to announce the Good News
I am willing to publicly affirm my faith in Christ—at school or work. I find it easy to talk about my personal faith.

1　2　3　4　5　6　7　8　9　10

Faith
I am prepared to step out with Christ—to risk my life, my fortune and my future to him whatever the cost or consequences. I am willing to build my whole life around God's will.

1　2　3　4　5　6　7　8　9　10

Salvation
I know that I am part of the family of God because of Jesus Christ. I have a strong inner peace because I am at peace with God.

1　2　3　4　5　6　7　8　9　10

Word of God
I actively seek to know more about God and his will for my life through an ongoing study of his guidebook, the Bible. I discipline myself to study daily.

1　2　3　4　5　6　7　8　9　10

Prayer
I set aside time regularly to talk with God and to let him speak to me. I consciously try to submit every decision in my life to God.

1　2　3　4　5　6　7　8　9　10

GOING DEEPER

1. If I were thrown into a tough spiritual contest today, I would probably *(circle one)*:
   a. collapse before the game even started
   b. tire out before the first quarter was over
   c. barely make it through
   d. find reserves I didn't know I had
   e. rise to the occasion

2. From my own experience, I seem to grow in my spiritual life when *(circle one)*:
   a. the pressure is on
   b. I am around others who are serious
   c. I have plenty of time to devote to it
   d. I am away from home
   e. I am really serious about it
   f. someone is checking up on me

3. In my own personal habit of Bible study and prayer, the hardest thing for me is *(circle two)*:
   a. getting time alone
   b. consistency
   c. concentration
   d. desire
   e. getting to bed the night before
   f. finding some privacy at home
   g. knowing how to get something out of the Bible
   h. keeping from falling asleep
   i. ...what habit?

ment in the Warm-up. Take the first part and both share your responses and why. Then take the second part and explain how you checked yourself, etc., through the series. *(Explain how you ranked yourself on the first part "truth." Then ask each person to explain his answer to his partner. After 15 minutes call time and move on.)*

Going Deeper / 4's / 10 min.

With your partner get together with another pair from your group of 8. Go around, each one giving his answer to the first question in Going Deeper and explaining why. If there is time, go around on the next question, etc. *(Explain your answer to the first question and set the pace for real soul-searching in the support groups. After 10 to 15 minutes call time and move on to the Close-out.)*

Close-out

In your groups of 4, spend a few moments in prayer for one another, mentioning in particular any needs that have been shared. After a couple of minutes I will break in and close with a prayer for the whole group. *(Pause two or three minutes. Then break in with a closing prayer. Pick up the books.)*

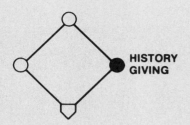

**HISTORY
GIVING**

Where do you stand?

DANGER
HIGH VOLTAGE

Objective: To take inventory of your personal conduct in your relationships in light of the Sermon on the Mount, and to use your insights as the basis for a sharing experience in your support group.

PROCEDURE

The instructions are given in the words you can use in leading the group.

Silent Preparation / 5 min.

fill out the questionnaire.

Warm-up / 2's / 15 min.

Get together in 2's—with someone from your support group—and share how you ranked yourself on each question in the Warm-up. Take the first question and let each person explain his answer. Then

TEACHING ABOUT ADULTERY

"You have heard that it was said, 'Do not commit adultery.' But now I tell you: anyone who looks at a woman and wants to possess her is guilty of committing adultery with her in his heart."

TEACHING ABOUT REVENGE

"You have heard that it was said, 'An eye for an eye, and a tooth for a tooth.' But now I tell you: do not take revenge on someone who does you wrong. If anyone slaps you on the right cheek, let him slap your left cheek too....when someone wants to borrow something, lend it to him."

LOVE FOR ENEMIES

"You have heard that it was said, 'Love your friends, hate your enemies.' But now I tell you: love your enemies, and pray for those who persecute you, so that you will become the sons of your Father in heaven. For he makes his sun to shine on bad and good people alike, and gives rain to those who do good and those who do evil. Why should God reward you if you love only the people who love you? Even the tax collectors do that!"

MATTHEW 5:27-46 GNFMM

WARM-UP

If you were to ask yourself the following questions, how would you answer? *(Read over the Scripture passage. Then on each line put a dot somewhere between the two extremes*

Adultery

1. Am I willing to live a clean life sexually?
not willing _____very willing

2. Is my talk about the opposite sex dirty or clean?
dirty _____clean

3. How strong is my self-discipline when it comes to sexual opportunities?
very weak _____very strong

4. Do I seek in my relationships God or self-satisfaction?
self _____God

Revenge

1. When someone is mean to me and tries to hurt me, do I seek revenge or turn the other cheek?
revenge _____turn cheek

2. Do I use my moods to punish people?
punish _____never punish

3. Do I protect myself from hurt by threatening others?
threaten _____never threaten

4. Do I seek punishment of those who are wrong as my job or God's?
my job _____God's job

Love for enemies

1. Do I go out of my way to reach people who are not my close friends?
no reach out _____reach out

2. Is my relationship with others as important as my relationship with Christ?
as important _____not as important

3. When I see people I don't like, do I reject them or try to understand them?
reject _____understand

4. Do I enjoy the failure of enemies or offer them support and encouragement?
enjoy their failure _____support

GOING DEEPER

1. Who or what influences the decisions you make every day? *(Place one or more of the following symbols beside each category to indicate who/what has the most influence in your decisions. For instance, in the area of "clothes," you might put an "F" because your friends are the biggest influence.)*

P pals   S school
F family   TV television
C church   EX experience

_____ clothes—what to wear
_____ time/leisure—how to use it
_____ money—how to spend it
_____ grades—their importance
_____ reading matter—what to read
_____ sex/love—what is OK
_____ engagement/marriage—when and how
_____ family/children—their importance
_____ work/job—what to do
_____ success—what it means to you
_____ happiness—what it is to you

2. From this exercise, I discovered that the most important influences in my life are *(rank 1, 2, 3, etc., in order of importance)*:

_____ pals   _____ school
_____ family   _____ television
_____ church   _____ experience

take the next question, etc., through the Warm-up. *(Explain how you marked yourself on the question, "Am I willing to live a clean life sexually?" Then ask each person to explain his answer to his partner. After 15 minutes call time and move on.)*

Going Deeper / 4's / 10 min.

With your partner get together with another pair from your original group. Go around and share how you marked the second part of Going Deeper, telling who influences your conduct most —and why. If there is time, go back to the individual items and share your answers, beginning with who influences your decisions on clothes. *(Take a moment and tell who or what you ranked as the most important influences in your life. Explain why. Then turn the groups loose. After 10 minutes call time and move on to the Close-out.)*

Close-out

In your same groups. spend a few moments in prayer for one another, mentioning in particular any needs that have been shared. After a couple minutes, I will break in and close with prayer for the entire group. *(Wait a bit. Then pray for the group. Pick up the books.)*

AFFIRMATION

Where's the beef?

WARM-UP

How would you evaluate the positive qualities in your life? *(Read over the Scripture passage. Then rank yourself on each of the fruits of the Spirit by circling a number from 1 to 10—1 being very weak and 10 being very strong. For instance, for the fruit of love, you might circle "8" because you feel you are sensitive and caring, but you could do even better.)*

THE SPIRIT AND HUMAN NATURE

What human nature does is quite plain. It shows itself in immoral, filthy, and indecent actions; in worship of idols and witchcraft. People become enemies, they fight, become jealous, angry, and ambitious. They separate into parties and groups; they are envious, get drunk, have orgies, and do other things like these. I warn you now as I have before: those who do these things will not receive the Kingdom of God.

But the Spirit produces love, joy, peace, patience, kindness, goodness, faithfulness, humility, and self-control. There is no law against such things as these. And those who belong to Christ Jesus have put to death their human nature, with all its passions and desires. The Spirit has given us life; he must also control our lives. We must not be proud, or irritate one another, or be jealous of one another.

GALATIONS 5:19-26 GNFMM

Objective: To take inventory of the qualities of your life in the light of the fruits of the Spirit, and to use your insights as the basis for a sharing experience.

PROCEDURE

The instructions are given in the words you can use in leading the group.

Silent Preparation / 5 min.

(Have the groups of 8's sit together so that they can see each other while completing the questionnaire.)
fill out the questionnaire.

THE FRUIT OF THE SPIRIT

Love
I am quick to sense the needs of my friends, classmates and family, and I respond—just as Christ would.

1 2 3 4 5 6 7 8 9 10

Joy
I can celebrate life even in the midst of pain and confusion because of deep, spiritual reservoirs.

1 2 3 4 5 6 7 8 9 10

Peace
I have a quiet, inner confidence in God's care of my life that keeps me from feeling uptight and anxious.

1 2 3 4 5 6 7 8 9 10

Patience (endurance)
I have a staying power that helps me to handle frustration and conflict without blowing my stack.

1 2 3 4 5 6 7 8 9 10

Kindness
I act toward my friends, classmates and family as I want them to act toward me—warm, considerate, generous with praise—always trying to see the best in others.

1 2 3 4 5 6 7 8 9 10

Goodness
I have a real desire to live a clean life, to set a good example by my conduct wherever I am. I want to be God's man!

1 2 3 4 5 6 7 8 9 10

Faithfulness (fidelity)
I stick to my word; I stand up for my friends; I can be counted on to stay firm in my commitment to God and others.

1 2 3 4 5 6 7 8 9 10

Humility (gentleness)
I have an inner strength that permits me to be gentle in my relationships; open; aware of my own abilities without having to make a show of them.

1 2 3 4 5 6 7 8 9 10

Self-control
I am learning to discipline my time, energy and desires to reflect my spiritual values and priorities.

1 2 3 4 5 6 7 8 9 10

GOING DEEPER

What qualities do you appreciate most in the members of your group? *(In the circles write the names of your support group. Then go back to the list of fruit of the Spirit and jot down a fruit beside each name—the one most appropriate for each person. For instance, beside Tom's name you might jot down "peace" because you have observed an inner peace in his life lately—even in the midst of storms.)*

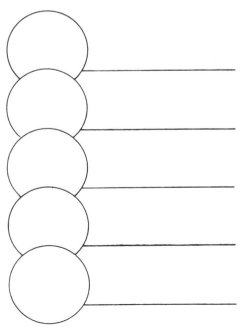

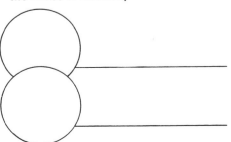

Warm-up / 2's / 15 min.

Get together with one other person from your group of 8 and share the Warm-up. Take the first fruit and each of you explain how you ranked yourself and why. Then take the next fruit and do the same, etc., until you have covered them all. *(Share how you ranked yourself on the first fruit. Set the pace for painful honesty. After 10 minutes call time and move on.)*

Going Deeper / 8's / 15 min.

Regather your group of 8. While one person remains silent the others explain the fruit they feel is the strongest in this person's life. Repeat the process for each person in the group. *(Choose one person and explain the fruit you would put down for him and why. Set the pace for beautiful, sincere affirmation. Then turn the groups loose.)*

Close-out

Stand together in a close circle and have a time of prayer for each other. After a couple minutes I will close in prayer for all of the groups. *(Wait about 2 minutes. Then break in and give a short prayer. Pick up the books.)*

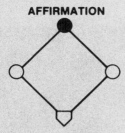

AFFIRMATION

Are you pulling your weight?

WARM-UP

To what degree do you feel strong or weak in the various spiritual gifts? *(Read over the Scripture passage. Then rank yourself from 1 to 10 on each of the spiritual gifts—1 being very weak and 10 being very strong. For instance, on the gift of "speech" you might circle number 3 because you feel that you are rather weak in communicating the Gospel verbally.)*

Speak God's message (speech)
God has given me a gift for communicating the Gospel. When I explain the Good News, God seems to use my words to bring insight and understanding about his grace.

1 2 3 4 5 6 7 8 9 10

Serve (service)
God has given me a special knack for helping out when a need arises. I am sensitive to other people and find it easy to respond to their needs.

1 2 3 4 5 6 7 8 9 10

Teach (teaching)
God has given me a skill for helping others to learn. I am good at getting other people motivated.

1 2 3 4 5 6 7 8 9 10

Objective: To take inventory of the qualities in your life in light of the spiritual gifts mentioned in Romans 12, and to affirm the qualities you have observed in your support group.

PROCEDURE

The instructions are given in the words you can use in leading the group.

LIFE IN GOD'S SERVICE

"...Do not think of yourselves more highly than you should. Instead, be modest in your thinking, and each one of you judge himself according to the amount of faith that God has given him. We have many parts in the one body, and all these parts have different functions. In the same way, though we are many, we are one body in union with Christ and we are all joined to each other as different parts of one body. So we are to use our

Encourage others

God has given me the disposition to see the best in others. I find it easy to compliment people—to point out their strengths, to "call forth" their best.

1 2 3 4 5 6 7 8 9 10

Generosity

God has given me a freedom to share myself with others. I find it easy to give, to reach out, to touch and care whenever there is a need.

1 2 3 4 5 6 7 8 9 10

Authority (leadership)

God has given me a gift for organization. I can get things done. I find it easy to take responsibility and direct others.

1 2 3 4 5 6 7 8 9 10

Kindness

God has given me the ability to be compassionate—warm and tender—whenever someone is in trouble or needs help. I can enter into people's pain—feel with them—and minister.

1 2 3 4 5 6 7 8 9 10

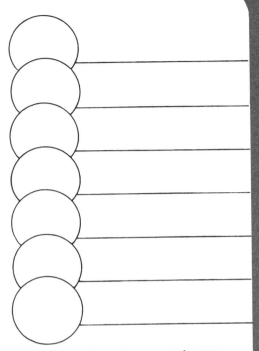

GOING DEEPER

1. What gifts have the members of your group shown during these sessions? *(In the circles write the names of the people in your group. Then think over the list of "gifts" and jot a gift beside each name. For instance for Tom you might put down "speech," because with his explanation you really understand the Gospel. For Bea you might put down "encouragement," because he has been the one to call forth the best in you.)*

2. If God were to grade you on the use you have made of his gifts, what would he probably give you? *(Circle one.)*
   a. A+   c. B+   e. C   g. F
   b. A-   d. B-   f. D-

3. When it comes to "affirming your own gifts," what do you tend to do? *(Circle one.)*
   a. think I have no gifts
   b. downgrade my gifts
   c. overestimate my gifts
   d. pooh-pooh the whole idea of spiritual gifts
   e. shy away from thinking about it

Silent Preparation / 5 min.

(Ask the groups of 8 to sit together so that they can see each other while filling out the questionnaire.) fill out the questionnaire.

Warm-up / 4's / 10 min.

Get together in 4's—with others from your support group—and share two of the gifts of the Spirit: (a) the gift on which you ranked yourself the highest, (b) the gift on which you ranked yourself the lowest. *(Take a moment and explain the gifts on which you ranked yourself highest and lowest. After 10 minutes call time and move on.)*

Going Deeper / 8's / 15 to 20 min.

Regather your group of 8. Have one person remain silent while the others share the gifts they would give him and why. After everyone is through, he tells how he answered the last two questions in the questionnaire and explains why. Repeat the procedure until everyone in your group has had a turn. *(Pick out one person and explain to everyone the gift you have observed in this person. Then let the groups proceed.)*

Close-out

Stand together in a close circle and have a time of prayer for each other. Remember the high points of our time together. *(Wait a few moments to give everyone an opportunity to pray. Then break in with thanks to God for his many blessings.)*

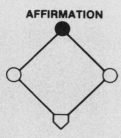

AFFIRMATION

When do you blow it?

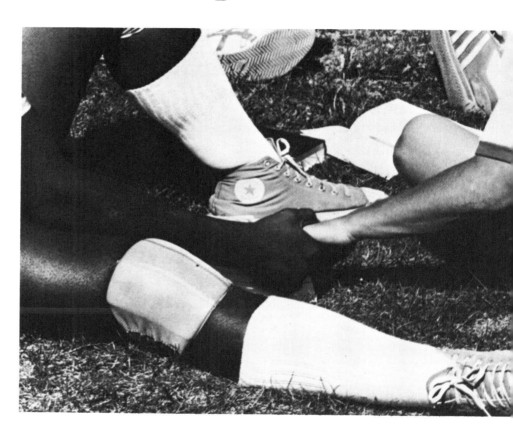

Objective: To take inventory of your family life in light of the teachings of Jesus about criticism "murdering your brother," and then to find out from those in your support group what they appreciate most about you.

PROCEDURE

The instructions are given in the words you can use in leading the group.

Silent Preparation / 5 min.

(Ask the groups of 8 to sit together so that they can see each other while filling out the questionnaire.)
fill out the questionnaire.

Warm-up / 4's / 10 min.

Get together in 4's—with people from your support group—and share the Warm-up in the questionnaire. Go around on the first question, each one explaining his

TEACHING ABOUT ANGER

"You have heard that men were told in the past, 'Do not murder; anyone who commits murder will be brought before the judge. But now I tell you: whoever is angry with his brother will be brought before the judge; whoever calls his brother 'You good-for-nothing!' will be brought before the Council; and whoever calls his brother a worthless fool will be in danger of going to the fire of hell. So if you are about to offer your gift to God at the altar and there you remember that your brother has something against you, leave your gift there in front of the altar and go at once to make peace with your brother; then come back and offer your gift to God."

MATTHEW 5:21-24 GNFMM

WARM-UP

After reading the Scripture how would you complete the following?

1. Murder is defined in the Scripture passage as *(circle one)*:
   a. killing your brother
   b. slandering your brother
   c. tearing down your brother's self-worth
   d. making it difficult for your brother
   e. not giving in to your brother

2. According to the passage God expects *(circle one)*:
   a. the person who has done wrong to go to God and make it right
   b. the person who has been wronged to go to God and make it right
   c. the person who has done wrong to go to the person and make it right
   d. the person who has been wronged to go to the person and make it right

3. If I were to describe my relationship with each person with whom I live now, I would use the following symbols. *(Write the names of the people on the lines Then beside each name place one of the symbols.)*

   ○ Our relationship is completely affirming. I build this person up and he builds me up. We help each other to win.

   ◑ Our relationship is half affirming. I try to build this person up but he refuses to build me up.

   ◐ Our relationship is half affirming in the other direction. This person tries to build me up, but I do not know how to build him up.

   ◓ Our relationship is mutually destructive. I tear this person down and he tears me down, We are destroying each other.

GOING DEEPER

What do you appreciate most about each member of your group? *(Write the names of your group in the circles. Then beside each name write what you appreciate most about him—or his "most outstanding strength." For instance, for Tom you might put: "warmth" or "moral courage." Be honest. Here is your chance to do what the Scripture passage is all about.)*

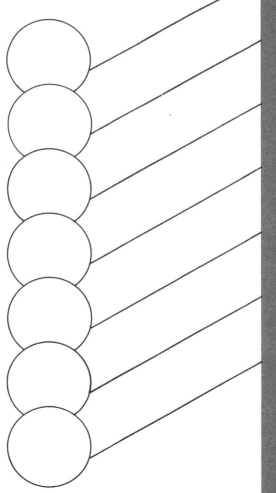

answer and why. Then go around on the next question, etc. *(Take a moment and explain your answer to the first question. Then turn the groups loose. After 10 minutes call time and move on.)*

Going Deeper / 4's or 8's / 15 min.

(You will have to decide whether to use groups of 4 or 8, depending upon the time available. If there is plenty of time, move into groups of 8. If not, stay with groups of 4 so the participation can be greater.)

This is what might be called a "strength bombardment" experience. Let one person sit in silence while the others explain what they appreciate most about him—or what they feel is his most outstanding strength. When everyone is finished, let the person finish the sentence. "The thing I would most like to change about myself is..."

Then another person remains silent while the others share what they appreciate most about him, etc., until everyone in your group has been covered. *(Choose a person and explain in all honesty the thing you appreciate most about him. By your own example set the pace for deep sharing. When all of the groups are through, call time and move on to the Close-out.)*

Close-out

Spend a few moments in prayer for one another mentioning particular needs that have been shared. After a few minutes I will break in and close with a prayer for the whole group. *(Wait a bit. Then pray for the entire group. Collect the books.)*

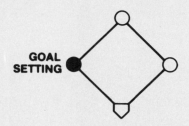

GOAL SETTING

How's it with your community?

Objective: To take inventory of your personal attitudes and lifestyle in light of the creed for the personal behavior of a Christian as suggested in Romans 12, and to use your insights as the basis for a sharing experience.

PROCEDURE

The instructions are given in the words you can use in leading the group.

Silent Preparation / 5 min.

fill out the questionnaire.

Warm-up / 2's / 15 min.

Get together with someone from your group of 8 and share the Warm-up—one phrase at a time. Take the first phrase and explain to each other how you rated your life. Then take the next phrase and each explain his rating, etc. *(Honestly share how you ranked*

WARM-UP

Where do you stand in view of Romans 12? *(Read over the Scripture. Then measure your life against the passage —phrase by phrase—by circling a number between 1 and 10—1 being very weak and 10 being very strong. For instance for "love must be completely sincere," you might circle "4" because you find you're likely to play that you love a person when you really don't.)*

Love must be completely sincere
I am able to really give myself to other Christian brothers and sisters, not in some phony way, but with real meaning.

1 2 3 4 5 6 7 8 9 10

Hate what is evil, hold on to what is good
I am learning to stand up for my convictions; to say no to something I know is wrong and yes to God's thing.

1 2 3 4 5 6 7 8 9 10

Love one another warmly as brothers in Christ...and show respect for one another
I am learning how to reach out and hug my Christian brothers and sisters warmly—in the right way—and for purely spiritual reasons.

1 2 3 4 5 6 7 8 9 10

Work hard and do not be lazy
I have a deep desire to pitch in at home and school and at work without having to be asked.

1 2 3 4 5 6 7 8 9 10

Serve the Lord with a heart full of devotion
I am eager and enthusiastic to do anything I can for Christ because my heart is full of gratitude for what he did for me.

1 2 3 4 5 6 7 8 9 10

Let your hope keep you joyful
I am experiencing a new freedom that overflows in praise because I know that God is in control.

1 2 3 4 5 6 7 8 9 10

Be patient in your troubles
Problems don't get me down any more. I can take the heat. Under pressure I can stay cool.

1 2 3 4 5 6 7 8 9 10

LIFE IN GOD'S SERVICE

Love must be completely sincere. Hate what is evil, hold on to what is good. Love one another warmly as brothers in Christ, and be eager to show respect for one another. Work hard, and do not be lazy. Serve the Lord with a heart full of devotion. Let your hope keep you joyful, be patient in your troubles, and pray at all times. Share your belongings with your needy brothers, and open your homes to strangers.

Ask God to bless those who persecute you; yes, ask him to bless, not to curse. Be happy with those who are happy, weep with those who weep. Have the same concern for all alike. Do not be proud, but accept humble duties. Do not think of yourselves as wise.

If someone does evil to you, do not pay him back with evil. Try to do what all men consider to be good. Do everything possible, on your part, to live at peace with all men. Never take revenge, my friends, but instead let God's wrath do it. For the scripture says, "I will take revenge, I will pay back, says the Lord."

Instead, as the scripture says: "If your enemy is hungry, feed him; if he is thirsty, give him a drink; for by doing this you will heap burning coals on his head." Do not let evil defeat you; instead, conquer evil with good."

ROMANS 12:9-21 GNFMM

Pray at all times
I have learned to turn over every need to Christ and to share every decision I have to make with him. I have learned to "wait on God" and let him work things out.

1   2   3   4   5   6   7   8   9   10

Share your belongings with the needy ...open your homes to strangers
I have learned that my possessions, my time, my whole being, belongs to God— to be shared with those in need.

1   2   3   4   5   6   7   8   9   10

Ask God to bless those who persecute you
I have learned to respond with kindness to those who put me down—and to pray on their behalf. I am no longer defensive about my life.

1   2   3   4   5   6   7   8   9   10

Be happy with those who are happy, weep with those who weep
I have learned to roll with the punches; to celebrate life when the occasion is right, and to grieve openly when the occasion demands. I am not afraid to show my feelings.

1   2   3   4   5   6   7   8   9   10

GOING DEEPER

1. If this passage is a picture of what a Christian ought to be, then I am *(circle one)*:
   a. really in trouble
   b. a poor specimen
   c. moving in the right direction
   d. doing OK, but...
   e. going to have to change some things
   f. _____

2. Since being in this program, I feel that in my Christian life I have *(circle one)*:
   a. slipped back
   b. started to move
   c. only just begun
   d. come a long way
   e. really grown
   f. a long way to go
   g. changed

3. The greatest change in my Christian life since starting in this program has been in my *(circle two)*:
   a. sense of freedom
   b. feeling of what is important
   c. own self-acceptance
   d. personal devotional habits
   e. desire to clean up my life
   f. feeling of really belonging to God's family
   g. commitment to follow God's will

yourself on the first phrase. Then turn the people loose. After 15 minutes call time and move on.)

Going Deeper / 4's / 15 min.
With your partner get together with 2 others to form a group of 4. Go around and explain your answer on the first point in Going Deeper. Then go around on the second question, etc. *(Explain your answer to the first question and set the pace for openness and honesty.)*

Close-out
Stand together in a close circle and have a time of prayer for each other. Remember the high points of our time together. *(Wait a few moments to give everyone an opportunity to pray. Then break in with thanks to God for his many blessings.)*

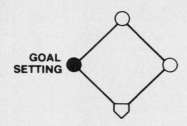

GOAL SETTING

What's the scoop?

Objective: To take inventory of your life during the time you have been in this program, and to share the results with your support group.

PROCEDURE

The instructions are given in the words you can use in leading the group.

GOD OUR FATHER

As for us, we have this large crowd of witnesses around us. Let us rid ourselves, then, of everything that gets in the way, and the sin which holds on to us so tightly, and let us run with determination the race that lies before us. Let us keep our eyes fixed on Jesus, on whom our faith depends from beginning to end. He did not give up because of the cross! On the contrary, because of the joy that was waiting for him, he thought nothing of the disgrace of dying on the cross, and is now seated at the right side of God's throne.

HEBREWS 12:1-2 GNFMM

WARM-UP

How have you progressed while in this program? *(Read over the Scripture passage. Then rank your progress. Circle a number between 1 and 10—1 being very low and 10 being very high. For instance, for the first one you might circle number 3 because you have made a little progress but you still have a long way to go.)*

In my prayer life

1　2　3　4　5　6　7　8　9　10

In my regular study of Scripture

1　2　3　4　5　6　7　8　9　10

In sorting out my priorities

1　2　3　4　5　6　7　8　9　10

In understanding God's will for my life

1　2　3　4　5　6　7　8　9　10

In developing my own value system

1　2　3　4　5　6　7　8　9　10

In standing up for what I believe

1　2　3　4　5　6　7　8　9　10

In disciplining my leisure for the best use

1　2　3　4　5　6　7　8　9　10

In controlling my temper

1　2　3　4　5　6　7　8　9　10

In my own inner peace of mind

1　2　3　4　5　6　7　8　9　10

In my personal habits

1　2　3　4　5　6　7　8　9　10

In my determination to do what is right

1　2　3　4　5　6　7　8　9　10

In appreciating what Jesus has done for me

1　2　3　4　5　6　7　8　9　10

In sharing the Gospel

1　2　3　4　5　6　7　8　9　10

In submitting wholeheartedly to God

1　2　3　4　5　6　7　8　9　10

In realizing God's love

1　2　3　4　5　6　7　8　9　10

In being sensitive to other people

1　2　3　4　5　6　7　8　9　10

In using my energy for God

1　2　3　4　5　6　7　8　9　10

In resisting temptation to waste myself

1　2　3　4　5　6　7　8　9　10

In determining to use the gifts God has given me

1　2　3　4　5　6　7　8　9　10

GOING DEEPER

In what areas do you have strong feelings? *(Below are a series of statements. Choose five that really mean something to you. Rank them in the order of their importance in your life right now. For instance you might rank "Pain has meaning" number 1, because God has taught you something special through a painful experience.)*

_____ Those who give themselves will receive God.

_____ Caring for others is caring for God.

_____ God's love is unearned.

_____ We should obey authority, but not imitate those in authority.

_____ Pain has meaning.

_____ Death has no permanent hold over us.

_____ God makes up the difference in my efforts.

_____ Knowing God is different from knowing about God.

_____ I need to be quietly receptive to God's speaking to me.

_____ God dispenses his power to us to use.

_____ Through Jesus, God is made visible in people like us.

_____ I can do anything through Jesus Christ.

_____ Nothing can separate me from the love of God.

_____ We should do everything to the glory of God.

_____ No temptation that we have, need overcome us.

Silent Preparation / 5 min.
fill out the questionnaire.

Warm-up / 2's / 10 min.
Get together in 2's—with someone from your support group—and share how you ranked yourself in the Warm-up. Take the first point and let each person explain how he ranked himself and why. Then take the second, etc. *(Take a moment and explain how you ranked yourself on the first point. After 10 minutes call time and move on.)*

Going Deeper / 8's / 15 to 20 min.
Get together with your entire support group and share your answers to Going Deeper. Take the first point and go around, letting each person explain his answer and why. If there is time, go around on the second question, the third, etc. *(Explain your answer to the first question and set the pace for real depth sharing. At the close call time and move on to the Close-out).*

Close-out
In your support groups, spend a few moments in prayer for one another, mentioning the particular needs that have been shared. After a couple minutes I will break in and close with prayer for the entire group. *(Wait two or three minutes. Then break in with a closing prayer.)*

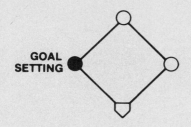

GOAL SETTING

Objective: To take inventory of your life during the time you have been in this program, and to share the results with your support group.

PROCEDURE

The instructions are given in the words you can use in leading the group.

Silent Preparation / 5 min.
fill out the questionnaire.

Warm-up / 2's / 10 min.
Get together in 2's—with someone from your support group—and share how you ranked yourself in the Warm-up. Take the first point

Give yourself a hand!

WARM-UP

How have you progressed while in this program? *(Read over the Scripture. Then in each area rank your spiritual progress from 1 to 10—1 being very low and 10 being very high. For instance, for your "prayer life" you might circle number 3, because you don't have much of a prayer life but you have more than when you started this program.)*

In living out my commitment to Christ

1　2　3　4　5　6　7　8　9　10

In reshaping my lifestyle around spiritual values

1　2　3　4　5　6　7　8　9　10

RUNNING TOWARD THE GOAL

I do not claim that I have already succeeded or have already become perfect. I keep going on to try to win the prize for which Christ Jesus has already won me to himself. Of course, brothers, I really do not think that I have already won it; the one thing I do, however, is to forget what is behind me and do my best to reach what is ahead. So I run straight toward the goal in order to win the prize, which is God's call through Christ Jesus to the life above.

All of us who are spiritually mature should have this same attitude. If, however, some of you have a different attitude, God will make this clear to you. However that may be, let us go forward according to the same rules we have followed until now."

PHILIPPIANS 3:12-16 GNFMM

In working for justice for all peoples
1 2 3 4 5 6 7 8 9 10

In thinking of my long-range goals
1 2 3 4 5 6 7 8 9 10

In experiencing God's inner peace
1 2 3 4 5 6 7 8 9 10

In discovering my own special gifts
1 2 3 4 5 6 7 8 9 10

In dealing with feelings of insecurity and inadequacy
1 2 3 4 5 6 7 8 9 10

In dealing with sexual hangups
1 2 3 4 5 6 7 8 9 10

In experiencing God's forgiveness
1 2 3 4 5 6 7 8 9 10

In believing in myself
1 2 3 4 5 6 7 8 9 10

GOING DEEPER

1. Five years from now, I will probably look back upon the time in this program as *(circle one)*:
   a. a waste of time
   b. the beginning of my spiritual life
   c. the first time I really got serious about God
   d. a time of fun and laughter with people who really came to mean a lot to me
   e. a beautiful experience, but...
   f. _____

2. If I had to put my finger on one thing in this program where God "touched" me, it would be *(circle one)*:
   a. the prayer time
   b. the sharing of our problems
   c. getting into Scripture for myself
   d. _____

3. The challenge in the Scripture to "forget what is behind me" and run "straight toward the goal" in Jesus Christ, strikes me as *(circle one)*:
   a. almost impossible
   b. what I am already doing
   c. what the Christian life is all about
   d. separating the men from the boys

In putting my money where my mouth is
1 2 3 4 5 6 7 8 9 10

In developing a daily devotional habit
1 2 3 4 5 6 7 8 9 10

In keeping thoughts under control
1 2 3 4 5 6 7 8 9 10

In standing up for what I believe
1 2 3 4 5 6 7 8 9 10

In controlling my temper
1 2 3 4 5 6 7 8 9 10

In dealing with family relationships
1 2 3 4 5 6 7 8 9 10

In managing my time for best use
1 2 3 4 5 6 7 8 9 10

In sharing my faith with my friends
1 2 3 4 5 6 7 8 9 10

and let each person explain how he ranked himself and why. Then take the second, etc. *(Take a moment and explain how you ranked yourself on the first point. After 10 minutes call time and move on.)*

Going Deeper / 8's / 15 to 20 min.

Get together with your entire support group and share your answers to Going Deeper. Take the first point and go around, letting each person explain his answer and why. If there is time, go around on the second question, the third, etc. *(Explain your answer to the first question and set the pace for real depth sharing. At the close call time and move on to the Close-out).*

Close-out

In your support groups, spend a few moments in prayer for one another, mentioning the particular needs that have been shared. After a couple minutes I will break in and close with prayer for the entire group. *(Wait two or three minutes. Then break in with a closing prayer.)*

Special Events

7-hour staff training day

OBJECTIVE: (1) To build a close-knit community within your Youth Ministry Team, and (2) To plan the youth program for the coming months.

TIME: 7 hours. If you combine this training event with recreation, make sure that the quality prime time is given to training.

PLACE: A cabin out of town, away from the phone and away from interruptions.

MATERIALS REQUIRED: Photocopy the exercises that are needed from this Encyclopedia, or provide this Encyclopedia for each member of your Youth Ministry Team. (This would be a good investment if you are planning on using this Encyclopedia through the year in planning the weekly youth meetings.)

LEADERSHIP: The Youth Pastor or Leader should be familiar with the philosophy of the Youth Ministry Team (pages 210-211) and the philosophy behind the Serendipity ''group-building'' model (pages 8-11 and 216-217).

The design of the the the four sessions of this ''7-hour training day'' will use the C-Group model for each sharing experience so that the Youth Ministry Team can *experience*

what the Serendipity model is all about.

After each session, take a moment and summarize for the Team what you have done.

AGENDA:

Session 1 (90 Minutes)
Team Building

Coffee Break

Session 2 (90 Minutes)
Bible Study / C-Groups

Lunch

Session 3 (90 Minutes)
Goal Setting

Coffee Break

Session 4 (90 Minutes)
Summation

P.S. If you are spreading the training day over an overnight, try to get the first two sessions on the first night and the last two sessions on the next morning. Then take off for your fun.

SESSION 1

Team Building

Game Plan
☐ Orientation / 10 Minutes
☐ Crowd Breakers / 20 Minutes
☐ C-Groups
  • Communication Exercise / 20 Minutes
  • Bible Study / 30 Minutes
☐ Wrap Up / 10 Minutes

Orientation
Explain the two objectives: (1) To build a close-knit fellowship out of the Youth Ministry Team and (2) To plan the youth program for the next few months. The first objective is what this session is all about.

Crowd Breakers
Choose *one* of these three options and collect the equipment or pass-outs for the option you choose.

Option 1 / Crowd Games. If you have 20 to 30 people on this training day, pick one or two of the Games on pages 17-35. Divide into two teams for this.

Option 2 / Concentration Games. If you have 10 to 20 people, divide into groups of 6 to 8 and play some of the Concentration Games on pages 44-45.

Looking into the Story *Luke 10:38-42*

Go around and have each person share their response to these questions — one question at a time.

1. Why do you think Jesus went to Mary and Martha's home?
 a. they were close friends
 b. he had nowhere else to go
 c. he needed their fellowship
 d. he wanted to help Mary
 e. he wanted to help Martha
 f. other _____

2. What do you think Jesus meant when he said to Martha that *"Mary has chosen what is better"*?
 a. she needed to get her priorities straightened out
 b. people are more important than a nice home
 c. spiritual fellowship is more important than food
 d. fussing over little things is a sign of spiritual immaturity
 e. people who let their homework go are more spiritual
 f. other _____

3. If you had been Martha, how would you have responded to Jesus' remarks?
 a. gotten mad
 b. been embarrassed
 c. thought to myself, "Who does he think he is to tell me how to be a hostess?"
 d. accepted the rebuke
 e. gone to my bedroom and cried
 f. sat down with Jesus and let the supper burn
 g. other _____

4. Why do you think Jesus said what he did to Martha?
 a. she was picking on her little sister
 b. she was getting on his nerves
 c. he knew her well enough to say this without hurting her
 d. he really wanted to help her rearrange her priorities
 e. he enjoyed putting people down
 f. he knew that he had only one more week to live and he wanted to spend the time with her

IF I HAD TO CHOOSE: If you had to choose between Mary and Martha in the following situations, which would you choose (check one):

MARY	MARTHA	
☐	☐	**As a roommate**
☐	☐	**For a close friend**
☐	☐	**To leave in charge of my estate**
☐	☐	**To go to when I have a problem**

MARY	MARTHA	
☐	☐	**To work for**
☐	☐	**To work for me**
☐	☐	**To be my next-door neighbor**
☐	☐	**To be my pastor**

I AM SOMEWHERE BETWEEN: Put a dot on the line in each category to indicate how you see yourself. For Example:

On Housework, I am....
 Dirty dishes everywhere   Slippers at the door
 Mary _____Martha

On Temperament, I am....
 Easy going   Pistol packing
 Mary _____Martha

On Taking Responsibility, I am....
 Little sister   Take charge
 Mary _____Martha

On Spiritual Priorities, I am....
 Guilty if I don't start   Doing good if I open
 the day with God   the Bible once a week
 Mary _____Martha

Option 3/Table Games. If you have under 10 on the training day, use the "get acquainted" game that starts off the first session in the Counselor Training Program on pages 208-209. Photocopy these pages for each person.

C-Groups
Divide the group into smaller groups of 4 each. Then pass out these *two* handouts to everyone.
 ☐ *Music in My Life* (page 57). Ask the small groups to explain where they would put the dots and why. Give 10 minutes to share this exercise.
 ☐ *Bible Study* (page 192). Read the Scripture passage aloud — Luke 10:38-42 — and ask the small groups to share their responses to question #1. Then question #2, etc. Give 20 minutes to share the Bible study.

After 20 minutes call time and ask all groups to reassemble for your Wrap Up.

Wrap Up
Put the following on the blackboard or ask everyone to turn to pages 12-13 in this *Encyclopedia.* Explain how their session

was a taste of the Serendipity model for a typical youth meeting:

☐ Meal (30 Minutes)
☐ Fun Games (30 Minutes) All Together
☐ C-Group (45 Minutes) Two Stages
  • Communication Game—to start the conversation—"Music in My Life."
  • Bible Study—to walk through a Scripture story and share their "stories."

SESSION 2
Bible Study / C-Groups

Game Plan
☐ Orientation / 10 Minutes
☐ Crowd Breakers / 20 Minutes
☐ C-Groups / 50 Minutes
  • Communication Exercise / 20 Minutes
  • Bible Study / 30 Minutes
☐ Wrap Up / 10 Minutes

Orientation
With the Baseball Diamond on the blackboard or everyone looking at pages 10-11 in the *Encyclopedia*, explain briefly the concept of "group building." A fuller explanation is found on pages 216-217. Then go back to First Base and explain that "telling your spiritual story" is what this session is all about. . . . HISTORY GIVING.

Crowd Breakers
Again choose *one* of the three options below, depending upon the size of your group.

Option 1 / Crowd Game. For groups of 20 or more, choose something from pages 17-35.

Option 2 / Concentration Game. For groups between 10 and 20, choose another one of the Concentration Games—pages 44-45—and divide into groups of 6 to 8.

Looking into the Story *Luke 5:1-11*

1. Do you think it was merely coincidental that Simon Peter was *"washing his nets"* when Jesus needed a boat and chose Simon's . . . or was this all part of the plan and purpose of God?
   a. merely coincidental
   b. more than coincidental
   c. a little bit of both
   d. other _____

2. If you had been Simon Peter when Jesus asked him to *"Put out into deep water, and let down the nets for a catch,"* how would you have responded?
   a. just about like Peter did
   b. wondered who this person thought he was
   c. probably made some excuse
   d. politely told Jesus to stick to his preaching
   e. suggested they try fishing tomorrow morning when there was a greater chance to catch something
   f. gone ahead with the idea but grudgingly
   g. other _____

3. When they *"caught such a large number of fish that their nets began to break,"* how do you think Simon Peter felt?
   a. ecstatic / elated / overjoyed
   b. terrible about what he said to Jesus
   c. dumbfounded

My Own Story

1. In comparison to Simon Peter's call, my own spiritual beginning with God has been:
   a. tame
   b. more intellectual
   c. just as confusing
   d. even more crazy
   e. different, but just as real
   f. not sure
   g. other _____

2. My spiritual "boat" right now is: (choose two)
   a. sinking
   b. out for repairs
   c. dead in the water
   d. sailing at a fast clip
   e. sailing in the wrong direction
   f. afloat, but just barely
   g. other _____

   d. aware that Jesus was everything he said he was and more
   e. completely confused
   f. other _____

4. When Simon Peter said, *"Go away from me, Lord; I am a sinful man!"* what was he really saying?
   a. "You embarrass me because you know more about fishing than I do"
   b. "I feel uncomfortable being around you because of the life I've lived"
   c. "I know you are all that you say you are, but I am not ready to follow you"
   d. "Stop bugging me. Get out of my life"
   e. "I'm not your kind of follower. I'm just a fisherman"
   f. "I'm confused. If I say 'yes,' I know that it will mean changing my lifestyle . . . and I don't think I can measure up"

5. What did it mean to Simon Peter to leave *"everything and follow Jesus"*?
   a. become a hermit
   b. leave behind his sinful ways and follow Jesus
   c. go into the Christian ministry
   d. turn over the keys of his life to Jesus and let Jesus do the driving
   e. give up his occupation
   f. start a risky "faith adventure," not knowing what the outcome would be
   g. other _____

3. The idea of *"pushing out into the deep water"* with Jesus sounds: (choose two)
   a. scary
   b. crazy
   c. okay, but
   d. too mystical
   e. fine, if others will join me
   f. not sure what you mean
   g. just the invitation I've been waiting for
   h. other _____

4. Before I can honestly join in this venture, I need to:
   a. get myself together
   b. think it over
   c. consider the cost
   d. straighten out a few things
   e. deal with my fear of failure
   f. clean up my life
   g. other _____

Looking into the Story *Acts 2:42-47*

1. SPIRITUAL NURTURE/GROWTH: *"They devoted themselves to the apostles' teaching and to the fellowship, to the breaking of bread and to prayer."*

We give PRIORITY to studying the Scripture, to meeting with other believers for the purpose of learning more about our faith and to prayer for one another.

1   2   3   4   5   6   7   8   9   10

2. SPIRITUAL HEALING: *"Everyone was filled with awe, and many wonders and miraculous signs were done by the apostles."*

We expect and anticipate the healing ministry of the Holy Spirit in our midst, and we see God's healing power in people and relationships all the time.

1   2   3   4   5   6   7   8   9   10

3. SPIRITUAL CARETAKING: *"All the believers were together and had everything in common. Selling their possessions and goods, they gave to anyone as he had need."*

There are no needs in our community because we look after one another. If someone is out of food, out of work, or in need in other ways, we do what we can to support each other.

1   2   3   4   5   6   7   8   9   10

4. CORPORATE WORSHIP: *"Every day they continued to meet together in the temple courts."*

We meet regularly for worship with the larger body of believers—to celebrate Christ's resurrection and his triumph over sin.

1   2   3   4   5   6   7   8   9   10

5. SMALL SHARING GROUPS: *"They broke bread in their homes and ate together with glad and sincere hearts, praising God and enjoying the favor of all the people."*

We also meet regularly in small Bible study and support groups to praise God, study the Bible, share our needs, and support one another.

1   2   3   4   5   6   7   8   9   10

6. NUMERICAL MULTIPLICATION: *"And the Lord added to their number daily those who were being saved."*

We keep our groups open to new people that have become believers and need a Bible study and support group . . . and the Lord continues to add to our number each week.

1   2   3   4   5   6   7   8   9   10

My Own Story

If you could have any wish you wanted for your group, what would it be? Think a moment . . . and fill in the wishing well below.

In the first box, jot down two concerns you have about your group, such as "I am concerned about the kids on the sidelines in our group. . . ."

In the second box, make two "wishes" about this concern, such as "I wish we could have an overnight retreat. . . ."

In the third box, spell out two practical steps for putting your wish into action, such as "I will bring this up at our next meeting. . . ."

```
I AM CONCERNED ABOUT
```

```
I WISH WE COULD
```

```
I AM GOING TO
```

Option 3/Table Game. If you have 10 or less in your meeting, split into groups of 4 or 5 and use the Table Game on pages 214-215. You will need two things for each group to play this game:

☐ A photocopy of the Game—"The Way We Were."

☐ A die (one dice) for each group.

C-Groups

Divide into the same C-Groups (groups of 4 or 5) that you were in for the first session. Then pass out these two handouts to everyone.

☐ *My Coat of Arms* (page 56). Ask everyone to fill in the blanks and then share his/her "Coat of Arms" with the group.

☐ *Bible Study* (page 193). Read the Scripture passage aloud—Luke 5:1-11—and ask the small groups to share their responses to question #1. Then, question #2, etc. Give 20 minutes for sharing.

After 20 minutes, call time and ask all groups to reassemble for your Wrap Up.

Wrap Up

Put on the blackboard the diagram on page 8. Explain how the three parts of an effective Youth Ministry Program (Content, Group Building and Mission) are integrated. Then put the baseball diamond on pages 10-11 on the blackboard again and explain that they have just completed a session built around HISTORY GIVING, or first base on the baseball diamond.

SESSION 3
Goal Setting

Game Plan
☐ Orientation/10 Minutes
☐ Crowd Breakers/20 Minutes

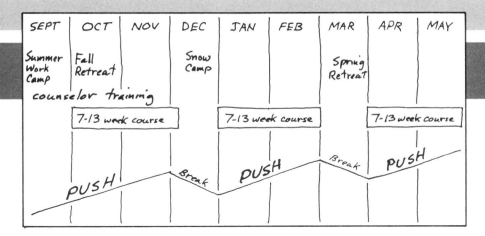

SEPT	OCT	NOV	DEC	JAN	FEB	MAR	APR	MAY

Summer Work Camp — Fall Retreat — Snow Camp — Spring Retreat

counselor training

7-13 week course   7-13 week course   7-13 week course

PUSH   Break   PUSH   Break   PUSH

□ C-Groups/50 Minutes
  • Communication Exercise/20 Minutes
  • Bible Study/30 Minutes
□ Wrap Up/10 Minutes

Orientation

With the calendar (like the sample above) on the blackboard—NOT filled in—explain that the objective of this session is to start planning the long-range program of the youth group. In this session, you will work on the "big picture." In the next session, you will work on the next few weeks.

Crowd Breakers

Choose *one* of the three options below, depending upon the size of the group.

Option 1/Crowd Game. For groups of 20 or more, choose something from pages 17-35.

Option 2/Concentration Game. For groups of 10 to 20, choose one of the Concentration Games—pages 44-45—and divide into groups of 6 to 8.

Option 3/Table Game. If you have 10 or less, use the "Guess Who" game on pages 220-221. You will need two things for every person in the group:
• A small slip of paper
• A photocopy of the game on pages 220-221.

C-Groups

Divide into the same C-Groups (groups of 4

or 5) that you were in before. Then pass out these two handouts to everyone.
□ *Job Placement Exercise* (page 73). Ask everyone to jot down the names of the others in the group next to the "perfect" job. Then ask one person to sit in silence while the others explain the job they picked and why, etc.
□ *Bible study* (page 194). Read the Scripture passage aloud—Acts 2:42-47—and let the small groups complete the questionnaire *before* they start to share.

After 20 minutes, call time and ask all groups to reassemble for your Wrap Up.

Wrap Up/Brainstorming

In the large group, ask one or two from each group to share any "dreams" that were mentioned in their Bible studies. Then, with the blank calendar on the blackboard, start to pencil in the *long-range* goals on the calendar, such as:
• Fall, winter and spring time blocks
• Subjects, curricula needs
• Retreats, trips, mission plans
Work on the "big picture." Leave the specifics to the next session. (Note in the Sample how we would break the 9-month school into three major "pushes"—with a "change of pace" or "break" between periods.)

Call attention to the fact (if they have not realized it) how easy it is to get to know people in small, intimate sharing groups like you have been using throughout the day.

Game Plan
□ C-Groups/20 Minutes
□ Brainstorming/40 Minutes
□ Worship/30 Minutes

C-Groups

Explain that this last session will be a little different—that you are skipping the Crowd Breakers to make time for worship at the close.

Then divide into the C-Groups and give the two exercises on page 77 (Funny Faces and Redecorating My Life) to everyone. Photocopy the exercises out of the book.

On the "Funny Face" exercise, let each person "show and tell" the drawings.

On the "Redecorating My Life" exercise, ask persons to share only the "two or three areas in their lives where they need a little redecorating."

Brainstorming/20 Minutes

Regather all of the groups and explain the rules for brainstorming. The topic will be: "What can we do in the next three months to make the youth group better?"

Worship/40 Minutes

Close the day with a time of common worship . . . and dedication. Here are some possibilities:
• *Quaker Meeting:* Silent time with opportunity for anyone to share something on his/her heart.
• *Commissioning Service:* One person at a time, give everyone in the group a chance to share where he/she needs to "get out of the boat" and commit his/her life to God.
• *Communion Service:* The group takes the "Lord's Supper" together.

Weekend retreat

OBJECTIVE: (1) to build a close-knit community inside of the youth group, and (2) to deepen the spiritual life of the youth group.

TIME: Friday night through Sunday noon.

PLACE: A cabin or retreat center away from the church, with suitable recreation facilities nearby.

MATERIALS REQUIRED: Study the four sessions carefully for the recommended pass-out exercises, which you are free to photocopy from this book. Also, make a checklist of athletic equipment that will be needed for the crowd breakers before each session.

LEADERSHIP: The Youth Pastor should build a Youth Ministry Team to assist on this retreat . . . by having a counselor for each C-Group. A quickie course for the Youth Ministry Team is laid out on pages 190-195 under "7-hour staff training day." A more extensive training program for a Youth Ministry Team is laid out on pages 207-235. Here is a minimum staff for a weekend retreat:
- ☐ Retreat Director
- ☐ C-Group Counselors—a counselor for every 4 to 7 kids
- ☐ Recreation Coordinator
- ☐ Cook
- ☐ Music Director

AGENDA:

Friday night / 90 Minutes
Group Building

Saturday morning / 90 Minutes
C-Groups / Bible study

Saturday night / 90 Minuites
Affirmation / Bible study

Sunday morning / 90 Minutes
Worship / Commissioning

P.S. If possible, keep the C-Groups together for recreation periods . . . so that they can continue to build their relationships with sports, etc. If you need two teams, combine C-Groups . . . but keep them together.

FRIDAY NIGHT
Group Building

Game Plan
- ☐ Crowd Breakers / 40 Minutes
- ☐ C-Groups / 50 Minutes
  - • Group Building Games
  - • Communication Games
- ☐ Singing / Wrap Up Talk

Crowd Breakers / 40 Minutes
Choose 3 or 4 exercises from *one* of the options and collect the equipment for this option. The purpose of this time is to use up the energy of the kids with high energy games.

Option 1/For Large Groups. If you have 50 or more on the retreat, pick one or two of the Crowd Breakers from pages 18-21 (with the whole crowd together,) and then divide into two teams and pick one of the Outdoor or Indoor Sporting Events on pages 24-33.

Option 2/For Medium Size Groups. If you have from 20 to 50 on the retreat, divide into two teams immediately and use some of the Outdoor or Indoor Sporting Activities on pages 24-33.

Option 3/For Small Numbers. If you have only 8 to 20 on the retreat, find three or four games from pages 18-47 that would be suitable for your small group, but choose games with high energy output.

C-Groups/50 Minutes
Divide the entire group into small groups of 4 to 7 kids in each group, plus a counselor from the Youth Ministry Team. Try to split up cliques by assigning the kids by name or by counting off.
☐ *Group Building Games:* Pick two or three fast-moving games from pages 34-47 that allow the C-Groups to work together as teams—with the counselors of the C-Groups cheering them on.
☐ *Communication Games:* Pick two or three "hello" kind of games from pages 52-68 that help the C-Group to get better acquainted with each other in fun ways. Photocopy the exercises so that everyone can have a copy of the exercise.

Singing/Wrap Up Talk
Bring all of the C-Groups together for a few familiar choruses (give out a songsheet). Start off with a rousing chorus and gradually move to something more mellow.
   Close with a very brief talk from the Director or Speaker about the reason for the

retreat and "some hopes you have for the weekend."

C-Groups/Bible Study

Game Plan
☐ Singing/Calisthenics/10 Minutes
☐ C-Groups/50 Minutes
   • Concentration Games
   • Communication Games
   • Bible Study
☐ Wrap Up Talk/20 Minutes

Singing/Calisthenics
Wake up the kids with some crazy calisthenics that will get the blood circulating. Pass out the song sheets and sing a couple choruses.

C-Groups
☐ *Concentration Games.* Regather the C-Groups from the previous session and try some of the Concentration Games on pages 44-45. Demonstrate the game first before turning the C-Groups loose.
☐ *Communication Games.* Pick one of the History-Giving Games (pages 52-68) and give the C-Groups a chance to get to know each other better with this exercise. Photocopy the exercise for everyone.
☐ *Bible Study.* Pick one of the Bible Studies from the History Giving sections of the Red, Blue, or Green sections (pages 85-187). Photocopy the Bible Study so that everyone can have a copy. Discuss the Bible Study in the small groups, with the counselor leading the way.

Wrap Up Talk/20 Minutes
Regather all of the groups for a brief talk from the Director or Speaker. Build on what the groups have been experiencing together—i.e., "becoming a caring group for one another."

DOGPATCH OLYMPICS

Before lunch (or right after lunch) pull out the stops and have some large crowd activity, such as the Dogpatch Olympics (pages 48-49), complete with a giant scoreboard, trophies, etc. Really play up the deal!

Combime C-Groups to make either two teams or several teams if you have a large crowd.

Have the Olympics well organized so that no time is wasted finding the equipment, etc. The C-Group counselors and camp speaker should be involved directly in some way.

SATURDAY NIGHT
Affirmation / Bible Study

Game Plan
☐ Party Time/Skits
☐ C-Groups
  • Group Building Games
  • Affirmation Games
  • Bible Study
☐ Wrap Up Talk

Party Time/Skits
Start off the evening with some crazy skits by the staff (pages 40-41) or some Competitions/Contests (pages 36-39) with everyone participating. If possible, keep the C-Groups in the Competitions/Contests together. (You might even announce the Competitions ahead of time and give the people time to prepare.)

C-Groups
☐ *Concentration Games.* Regather the C-Groups and try another one of the Concentration Games (pages 44-45). Be sure to demonstrate the game before turning the C-Groups loose.
☐ *Affirmation Games.* By now the C-Groups should know each other well enough to try one or two of the Affirmation Games (pages 69-76) where they respond to one another with *positive* feedback. (See the explanation on pages 216-217.) Photocopy the exercise you choose so that everyone has a copy.
☐ *Bible Study.* Pick one of the Bible Studies at Second Base (note the Baseball Diamond at the top) from the Red, Blue, or Green Bible Study sections. Photocopy the study for everyone.

Wrap Up Talk
Regather the C-Groups for the talk from the Director or Speaker. Talk about the meaning of "affirmation"—seeing the beautiful things in each other. Draw upon the examples of Jesus:
• Peter: "I see you as a *rock*." (A person with great strength.)
• Zacchaeus: "I see you as the 'Son of Abraham.' " (A person of great worth.)
• Nathaniel: "Before you knew who you were, I knew who you were—a person without guile...." (A person with great integrity.)

Talk about how God sees people with new eyes, and ask "his community" to affirm this "new thing" in one another.

SUNDAY MORNING
Worship / Commissioning

Game Plan
☐ Singing/10 Minutes
☐ C-Groups/50 Minutes
  • Communication Games
  • Commissioning Time
☐ Final Talk or Lord's Supper

Singing/Calisthenics

Wake up the group with a few warm-up calisthenics or rousing songs. (The kids are probably very tired by this time and you need to start off slow.)

C-Groups

☐ *Communication Game:* Choose one of the Progress Report exercises on pages 80-83 for the kids to talk about what they experienced at the retreat. Photocopy the exercise for everyone.

☐ *Commissioning Bible Study:* Choose one of the Third Base Bible Studies (note the Baseball Diamond at the top) from the Red, Blue, or Green sections (pages 112-187). Photocopy and give out to everyone.

Final Talk/Lord's Supper

Close the retreat with all of the groups back together for the final talk and some kind of celebration, such as:

☐ Old Fashioned Dedication Service (with an opportunity to turn over your life to Christ).

☐ Quaker Service (sometimes called a "testimonial" meeting).

☐ Commissioning Service (where every kid gets a cross from their group).

☐ Lord's Supper/Eucharist.

Weeklong Camp

OBJECTIVE: (1) to build deep, spiritual, caring relationships within small groups, and (2) to deepen the spiritual life of each person.

TIME: 5 to 7 days

PLACE: A setting that lends itself to the objectives. This could be a wilderness camp setting, a ''work camp'' mission trip, or a large youth convention where the emphasis is upon building relationships.

MATERIALS REQUIRED: The small group sessions will need one or two pass-outs for each person per session, which you are free to photocopy from this book. (See the permission release inside of the front cover of this book.) In addition, you will need equipment for all of the crowd breakers and sporting activities each day.

LEADERSHIP: A Leadership Team should be recruited and trained for this experience. A quickie course for the Team is laid out on pages 190-195. A long and more extensive course for this Team is given on pages 207-235.

A trained counselor will be needed for every 4 to 7 kids. This C-Group will meet at least twice a day and should be teamed together for various activities throughout the day. The counselor for each C-Group is absolutely essential for this kind of camp experience. ''Don't leave home without them.''

A TYPICAL DAY'S AGENDA

7:00 Calisthenics/Breakfast
9:00 Morning Session
   • Rousing Songs/15 Minutes
   • C-Groups/60 Minutes
10:15 Morning Talk (Make it short)
10:30 Major Morning Event (Something Different every morning—like Dogpatch Olympics—pages 48-49)
12:00 Lunch
1:30 Organized sports/hikes/work
5:30 Supper
7:00 Big Meeting
   • Skits (from the staff)/stunts (with everyone)
   • Songs
   • Talk (same speaker every night)
9:00 C-Groups (same groups as in the morning)

FIRST NIGHT
Game Plan
☐ Crowd Breakers/30 Minutes
☐ C-Groups/60 Minutes
   • Concentration Games
   • Communication Games
☐ First Talk/15 Minutes

Crowd Breakers
Choose three or four large crowd activities from pages 18-33.

C-Groups
☐ *Concentration Games.* Divide into C-Groups (4 to 7 kids, plus a counselor) and

pick one or two of the Concentration Games on pages 44-45. Demonstrate the game before letting the C-Groups loose.

☐ *Communication Games.* Choose one "get acquainted" exercise from pages 52-68. Photocopy the exercise for each person.

First Talk
Explain that one of the thrills of the camp will be getting to know some kids on a deeper level and becoming a "caring community" for one another.

MORNING C-GROUPS
Game Plan
☐ *Group Building Games:* Pick one or two Concentration Games on pages 44-45 to break the tension in the C-Groups.

☐ *Communication Games:* Pick one or two Communication Exercises from pages 52-68 to get acquainted within C-Groups. Photocopy the exercise for everyone.

☐ *Bible Study:* Choose one of the Bible Studies from the Red, Blue, or Green sections with a First Base indication on the Baseball Diamond in the top corner. These Bible Studies are designed for getting acquainted—History Giving. Photocopy the exercise for everyone.

EVENING C-GROUPS
Game Plan
☐ *Communication Game:* Choose very carefully an exercise that would follow up on the talk of the evening. Photocopy the exercise for everyone.

□ *Bible study:* Choose a Bible Study from the Red, Blue, or Green section that would follow up on the talk of the evening. Photocopy the Bible Study for everyone.

□ *Prayer:* Keep the prayer time to "one sentence" prayers until the group feels more comfortable praying aloud. The counselor may choose to use "silent" prayer for the first two or three nights.

PARTY NIGHT

The night *before* the last night at camp, plan a big party. The game plan for this night might include:

□ Skits/Stunts (pages 40-41)

□ Competitions/Contests (pages 36-39)

□ Crowd Breakers (pages 18-21)

□ Dogpatch Olympics (pages 48-49)

LAST NIGHT

The last night of camp should be a special night and have a special game plan. Some of the options might include:

□ Dedication service (opportunity for kids to commit or recommit their lives to Christ).

□ Quaker Service (old fashioned "testimonial" service).

□ Commissioning (each person receiving a cross from his/her C-Group).

□ Lord's Supper/Eucharist.

6 training sessions for your youth ministry team

NOTE: This training program refers to the Youth Bible Study Series (shown on the back cover) but it can be used to train youth leaders for any program.

ORIENTATION: What is a Youth Ministry Team?

Objective: To get acquainted, introduce the concept of team ministry and agree on a contract for the next 5 training sessions.

Setting: Informal—youth leader's office or home.

Time: About 90 minutes.

- ☐ Group Building Game/25-30 Minutes
- ☐ Content/15-20 Minutes
- ☐ Group Sharing/20-25 Minutes
- ☐ Wrap-up/20-25 Minutes

Materials required: Leader's Guide and pencil for everyone.

Leadership: The youth leader should direct the first two sessions. To introduce the concept of team ministry, the youth leader must be familiar with the flow for all 6 training sessions.

End results: At the conclusion of this session, participants should be: (1) familiar with the philosophy of team ministry, (2) committed to spending 5 more sessions in the team training, and (3) open to serving on the Youth Ministry Team *if* God directs them to this mission after the 6 training sessions.

> NOTE: This training program refers to the Youth Bible Study Series (shown on back cover) but it can be used for training leaders in any youth program.

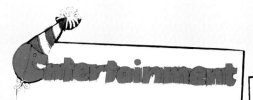

Entertainment

FOR $1: I would likely:
a. go out for first run movie
b. stay home for TV re-run

FOR $2: On TV, I would choose:
a. Sesame Street
b. soap opera
c. Evening News

FOR $3: If a movie gets scary, I usually:
a. go to bathroom
b. close my eyes
c. clutch a friend
d. love it

FOR $4: In movies, I prefer:
a. musical comedy
b. horror film
c. shoot-em-up cowboy
d. science fiction
e. Walt Disney
f. serious drama

FOR $5: My idea of a good family time is:
a. family picnic
b. camping trip
c. playing in yard
d. sitting around the fire

ideals

FOR $1: If I had a choice, I would:
a. inherit a million dollars to spend
b. make a million to give away

FOR $2: I would choose a life of:
a. happiness
b. success
c. riches
d. adventure

FOR $3: The person who represents my ideals is:
a. John Wayne
b. Mother Teresa
c. Archie Bunker
d. Jackie Kennedy Onassis

FOR $4: If I chose a TV commercial for my life, it would be:
a. Reach out and touch someone
b. You only go around once in life, so reach for the gusto
c. Sensual but not too far from innocence
d. It's the real thing

FOR $5: In my family, I see myself as the:
a. funny bone
b. wish bone
c. back bone
d. neck bone (sticking my neck out)

Clothes

FOR $1: For clothes, I am more likely to go to:
a. Sears
b. Saks Fifth Avenue

FOR $2: I feel more comfortable wearing:
a. formal clothes
b. sport clothes
c. casual clothes
d. grubbies

FOR $3: In buying clothes, I look first for:
a. fashion/style
b. name brand
c. price
d. quality

FOR $4: If I buy the expensive "top of the line" in anything, it is:
a. sox
b. underwear
c. shoes
d. suit/dress
e. sportswear

FOR $5: In buying clothes, I usually:
a. shop all day for a bargain
b. choose one store but try on everything
c. buy the first thing I try on
d. buy without trying it on

TASTE

FOR $1: In music, I am closer to:
a. Bach
b. Beatles

FOR $2: In furniture, I prefer:
a. Early American
b. French Provincial—elegant
c. Scandinavian—contemporary
d. Hodgepodge—little of everything

FOR $3: My choice of reading matter is:
a. science fiction
b. sports
c. murder mystery
d. romance
e. history

FOR $4: If I had $1,000 to splurge, I would buy:
a. one original painting
b. two numbered prints
c. three reproductions and an easy chair
d. four cheap imitations, easy chair and color TV

FOR $5: In our family, we put a premium on:
a. good education
b. getting ahead
c. quality time together
d. simple life
e. culture

Romance

FOR $1: I would prefer:
a. blind date
b. my second choice

FOR $2: In dating, I prefer:
a. going steady
b. playing the field
c. being close friends

FOR $3: I prefer to marry someone who is:
a. rich
b. generous
c. beautiful/handsome
d. has sense of humor
e. intelligent

FOR $4: I would choose for a honeymoon:
a. Niagara Falls
b. ten days in Vegas
c. South Sea island
d. Broadway theatre
e. backpacking in Tetons
f. save money for downpayment on house

FOR $5: My idea of a beautiful relationship is:
a. Kermit and Miss Piggy
b. Cinderella and Prince Charming
c. Mork and Minday
e. The Waltons
f. Don Quixote and Aldonza

TRAVEL

FOR $1: When it comes to travel, I prefer:
a. excitement
b. enrichment

FOR $2: On a vacation, my lifestyle is:
a. go, go all the time
b. party every night and sleep in
c. slow and easy

FOR $3: In packing for a trip, I include:
a. toothbrush and change of underwear
b. light bag and good book
c. small suitcase and nice outfit
d. all but the kitchen sink

FOR $4: If I had $100 to blow, I would choose:
a. one glorious night in luxury hotel
b. weekend in a nice hotel
c. full week in cheap hotel
d. two weeks camping in boondocks

FOR $5: My idea of a great family vacation is:
a. Disneyland
b. rafting down the Colorado River
c. going to see the Grandparents
d. ski weekend
e. staying home and having fun together

HABITS

FOR $1: I am more likely to take a:
a. shower
b. bath

FOR $2: I am more likely to squeeze the toothpaste:
a. in the middle
b. from the end
c. roll it up

FOR $3: If lost, I will probably:
a. stop and ask directions
b. check the map
c. find the way by driving around

FOR $4: I read the paper, starting with:
a. funnies
b. sports
c. world news
d. local news
e. editorial
f. amusements
g. cross word puzzle

FOR $5: when I undress at night, I put my clothes:
a. on a hanger in closet
b. folded neatly over chair
c. stuffed into hamper
d. tossed in corner
e. left on floor

CARS

FOR $1: My car is likely to be:
a. spotless
b. messy

FOR $2: The part of my car that I keep in the best condition is:
a. outside paint job
b. interior
c. engine

FOR $3: I am more likely to buy a:
a. luxury car—10 mpg
b. sport car—20 mpg
c. economy car—30 mpg
d. tiny car—40 mpg

FOR $4: If I had a choice of antique cars, I would choose:
a. 1955 pink T-Bird
b. 1952 red MG-TD convertible
c. 1937 silver Rolls Royce
d. 1929 Model A Ford

FOR $5: I think the best car for our family would be:
a. Luv Bug
b. Chitty Chitty Bang Bang
c. Turbo Charged Ferrari
d. Flowering Gypsy Wagon
e. Circus car

WORK

FOR $1: I prefer to work at a job that is:
a. too big to handle
b. too small to challenge

FOR $2: The job that is like work is:
a. cleaning house
b. working in yard
c. balancing checkbook

FOR $3: In choosing a job, I look for:
a. salary
b. security
c. fulfillment
d. working conditions

FOR $4: If I had to choose between these jobs, I would choose:
a. pickle inspector at processing plant
b. complaint office at department store
c. bedpan changer at hospital
d. garbage collector
e. personnel manager in charge of firing

FOR $5: If my family could start a business, we would be good at:
a. small general store
b. family run restaurant
c. day care center
d. circus troupe
e. disco

FOOD

FOR $1: I prefer to eat in:
a. drive in
b. fancy restaurant

FOR $2: On the menu, I look for something:
a. familiar
b. different
c. way out

FOR $3: When eating chicken, I pick first:
a. drum stick
b. breast
c. gizzard
d. liver

FOR $4: I draw the line when it comes to eating:
a. frog legs
b. pickled pigs feet
c. sweet bread
d. snails
e. raw oysters
f. Rocky Mountain oysters

FOR $5: When my family eats at home, I prefer:
a. spaghetti
b. meat and potatoes
c. hamburgers
d. steak
e. casserole

GROUP BUILDING GAME
Groups of 4 to 8/25-30 Minutes

Kwiz

Rationale: Getting acquainted is twice the fun if you can do it in a guessing game. In Kwiz, the others in your group try to guess what your answer will be BEFORE you explain.

Instructions:

1. If a large class, divide into smaller groups of from 4 to 6 each.

2. FIRST PERSON: Choose ONE category, such as Entertainment.

3. Read the $1 question aloud to the group.

4. Everyone tries to GUESS your answer BEFORE you explain.

5. All who guessed RIGHT win $1 each. Keep score of the money you win in the margin of your book.

6. Read the $2 question and ask the group to guess. Those who guess right get $2.

7. Read through all questions in the category. Those who guess right on any question get the specified dollars.

8. NEXT PERSON: Choose another category.

9. Read the $1 question. Before you explain, let others try to guess. Those who guess right win $1.

10. WINNER: When everyone in your group has read a category, add up the individual scores. The person with the most money wins.

HINT: *To make the game even more fun, divide your group into two teams and combine the individual scores within your team to determine the team winner.*

CONTENT
All Together/15-20 Minutes

What is a Youth Ministry Team?

1. A Hand-Picked Group
The Youth Ministry Team (YMT) is a hand-picked group of people who have been personally recruited to assist in the youth ministry of the church. Team members must be at least two years older than the youth they are serving. This means that juniors and seniors in high school can serve on the youth team for the younger teenage group, that college-age people can serve on the senior high youth ministry team, and that young adults can serve on the college team.

AT A GLANCE

YOUTH LEADER
A professional or lay person designated by the church to direct and coordinate the youth ministry

YOUTH MINISTRY TEAM (YMT)
A study, support, and mission group of older youth and adults who are committed to Jesus Christ and to loving and serving inside and outside the church.

WEEKLY YOUTH MEETING
After the meal/recreation/songs, the kids are divided into C-Groups—small, sharing units of from 4 to 7 kids and a counselor from the YMT. The central focus of the youth meeting is the small, caring C-Group.

RECREATION/RETREATS
Once or twice during the 7-week series, the youth group gathers for a special evening . . . and for an overnight retreat once a quarter, with the YMT serving as counselors and sponsors. The purpose will determine the agenda.

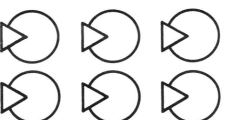

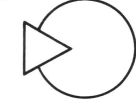

2. Gathered to Study and Support

The YMT is first and foremost a study and support group for team members' own spiritual growth. The YMT meets weekly—first to share in their own Bible study and then to plan the youth meeting. Ministry to youth must be the "journey outward" of team members' "journey inward," and the weekly study and support time is essential to personal, spiritual growth.

3. Then Sent Out to Share and to Serve

The YMT is made up of people with differing "spiritual gifts" in a common mission. At the close of the 6 training sessions, the YMT will divide the functional needs of the youth program based on the recognition and acceptance of each member's special gifts. Some people will serve as counselors for small "C-Groups," some will coordinate recreation, or lead singing or coordinate meals or help organize transportation or lead an outreach program.

The goal of the youth leader is to train and turn over to the YMT the actual running of the program. If the youth leader feels "overloaded," it is probably an indication that he or she has not sufficiently delegated to the YMT the various responsibilities. A good leader is one who sees that the job is done . . . through other people.

What Is the Youth Ministry Model?

1. Small "C-Groups"

The weekly youth meeting is built around small subgroups called "C-Groups," where every kid can belong to a close-knit, family caring group. (The "C" stands for caring, close-knit, concerned, community, core group . . . or any other c-word for that matter). Every C-Group has 4-7 students, a counselor from the YMT, and "an empty chair" for the newcomer who's always welcome.

The size of the C-Group really depends on the makeup of the youth group. For

QUESTIONS and ANSWERS

These questions refer specifically to the Youth Bible Study Series (shown on back cover).

1. *What does the word "serendipity" mean?* One surprise after another.

2. *What is so unique about the Serendipity Youth Ministry Model?* The small C-Groups, the Youth Ministry Team (YMT), the 7-week "travel and rest" course design.

3. *What's a C-Group?* Small, caring units—4-7 kids plus a YMT counselor—that develop into a sharing, supportive unit.

4. *How are the C-Groups transformed into this sharing, supportive unit?* Through a carefully designed system in each course that encourages and enables C-Group members to get to know one another, to share their stories, to be affirmed by one another, to talk about their hopes, dreams, concerns and pains and finally to agree together to help one another.

5. *Where does Bible study come in?* In every session in every course, there are two kinds of Bible study. 1) Relational Bible Study—where students relate their story to the biblical story and 2) Overtime Challenge—where students can go deeper into the same subject.

6. *How much do you have to know about the Bible to lead this kind of Bible study?* The more you know, the better background you'll have, but you can start with very little biblical knowledge and still be effective. The key ingredient: a desire to continually learn and grow in your own understanding.

   With that attitude, you can easily follow the step-by-step instructions.

7. *Who leads the youth meetings?* The Youth Ministry Team.

8. *How do you get on the Youth Ministry Team?* Go through the training program for team members.

9. *If you go to the training sessions, do you have to commit yourself to be on the Youth Ministry Team?* No. You can take the training for your own benefit and decide after the training is over if you want to be on the team.

10. *If you agree to be on the Youth Ministry Team, what does this demand?* A commitment to (1) be at the weekly team meeting, (2) be at the weekly youth meeting, and (3) share in the special youth retreats, trips, and activities.

11. *What if you have never worked with teenagers?* Great, this is a good place to get started. All you need is a teachable, open spirit, a love for kids and a commitment to Jesus Christ.

12. *What will I do if I am on the Youth Ministry Team?* You will be able to use the gifts God has given you in specific ways to minister to kids. You may be a C-Group counselor or help with music or coordinate recreation or organize transportation or meals. You may just "be a friend" to kids in need—meeting them at school, visiting with their parents, etc. But always you will have an opportunity to use your special gifts.

13. *What is the goal of this ministry?* To bring kids to a personal relationship with Jesus Christ and into a caring community where their personal commitment can be nurtured and grounded in the Scripture.

14. *What is the denominational slant to the material?* None.

15. *What makes you think this youth ministry will succeed?* It is based on some tried and true principles: 1) a team of people who are committed to Christ, to each other, and to kids, 2) small, caring/sharing groups where kids can feel they belong, 3) a structured 7-week course that provides the tools and strategies for youth ministry.

16. *What is Serendipity House?* A small research and development community that is committed to the gospel of Jesus Christ, to the local church, and to the theology of incarnational Christianity.

instance, in a smaller youth group of 8 kids total, the YMT may decide to have just one C-group with a couple counselors instead of two C-groups if they tend to be a little introverted and withdrawn. On the other hand, if the group is composed of "talkers," two 4-person C-groups would be better. But that's a decision of the YMT.

2. Short, 7-Week Courses
Three times in the school year—fall, winter, spring—the youth group will go through a 7-week course, combining spiritual growth through Scripture study with group building through C-groups.

> The 7-week course model is referring to the Youth Bible Study Series (shown on back cover) but the model can be used in designing your own youth program.

3. Time Off Between Courses
The Serendipity Youth Ministry Model is like a travel tour catalog. There are 9 special trips (or courses) in the system covering 9 basic areas of spiritual growth.

After each trip, the youth group stops to rest. For instance, the fall trip may last from the first week in October until Thanksgiving. Then the youth group does "something different" until after Christmas.

At the beginning of the new year, the youth group starts on another 7-week trip—concluding just before Easter. Finally, after Easter, there is time for one more 7-week trip before the school year concludes.

This pattern of travel and rest, travel and rest, travel and rest allows for great variety—a key ingredient to a vibrant youth ministry.

4. One Surprise After Another
At least once a month, the YMT should plan a Special Event for the group—something different from the regular youth meeting. Retreats, ski weekends, wilderness trips, workdays, etc.

Members of the YMT can be selected who specialize in planning and coordinating these events so that C-Group leaders don't feel burdened by "one more thing."

These Special Events are designed not only for times of spiritual growth and fun but also as a means for reaching out to others in the community.

The YMT should plan at least one recreational event every month and one extended overnight or weekend event once during the 7-week course.

What does an Average Youth Meeting Look Like?

1. Hot Meal (Optional)
Since the beginning of the church two thousand years ago, shared meals have been an important part of learning and fellowship. If possible, the meeting should begin with a meal—a spaghetti feed, "sloppy joes," etc. The kids can pay $1.25 and a different parent can be asked each week to provide a simple meal. What the kids pay goes to the parent bringing the meal.

2. Crowd Breakers
After the meal, the group gathers for 30 minutes of high activity games. Sometimes the C-groups can be used as teams to compete with one another. The Leader's Guide will contain one or two Crowd Breakers for each meeting but other sources of Crowd Breakers can easily be obtained.

3. Warm-up
The agenda for the rest of the meeting is provided in the Serendipity Student Book

with instructions in the Leader's Guide. The Warm-Up is a short activity designed to help members of the C-Groups get reacquainted and ready for the Relational Bible Study.

4. Relational Bible Study
The Relational Bible Study is characterized by variety and involvement. Often, the C-Groups will subdivide into pairs to work quickly on a Bible study quiz and then regroup to share their results. Sometimes, group members will work solo. But always they will be interacting in such a way that the Bible relates to their own lives.

5. Overtime Challenge (Deeper Bible Study)
For those willing to "go deeper," each session provides a heavier Bible study which can be done in the context of a C-Group or at home. For more mature or older groups, the Overtime Challenge can be integrated into the normal Relational Bible Study time. Less time can be spent on the Relational Bible Study questions and more time on the Overtime Challenge ones.

 GROUP SHARING
Groups of 4 to 6/20-25 Minutes

Basic Assumptions
Leader: If you have more than 6 people in this session, divide the group into two or more groups. Ask each person to indicate their response to the 8 Basic Assumptions (page 6) by initialing each statement if they agree or putting a question mark (?) if they have a question or problem with the statement.

QUICK SURVEY: Turn back to page 6—to the 8 Basic Assumptions Behind Serendipity. After each statement, put your initials (like a contract) if you agree with the statement . . . or put a question mark (?) if you have a question or problem with the statement.

After you have read over the 8 Assumptions and jotted down your initials, get together in small groups and discuss your responses.

WRAP-UP
Total Group Together/20-25 Minutes

Questions/Commitment

Leader: Save a few minutes at the close of this session to bring everyone back together to answer any questions and to agree on the contract below.

YOUTH MINISTRY TEAM TRAINING CONTRACT

Now is the time to agree upon the guidelines for the next 5 sessions. What we need to do as individuals and as a group to prepare for the Youth Ministry Team. The contract is simple:

☐ To attend every session except in case of emergency
☐ To get involved at each session
☐ To be open to the leading of God to join the YMT *after* the last session

Initial: If you agree to this contract for the next 5 sessions: _____

(After discussion as to best times, etc., fill in the specifics below. The remaining training sessions will be):

Day of week: _____

Time: (minimum of 90 minutes) ____

Location: _____

P.S. Pass around your books and jot down your name/address/phone on pages 236-7.

JUNIOR HIGH CHARACTERISTICS AND HOW TO USE THEM

Physical Characteristics
They grow rapidly. Girls are about a year to eighteen months ahead of guys. Their coordination suffers because of rapid growth.

How To Relate
Be patient with their clumsiness. Don't make activities too competitive or overstrenuous.

They have altering periods of energy and fatigue.

Don't mistake laziness for fatigue; they may be doing their best.

Mental Characteristics
They like adventure and discovery, and have active imaginations.

How To Relate
Appeal to these characteristics. Help them use their imaginations to make the Bible come alive.

They are capable of serious thinking, and have a new ability to think abstractly as well as concretly. However, their knowledge is growing faster than experience.

Guide them in thinking through problems for themselves. Direct them to Scripture to find answers to tough questions.

They enjoy humor.

Learn to laugh with them. Use humor.

Social Characteristics
They want to be grown up and independent of adults. And yet in many ways they still act childish.

How To Relate
Never call them "children". Give them responsibilities, but don't be disappointed if they act irresponsibly.

They want to belong to the gang and have a strong sense of loyalty to peers.

Respect their peer loyalty. Expect cliques. Encourage them to choose good friends. Direct their loyalty to the Lord.

They are extremely self-conscious.

Avoid teasing or sarcastic remarks. They'll take them seriously. Show each teen that you like and care about them as individuals.

They are hero-worshippers.

Be worthy of their respect, but don't set yourself on a pedestal—you might fall off.

Emotional Characteristics
Their emotions are intense and frequently fluctuate. They have little control over their emotions because they are closely tied to the many changes taking place in their bodies.

How To Relate
Make a special effort to understand them. Avoid causing emotional disturbances. Don't schedule a rowdy game right before a serious devotion time; they won't be able to settle down that quickly.

They feel that no one understands them.

Take time to get to know each one personally. Show them that you appreciate their unique talents and interests.

Spiritual Characteristics
They want practical religion.

How To Relate
Always show that Biblical truths are relevant to their life situation.

They have many religious doubts.

Accept these doubts as part of the growing process. Welcome them as a sign that the teens are making their faith their own and not just part of the heritage from their parents. Meet the doubts with honest answers.

They seek ideals.

Direct this desire to Christ and the ideals he sets for us in Scripture.

C-GROUPS:
What is Serendipity all about?

Objective: To return to the time when you were 13 years old and learn from your own experience how much a youth group needs small, intimate caring units; to understand the theory behind the Serendipity group-building model, and to share your spiritual history with one another.

Setting: Informal—youth leader's office or home (or a home of another Youth Ministry Team member).

Time: About 90 minutes

☐ Group Building Game / 25-30 Minutes

☐ Content / 15-20 Minutes

☐ Group Sharing / 25-30 Minutes

☐ Wrap-up / 10-15 Minutes

Materials required:

☐ Leader's Guide and pencil for everyone

☐ One die or spinner for each group of 4

☐ One cup of crayons for each group of 4

Leadership: The Youth Leader should probably lead this session. The content (baseball diamond) is extremely important. The leader needs to understand the concept BEFORE trying to explain it.

End result: At the conclusion of this session, participants should
(1) know each other's spiritual roots and early spiritual experience,
(2) understand the "baseball diamond"

concept of group building, and (3) be on their way to "first base" *as a group*.

GROUP BUILDING GAME
Groups of 4 to 8/25-30 Minutes

The Way We Were

Rationale: Possibly the best way to understand what the kids in your youth group are going through is to remember what it was like for you at age 13. This is a game to help you remember.

Instructions:

1. Get a mover (a penny, dime, key, etc.) and put it on START.

2. Roll the die or spinner and advance your mover. Stop and explain or answer the question you land on.

3. To cross the Finish Line you must roll exact number that puts you on the Finish Line.

HINT: For more fun, divide into partners or two teams and require that everyone on the team must finish before you win.

CONTENT
All Together/15-20 Minutes

Theory Behind the Serendipity Youth Ministry Model

The Serendipity Youth Ministry Model is based on the concept of C-Groups—small caring units within the youth group where kids can experience real love, trust, and acceptance as they study the Bible and grow in their faith.

Every program should have a built-in mechanism for building relationships within these C-Groups. This mechanism is based on an educational theory called "group building."

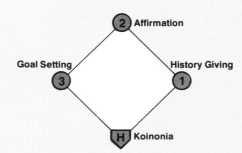

Like a Baseball Diamond

The best way to explain this theory is to picture a baseball diamond. The goal— Home Plate—is "koinonia." Koinonia is a Greek word used in the New Testament to describe a group of people who have arrived at a sense of oneness in Christ. It is similar to a marriage union—a spiritual relationship with one another in which there is total openness and freedom to be yourself, to share joy and pain without fear of being ridiculed or laughed at. And, most of all, to experience as "the body of Christ" the presence of the Holy Spirit.

First Base/History Giving

To get to Home Plate, a group has to go around the bases, which is another way of saying there is a "process" to becoming a C-Group that exhibits koinonia. First base in this process might be called "history giving."

This phase in group building is so basic that it's often forgotten until group members wake up months later and wonder why they feel like strangers to one another. In a word, history giving is "telling your story" to one another. It includes the:

☐ Past: where you have come from—your roots, heritage, significant people, places, and events in your past.

☐ Present: where you are right now—your interests, values, concerns and longings.

☐ Future: where you are headed—the

things you are looking forward to, dreaming about, etc.

The "history giving" phase in group building can be slow and tedious. This is the reason why each lesson plan should include "history giving" exercises that help the group members to give their history to each other almost without knowing it.

History giving is one of the primary goals in the first few sessions of the course. In fact, another term used for Relational Bible Study is "storytelling" Bible study; that is, telling your own story through a story in Scripture.

Second Base/Affirmation

After three weeks at first base, the group is ready to move on to second base. We call second base "affirmation," which is another word for saying *positive* feedback. Here, the group is given the opportunity to respond to each other's "story."

☐ *Appreciation:* "what I appreciate about you and your story"

☐ *Strengths:* "what I see as the strong points in your life and story"

☐ *Feelings:* "what I feel about you and your story"

Sharing *positive* feelings for one another should be a part of any relationship (especially in a small, caring group). This is doubly important in a group-building situation where everyone has shared the significant pages of his/her "story"— some of it painful or "never shared before."

Thus, in the fourth session, we reverse the process and have an entire session built around affirmation.

Jesus constantly used affirmation in his ministry, especially with people who were "down on themselves" or felt worthless. Look at the story of:

☐ *Simon* in John 1:40-42. Jesus saw in him a "rock" and changed his name to

Peter when Simon thought of himself as a "sinful man" (Luke 5:8).

☐ *Nathanael* in John 1:47-51. Jesus said of this lowly "nobody," ". . . Here is a true Israelite, in whom there is nothing false." Wow!

☐ *Zacchaeus* in Luke 19:1-10. Jesus called this "little guy" (up a tree) a "son of Abraham" . . . somebody I would like to get to know better over dinner. Look how his behavior changed after that dinner.

☐ *The prostitute* in Luke 7:36-47. The Pharisee saw this girl as "unclean," but Jesus saw in her a beautiful person . . . BECAUSE HE SAW WHAT THE GIRL WAS "BECOMING" (which is the real meaning of prophecy).

As the group moves deeper into sharing your "stories" at third base, the principle of affirmation will be more and more significant. In fact, the principle of affirmation underlies the whole of the sharing process as the group learns to do for each other what Jesus Christ is doing in our lives.

Hearing from the members of a group that you are "beautiful . . . appreciated . . . worthwhile . . . and a person of great potential" will enable you to say, "Yes . . . I am worthwhile . . . I have unique gifts . . . I can, I will be what I am called to be in Christ."

Third Base/Goal Setting

Third base in the group-building process is "goal setting." This is another way of saying "need sharing."

☐ Where are you struggling in your spiritual life?

☐ Where do you need to grow?

☐ Where do you need to be healed?

☐ What is God telling you to do?

If you asked these kinds of questions at the beginning of the group, you would scare everyone to death. You just don't talk about your needs to strangers. However, when you have established a trust and confidence in one another, it is only natural to share these things. In fact, if you withhold this information from the group, you have nullified the very purpose of the group—to support one another in your spiritual struggles.

So, in the fifth session the opportunity is given for you to share with the group the area in your life that needs some work. The optional conversation starters start the process, and the Bible study exercise allows you to walk through a Bible "story" into your own "story."

Once a person shares a goal or need, it is up to the group to support this person in this goal. This is the basis for the spiritual discipline of "accountability" in the covenant that every group member signs. Accountability means that you give permission to the group to hold you accountable to do what you said you would do.

Goal setting and accountability are what make a Serendipity group life-changing. When you start to get serious about your spiritual growth and are willing to commit yourself each week to deeper and deeper goals before God and the members of the group, and the group starts to take their responsibility seriously, a whole new ball game emerges. And the winner will be you.

Home Plate/Koinonia

This brings the group to home plate— "koinonia." Oneness, Spiritual union and communion—with Christ and with one another. This is the music of Pentecost that was heard when the broken followers of Christ got together in an "upper room" to bind up the wounds of one another, share their pain, shattered dreams, and feelings of failure. Not for *one* day like we celebrate in the church. But for 50 days—until something "happened."

This does not mean that the group will never experience conflict, any more than a happy marriage is without conflict. But there will be a new basis on which you will be able to deal with conflict: (1) understanding each other's story—the reason why you are who you are, (2) affirming each other's strengths, and (3) supporting each other in the goals you have set for yourselves.

This is what a Serendipity group is all about. Telling your "story" to each other. Supporting each other in your struggles. Rejoicing in your highs. Reaching out to each other in your lows. Being to one another the ministers of Jesus Christ.

Leader: Encourage questions and discussion about the baseball diamond concept of group building. Make sure everyone understands how a group goes around the bases in the first unit.

GROUP SHARING
Groups of 3 or 4/30 to 40 Minutes

My Spiritual Story

Leader: Before the session draw your own spiritual pilgrimage, using the instructions below. When the time comes for this exercise, "show and tell" your spiritual pilgrimage to the whole group. Go into great detail about your early spiritual beginnings. The "turning points" in your spiritual formation. And where you are right now. Set the pace for real openness and honesty by

SAMPLES

To draw your spiritual pilgrimage, you can choose from a number of art forms. Here are a few.

STICK FIGURES: Show the ups and downs in your spiritual life by drawing little stick figures in various positions and expressions.

ROAD MAP: Show your journey like a road map with the early beginnings, the mountain tops, the dark valleys, the fork in the road, and the place where you are right now. Then add symbols to tell the story.

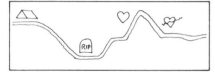

GRAPH LINE: This is probably the easiest way to tell your spiritual pilgrimage—with a line that goes up and down like a profit and loss statement.

SYMBOLS: Divide your spiritual life into three or four periods and describe each one with a symbol, such as a rainbow for happiness, a cloud for rainy days, a streak of lightning for crisis, and a question mark for doubt.

REMEMBER, USE COLORS TO DESCRIBE THE FEELINGS FOR EACH PERIOD IN YOUR SPIRITUAL LIFE. COLOR IS FEELING.

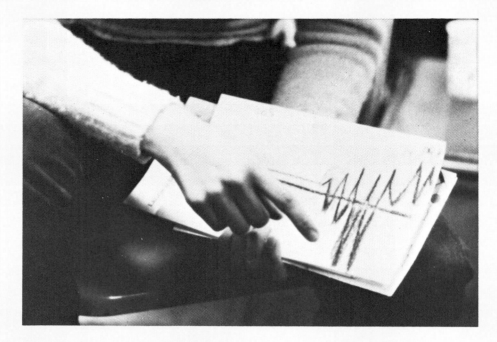

your model. Then, pass out the crayons and ask everyone to draw their spiritual pilgrimage IN SILENCE.

Instructions:

1. Think over the spiritual ups and downs in your life—from as far back as you can recall to the present—and try to tell the story of your spiritual life in a drawing on the next page.

2. Begin with the place where your first memories of God start. Draw a house, a church, or a symbol of this time in your life such as a flower. *Color* in the figure to represent the *feelings*—such as light green to represent early growth, or a bright orange to represent warm feelings.

3. Move to the next period in your spiritual pilgrimage. Think of a symbol or color to represent this period (such as a big question mark—colored in with gray).

   Try to portray every period in your spiritual life—and the TURNING POINTS—with a different *symbol* and color. Remember, color is FEELING.

4. *You will have 10 minutes IN SILENCE to draw your spiritual pilgrimage. Then, you will have an opportunity to "show and tell" your spiritual story.*

Leader: After 10 minutes, call time and explain the rest of these instructions.

5. Split into groups of 3 or 4. Rearrange your chairs—close together.

6. Turn your book around so that the others are looking directly at your drawing.

7. Start with the early beginnings. Explain your choice of symbol and color. Then, go to the next period in your spiritual story, etc., until you have explained your drawing in detail.

8. When the first person in your group has finished, stop and let the others

respond by finishing this sentence:

"The gift that you gave to me in your story was...."

For example: "The gift that you gave to me in your story was the part about growing up in an old fashioned Christian home where you read the Bible at the supper table." Or, "The gift that you gave to me was sharing some of your pain right now...."

(In responding this way, you are really AFFIRMING the person who has shared their story by responding with your *positive feelings* for the person.)

9. Then, move to the next person. Let this person share his/her story. Then, let the group respond to this person, etc.

10. Leader: Tell the group they have approximately _____ minutes (fill in the time) and this means everyone in your group will have _____ minutes. Move in close and proceed. [Allow at least 10 minutes per person for sharing.]

WRAP UP
All Together/10 Minutes

What I Learned

Leader: Get everyone together at the close for feedback. Go around and let everyone finish one of these two sentences:

☐ *In this session, I learned....*

☐ *In this session, I discovered....*

Take care of any unfinished business and close in prayer.

MY SPIRITUAL STORY: Described in a drawing ... showing my spiritual ups and downs.

session

YOUTH PROFILE
What are kids like today?

Objective: To understand the youth culture in general and the kids in your church in particular—their values, concerns, hot-buttons, and hang-ups.

Setting: Informal—youth leader's office or someone's home.

Time: About 90 minutes.

Materials required:

- ☐ Leader's Guide and pencil
- ☐ Small slips of paper for game
- ☐ Container for game (used to draw names)

Leadership: The youth leader or someone else on the team should prepare in advance to lead—especially to present the content on the youth culture.

End result: At the conclusion of this session, the youth team should know: (1) the youth culture in general, (2) the youth in your church in particular, and (3) the rationale for C-Groups in the youth program.

 GROUP BUILDING GAME
Groups of 4 to 8/25-30 Minutes

Guess Who?

Rationale: Affirmation—second base on the baseball diamond of group building—is often difficult for kids because they are not accustomed to "affirming" each other. Hence the need for affirmation exercises where affirmation "almost accidently" hap-

PLAYFUL PORPOISE
agile, intelligent, lively —
the life of the party.

COUNTRY COYOTE

PUPPY DOG
soft, furry, fun loving,
playful, irresistible —
disarmingly childlike.

TIRELESS TURTLE
slow and steady, persistent
plodder — willing to stick
out his/her neck.

CUDDLY TEDDY BEAR
lovable, warm, playful — that
brings out the "mother"
in all of us.

INNOCENT LITTLE LAMB
dressed in the skin of a
roaring lion with a big rough
exterior to cover up a gentle,
beautiful child inside.

1972 DUNE BUGGY
with sky blue sparkle paint
and balloon tires, roll bar and
bucket seats.

**SURREY WITH THE
FRINGE ON TOP**
with embroidery, tassles,
peek-a-boo curtains, the smell
of jasmine and all things nice.

1979 ULTRA TRANS AM
with side pipes, spider markings,
fancy seat covers and enough
horses under the hood to pull a
Sherman tank.

1962 PINK T-BIRD
with fur steering wheel,
leopard skin upholstery,
8-track tape deck and a
digital clock.

**1956 BELAIR HARDTOP
CHEVY**
with sidepipes and high jacks,
a mahogany steering wheel
and suicide nob — the radio
tuned to a '50's station and a
foxtail on the antenna.

**1929 MODEL T
FORD**
with rumble seat and genuine
leather upholstery, built to
last and just as fun as the day
it came from the factory.

TENACIOUS TUG BOAT
conscientious, unpretentious,
workhorse of the docks — capable
of pulling heavy loads and
guiding big ships.

TOY SAIL BOAT
with paper sail — original,
handmade, creative, childlike,
authentic.

HIGHSPEED MOTORBOAT
awesome power but low profile
— versatile and fun.

TOM SAWYER WOOD RAFT
unsinkable, homemade,
unpretentious — yet built for
lots of adventure.

CRUISING YACHT
sleek, posh, totally equipped
for luxurious travel and
deep sea sport.

VENETIAN GONDOLA
with love seat in the back and
a mustached oarsman to guide
through the romantic canals.

MOTHER HEN
warm, sensitive, sprightly, protective — always on the lookout for the well-being of others.

PEACEFUL, GENTLE DOVE
serene, calm in the midst of heavy storms.

WISE OLD OWL
quiet, thoughtful — with the appearance of being in deep contemplation.

FRIENDLY ROBIN
cheerful, perky, inquisitive, good humored — with a nesting instinct.

HONEY BEE
energetic, quick and tireless worker — nectar gatherer and pollen spreader.

LORDLY PEACOCK
colorful, spectacular — with a rainbow of plumage.

GRACEFUL SWAN
majestic, smooth-sailing, unruffled — always in command.

WILD EAGLE
untamed, noble — cherishes freedom and jealously guards independence.

HUNGRY CHEETAH
quiet, unassuming, sleek, on the prowl — usually gets his/her prey.

FAITHFUL SHEEP DOG
loyal, dependable, devoted — an abiding companion.

1941 RED MG RAGTOP
with bucket headlights and stick shift, Scotch plaid quilt and the hint of bagpipes in the air.

1975 HARLEY DAVIDSON MOTORCYCLE
with extended forks, double seat and custom sport bar.

WELLS FARGO STAGECOACH

with updated Monroe shocks and a strong undercarriage designed for rip-snortin' rough riding out West.

FLOWERING GYPSY WAGON

with eye-catching ornaments hanging from the sides and music and stories from a thousand romantic lands.

1977 ORIGINAL CUSTOMIZED LEVI VAN
with swivel seats and floor-to-ceiling carpet, a 40-channel CB and a waterbed.

VOLKSWAGEN WITH ROLLS ROYCE FRONT
with retread tires and white walls painted on, slightly incongruous and mischievous.

PORSCHE TURBO CARRARO
with air foils, spoilers and racing slicks, tuned to perfection and ready for the Le Mans.

SUGAR PLUM FAIRY MAKEBELIEVE CARRIAGE
with silvery wheels and diamond-studded trim, and a luggage rack of exotic magical items from far away lands.

RINGLING BROTHERS BARNUM & BAILEY CIRCUS CAR
with horns blaring, firecrackers exploding and Roman candles going off, and a musical calliope turning out a medley of fun songs.

ARISTOCRATIC QUEEN ELIZABETH II
dignified, well-endowed luxury — extravagently equipped but tasteful

MYTHICAL TREASURE SHIP
carrying hidden treasure and exotic spices, full of mystery and surprises and a little mischievous rum.

MISSISSIPPI RIVER FERRY BOAT
elegant, perfectly appointed, with minstrel music and the smell of perfume — quietly plying the waters.

OLD FASHIONED ROW BOAT
uncomplicated, but sturdy — made for fishing in quiet ponds with cane pole.

SLEEK HYDROFOIL
with jet engine for superfast gliding above rough waters or smooth sailing in calm waters.

AIRCRAFT CARRIER
sophisticated, awe inspiring, complex — equipped with the latest in technological advances.

RUBBER DINGY
with makeshift paddle, compact, transportable, inflatable — fun to be in.

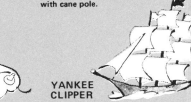
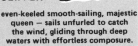

YANKEE CLIPPER
even-keeled smooth-sailing, majestic queen — sails unfurled to catch the wind, gliding through deep waters with effortless composure.

221

pens. "Guess Who?" is an affirmation game where a participant draws a name of another person and describes this person in terms of an animal, car, etc. Other members in the group then try to guess who was described. It's affirming and it's lots of fun.

Instructions:

1. Have everyone write their names on slips of paper. Fold them once and place them in a container in the center of the group.

2. Stir up the slips of paper. Reach in and draw one slip of paper. DO NOT LET ANYONE KNOW THE NAME YOU HAVE PICKED.

3. For the person you have chosen, think of an ANIMAL that best describes this person. (If you wish, look over the animals in the game—top section.)

ROUND ONE:

4. First person: Describe the person you have picked as an ANIMAL and let the others guess who this person is. Simply finish the sentence: "The person I have chosen is like a . . . ."

5. Next person: Explain the person you have picked as an ANIMAL and let the others guess.

6. Continue around your group until everyone has explained the person they have as an animal.

ROUND TWO:

7. Put all slips of paper back into the center of the group. Stir and pick a new slip of paper.

8. Go around and explain the person you picked as a CAR. ("This person reminds me of a . . . .") Then, the others try to guess who it is.

ROUND THREE:

9. Put all slips of paper back into bowl. Stir and pick a new slip.

10. Go around and explain the person you picked as a BOAT. ("This person reminds me of a . . . .") Let the others guess who it is.

CONTENT
All Together/20 Minutes

Youth Culture Today

In 1970 Merton Strommen surveyed over 7,000 teenagers—80 percent within the church. He identified what he called "five cries" that characterized teenagers then.* These basic cries are still evident today.

*Merton Strommen: *Five Cries of Youth,* Harper and Row, Publishers, 1974.

LONELINESS: Cry of self-hatred. This most commonly expressed cry is a mixture of self-criticism, lack of self-confidence, and low self-worth. They feel they are no good, unattractive, inadequate, worthless.

Four out of five of the youth surveyed indicated a low regard for themselves; one in five even entertained thoughts of suicide.

FAMILY TROUBLE: Cry of psychological orphans. The second most common cry was for family stability, support, and love. "I need to be part of a family where we love and accept and care about each other."

One in five youth lived in a distressing family situation: torn between parents, family disunity, distrust, open hostility, and physical abuse. Only one in four of the youth surveyed felt they were free to discuss openly their problems at home.

OUTRAGE: Cry of social protest. This cry ranked third among the common cries of youth. Among the junior high youth, the cry was usually me-centered: "Why isn't the world fair to me?" On the senior and college level, the cry was broadened to include others. "Why is the world so messed up? Why don't you do something about it?" Later in 1970s, the concern of youth turned inward. Thomas Wolfe coined the phrase "the ME generation" to describe this trend. However, in the 80s there is a new resurgence of concern and compassion for justice and social causes— especially among senior high youth.

CLOSED MINDS: Cry of the prejudiced. Big surprise was importance some youth gave to conformity, usually to the standards with which they had grown up. (Report in next column on shifting influences on youth may dispute this.)

Youth tended to accept the value system of a small segment of society (often their parents)—and quickly prejudged those who disagreed with them.

JOY: Cry of the joyous. Last (and most hopeful) finding of this survey was the overwhelming response of "joy" to life. The inner shout of celebration and hope contrasts with the despair and cynicism so often heard in the 20th century.

Vast majority of those surveyed were very specific about the source of their joy as Jesus Christ—and the sense of identity and mission as a result of their allegiance.

Shifting Influences upon Youth from 1960 to 1980

The Robert Johnston Company recently conducted a study for Junior Achievement on the Teen Environment. In this study they discovered a radical shift from 1960 to 1980.

The list below ranks in order the influences of youth in 1960. In the right column is the 1980 ranking. There are several major changes. The influence of friends and peers took over number 1; and television, radio, records, and movies jumped from number 8 to 3. On the other hand, the influence of youth club leaders, counselors, advisers, scoutmasters, and coaches dropped from number 5 to 9; and the influence of grandparents, uncles, and aunts shifted from number 8 to 10, indicating that the influence of the extended family has almost disappeared.

1960		1980
1	Mother, father	2
2	Teachers	4
3	Friends, peers	1
4	Ministers, priests, rabbis	6
5	Youth club leaders, advisers, counselors, scoutmasters, coaches, librarians	9
6	Popular heroes, idols in sports, music, etc.	5
7	Grandparents, uncles, aunts	10
8	Television, records, movies, radio	3
9	Newspapers, magazines	7
10	Advertising	8

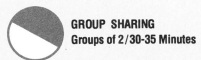

GROUP SHARING
Groups of 2/30-35 Minutes

Paper Dolls

Leader: Read over the instructions and think through the paper dolls before you begin. Set the pace for lots of fun and insight.

Instructions:

1. In a moment, get together with one other person and work together on specifying the appropriate "wear" for the average boy and girl teenagers in your youth group—complete with price tags, brand names, and anything else that is "in."

2. Beside each paper doll, jot down what they are saying: ☐ About themselves, ☐ About each other, and ☐ About the youth group.

3. Spend 5 minutes working with your partner on the paper dolls before discussing the "youth culture" as a group.

Leader: When you regroup, have each twosome "show and tell" their paper dolls. Then, move to a general discussion about (1) The Five Cries of Youth, (2) The Robert Johnston Survey and (3) The Junior High Characteristics and How To Use Them.

WRAP-UP
All Together/10-15 Minutes

Application

Leader: Finally, discuss this last item. First, have each person complete the sentence:

☐ *If we are going to counteract the influence of the youth culture upon our own kids, I think we need to. . . .*

PLANNING
How effective is our youth ministry now?

Objective: To evaluate the present youth program and brainstorm ways of improving it.

Setting: Informal—youth leader's office or someone's home.

Time: About 90 minutes.

Materials required:

☐ Leader's Guide and pencil

Leadership: The youth leader or someone else on the team should prepare in advance to lead—especially in sharing the content material on page 226.

End result: At the conclusion of this session, your Youth Ministry Team should: (1) know where your kids are itching, (2) know how to focus the youth ministry on their needs, and (3) know how to reach out to kids in your community who are outside of the church.

GROUP BUILDING GAME
Groups of 4 to 6/25-30 Minutes

Popcorn

Rationale: Your youth ministry strategy should grow out of an understanding of the particular interests and drives of your kids—which this quick quiz will bring out.

Instructions:
1. Gather in groups of 4 to 6.

OUR COMMUNITY

(Try to answer these questions—in one or two words—with the first thing that comes to mind)

WHERE DO THE KIDS IN OUR COMMUNITY . . .

1. hang out after school?
2. go to shop?
3. spend a lot of their time?
4. get their emotional support?
5. go to get away from it all?

WHAT DO THE KIDS IN OUR COMMUNITY . . .

1. do to get away from it all?
2. look at on TV?
3. read?
4. think about?
5. worry about?
6. joke about?
7. protest about?
8. dream about?
9. cry about
10. pray about?

WHO DO THE KIDS IN OUR COMMUNITY . . .

1. look up to?
2. blame for their problems?
3. listen to for advice?
4. go to when they are in trouble?

OUR KIDS IN OUR CHURCH

(Try to answer these questions—in one or two words—with the first thing that comes to mind)

WHERE DO THE KIDS IN OUR CHURCH . . .

1. hang out after school?
2. go to shop?
3. spend a lot of their time?
4. get their emotional support?
5. go to get away from it all?

WHAT IS IT . . .

1. about music that speaks to our kids?
2. on TV that appeals to our kids?
3. in magazines that grabs our kids?
4. that "turns on" our kids?
5. that concerns our kids?
6. that troubles our kids?
7. that our kids value most?
8. that our kids look forward to in life?
9. that our kids fear?
10. that sobers me when I think about our kids?

WHO DO THE KIDS IN OUR CHURCH . . .

1. look up to?
2. blame for their problems?
3. listen to for advice?
4. go to when they are in trouble?

OUR GAME PLAN

(Try to answer these questions—in one or two words—with the first thing that comes to mind)

WHERE CAN WE AS A YOUTH MINISTRY TEAM . . .

1. meet kids in the community?
2. go to study the youth culture?
3. spend some time getting to know kids?
4. provide support for kids?
5. reach out to kids?

WHAT CAN WE AS A YOUTH MINISTRY TEAM DO . . .

1. to appeal to the "hot buttons" of kids?
2. to make the kids in our community feel at home in our youth group?
3. to reach the kids in our church who do not feel at home in our youth group?
4. to speak to the real issues in our kids?
5. to expose the false gods in the youth culture?
6. to offer a radical alternative for our kids to the youth culture?
7. to make the youth program more exciting than anything in the youth culture?
8. to break down cliques in our youth group?
9. to give our kids a sense of belonging to something special?
10. to challenge our kids with the radical claims of Jesus Christ?

HOW CAN OUR YOUTH MINISTRY TEAM HELP OUR KIDS TO FEEL . . .

1. better about themselves
2. better about their youth group
3. better about their church
4. better about their future
5. better about their family

2. Appoint one person in each group to act as the reader.

3. Reader: Start with the first column—Our Community—and read the first question. Everyone answers instantly with the first thing that comes to mind. The answers should go off like popcorn the instant the question is read. **Don't stop to analyze the answers.**

4. Repeat this process for the questions in ALL three columns.

CONTENT
All Together/20 Minutes

What Makes for a Good Youth Ministry?

Why do certain youth groups flourish while most churches lose their youth in the crucial teenage years? It is hard to pinpoint the actual causes, but here are some characteristics of successful youth ministries.

People—not programs
First and foremost, a successful youth ministry is characterized by an emphasis on people, not programs. Getting to know kids. Making the kids *feel* important. Listening. Caring. Loving. When these ingredients are present, the youth ministry grows. When the emphasis is on a program—no matter how good the program is—the kids tend to lose interest.

One reason for this is the competition for time and energy with school activities. The church program simply cannot compete with the school for excitement. Unless the church youth ministry offers something different the kids are going to opt for school.

But the one thing that the school program usually does not offer is a personal interest in individual kids. If the church youth ministry majors in providing an atmosphere of love, trust, and acceptance, the kids will be there. Everyone wants to get in on love.

Christ—not creeds
Creeds are important. Super important. But kids are not usually high on catechism. Jesus Christ is another matter. Jesus Christ is the most exciting person who ever lived.

Kids can relate to Jesus Christ. They can quickly identify Jesus Christ as a person worth living for.

From the very outset, this unique difference should be brought out in direct and indirect ways: "Our youth ministry is dedicated to making Jesus Christ the Lord of life—our lives, our values, and our lifestyle."

A youth ministry that is timid about its purpose will ultimately lose kids to some other philosophy that is floating around.

The purpose does not need to be stated often but every member of the Youth Ministry Team and the student leaders in the group should understand and be committed to this distinctive.

Caring community—not a clique
A successful youth ministry must offer not only a radical commitment to Jesus Christ as Lord of life, but also a supportive, caring community where those who have made this commitment or are investigating and exploring this commitment can belong.

Kids, like adults, need a sense of belonging. Peer pressure is almost unbearable in the teenage years. And in most cases, the pressure is negative.

Therefore, a successful youth ministry must offer a counter peer group—an "extended family"—where youth can really belong.

Adult role models
Nearly one half of the kids in the average youth group come from single-parent families. Many of these can look to an uncle or aunt, scoutmaster, or coach as a role model for the missing parent. Some kids, however, have no one to look to. This is where the "extended family" of the youth group—with its positive role models—is so important.

In a recent study of Christian leaders, over 50 percent pointed to an adult person **in the church** as the most positive influence in shaping their Christian value system. Although the major source of influence for most teenagers today is the peer group, adult role models can still be significant.

Clearly defined priorities
In the rush of activity and the squeeze of time, it is easy to loose track of where the youth ministry is going. The following priorities for the YMT will help.

☐ Priority 1: spiritual growth and support for one another. This means meeting once a week to share your lives, needs and spiritual growth.

☐ Priority 2: weekly youth meeting—to share the responsibility for the youth program.

☐ Priority 3: social time with the kids. When the YMT sponsors a special event, be there. Or just show up at the school ball game to show your support.

Priority 3 is where the Youth Ministry *Team* comes in handy. At a crucial ball game, someone on the YMT is present. On another night, another team member shows up at the school play. "Showing up" says to the kids: "we care . . . you're important . . . what you do is important."

This is why the Youth Ministry Team is called a mission group. It is a group of people who are committed to "make time" for kids.

Leader: Now, discuss the elements for youth ministry and the priorities. What priorities would the team add?

GROUP SHARING
Groups of 4 to 6/25-30 Minutes

WRAP-UP
All Together/10 Minutes

Evaluation Questionnaire

Leader: Divide the group into the same small groups that played the game at the beginning of the session. Ask everyone to fill out the questionnaire in silence. Then, spend the rest of the time (30 minutes) discussing the questionnaire, point by point.

Brainstorming

Leader: Gather everyone at the close to brainstorm on this question:

☐ *What can we do in the next 30 days to put our dreams into action?*

Remember, in brainstorming, you do not stop to evaluate any suggestion. Don't let anybody pour "cold water" on an idea. Just keep brainstorming with better ideas.

At the close, deal with any business and close in prayer.

FEELINGS: Indicate how you feel about each statement below by circling a number from 1 to 10—1 being HO HUM and 10 being WHOOPEE.

Ho Hum   **Whoopee!**

Our youth ministry is really cooking.

1   2   3   4   5   6   7   8   9   10

I think we are doing a good job with the kids in the church.

1   2   3   4   5   6   7   8   9   10

I think we are doing a good job reaching out to kids outside the church.

1   2   3   4   5   6   7   8   9   10

BUMPER STICKERS: Choose two bumper stickers: (1) for the front of your church bus that advertises your youth group to those outside the church and (2) for the back of your church bus that advertises your youth group for those inside the church.

____Honk if you love Jesus
____Please have patience; God is not finished with me yet.
____To err is human . . . to forgive is out of the question.
____I found it.
____God loves you and I'm trying.
____If you're looking for a friend, I'd like to apply.
____I have abandoned my search for truth and am now looking for a good fantasy.
____I'm OK, you're so-so.
____I must hurry and catch up, for I am the example.
____Wise men still seek him . . . but not us.
____Don't bug me. I'm pedaling as fast as I can.

COMPARISONS: If you had to compare your youth group to the parables below, which would you choose? Circle one in each category.

Turbo-charged Ferrari . . . . Chitty Chitty Bang Bang
Love Boat . . . . The Brady Bunch
The Dallas Cowboys . . . . The New Orleans Saints
Bursting Sunflower . . . . Shy Violet
Fancy Restaurant . . . . Down Home Cooking
Day Care Center . . . . Marine Boot Camp

THE BOTTOM LINE: How would you evaluate your youth ministry in these two areas? Put a dot on the line—somewhere in between the two extremes—to indicate how you see your youth ministry.

On leading kids into a personal relationship with Jesus Christ.
Very weak _____Very strong

On providing a deep, caring community where kids can be nurtured in their faith.
Very weak _____Very strong

THE SMALL C-GROUP CONCEPT: How do you feel about the idea of providing small C-Groups within the youth ministry for kids to belong to? (Circle one)

    a. great idea   b. OK, but   c. what do we have to lose
                                   d. ask me tomorrow

GOAL SETTING: If you could make one wish for the youth ministry in your church, what would it be? Jot it down.

Now, take this wish and jot down one step—to start making this dream come true.

COUNSELING: How do you counsel kids?

Objective: To learn a number of counseling principles that can be applied by Youth Ministry Team members; to continue to become better equipped as individuals and as a team for youth ministry.

Setting: Informal—youth leader's office or someone's home.

Time: About 90 minutes.

Materials required:

- ☐ Die or spinner for game
- ☐ Markers for game
- ☐ Leader's Guide and pencils

Leadership: The youth leader or someone on the team should prepare in advance—especially for the presentation on counseling principles.

End result: At the conclusion of the session, team members should know (1) twelve principles of counseling, (2) in what areas of counseling they have strengths and weaknesses, and (3) how they want to be a more effective counselor.

 GROUP BUILDING GAME
Groups of 4 to 8/25-30 Minutes

The Youth Counseling Game

Rationale: The ability to listen to kids and help them with their problems is an important aspect of youth ministry. Unfortu-

nately, many people feel ill-equipped to counsel. This game, in a lighthearted way, helps youth workers get involved in a discussion on counseling and introduces several fundamental counseling concepts.

Instructions:
1. Each person selects a marker—a coin, key, etc., and places the marker on the starting line.

2. One person (e.g., the person with the largest shoe size) begins the game by spinning the spinner or throwing the die and proceeding to that space on the game board. The person does whatever that space indicates, moving forward or back, missing a turn or giving advice.

3. The second person then makes his/her move. The game continues with players taking turns until one person "wins."

CONTENT
All Together/25-30 Minutes

Counseling Kids

You don't have to be a professional to be an effective counselor. Counseling is not necessarily a mystical, magical, or professional process. It is simply one person in need reaching out to one person who cares and who has the love and the skills to help.

But there are certain principles of counseling that can help.

1. Love the kids
To be a counselor, it's important that you really love kids in general and *the* kid that comes to you for help in particular. A young person will not open up to you, in fact, he will not even seek you out if he knows that you don't care. If you don't have a genuine love for kids, you're probably in the wrong ministry. This love is not to be sugary-sweet. Nor does it have to be

adorned with a lot of hugs and "I love you's." But it does have to be genuine. Kids need to sense that you care.

2. Listen well . . . speak little
The art of listening is almost a lost art. Kids especially feel that adults don't listen to them. James writes, "Everyone must be quick to listen, but slow to speak and slow to become angry" (James 1:19). Those words should be written on the mind of every counselor. Listen with your ears. Listen with your eyes. But listen!

3. Don't overreact
Sometimes a teenager may test you by attempting to blow you away with a story that may contain very little truth. If you faint or call the Menninger Clinic, that may be the last time that young person comes to you. Sometimes the story is a smokescreen; sometimes it is a test, and sometimes it is the truth. But the principle is the same. Don't overreact.

4. Get the facts but hear the emotions
Remember there are always two sides to the story (this is especially true in the teenager-parent conflict). Recognize that like adults, kids can do a con job on you or anyone else. Expect the best but still get the facts. However, in your desire to know the facts, don't forget the emotional content.

5. Don't be totally non-directive
Several years ago the non-directive counseling approach was paraded as *the method* for helping people solve their own problems. The basic approach was to rephrase what the counselee had said and by so doing, you supposedly helped him/her see the problem, clarify the problem, and deal with the problem. But seldom, if ever, did the counselor give advice.

In counseling kids, it's important to be non-directive at times. But to be totally non-directive is to neglect the role God has given you in their lives. They have

come to you because they need outside help. And you have been called to the Youth Ministry Team because God wants to use you and your wisdom in helping kids. So, don't be totally non-directive. Don't overwhelm them with information and don't speak too quickly, but speak nevertheless.

6. Tell a few stories . . . share your "Life Message"
Storytelling is one of the most effective ways to help people learn to deal with their conflicts and problems. Jesus was the master storyteller as he shared parables of truth that people could remember and reflect on. So tell a few stories and let God use your life message—the important truths he has taught you on your spiritual pilgrimage. Kids can learn from mistakes—even yours. So share how God has taught you in the midst of personal failure and success.

Or tell a story of someone else's life or a Biblical story that will help convey the truth. Stories are less antiseptic than straight facts. Stories are more easily remembered, too.

7. Be Biblical
"All Scripture is God-breathed and is useful for teaching, rebuking, correcting and training in righteousness so that the man of God may be thoroughly equipped for every good work." (2 Timothy 3:16-17) When a young person comes to you for counseling, he or she knows at least two things: you care about kids and you are committed to Jesus Christ and the Word of God. That's what makes you unique. Use your uniqueness and the truth God has given in his Word. Teach about forgiveness when forgiveness is needed. Teach about avoiding every appearance of evil when that is required. Encourage them that the Holy Spirit indwells them as Christians and they are not alone in the temptations that come. Give them a sense of perspective and hope. Let them know the

truths of Romans 8:28 and 2 Corinthians 1:3-7. Let them sense the fact that God is never finished with them. That he loves them unconditionally. Bring God's perspective unapologetically, yet gently and lovingly to the situation. To do that means that you need to spend time with the Word yourself so that you can more effectively use this great tool.

8. Pray for the people you counsel
"The prayer of a righteous person is powerful and effective." (James 5:16) You may not "feel" righteous but you *are* righteous in Jesus Christ and you can expect your prayers to be powerful and effective. Personal care and personal prayer are a dynamite combination. Don't neglect either.

9. Don't be a parent substitute
God has called you to work *with kids*. And to work *with parents*. But he has not called you to be the *kids' parent*. God has given the parents the ultimate responsibility for the child and although you *can* help the kids better understand parents and vice versa, you *can't* take the parent's place. You don't have the authority and you don't really have the time.

Now there will be plenty of kids in need of a mother or a father. But you can't be either. It just doesn't work. You can, however, be a loving, supportive significant adult in their lives and you can affect them greatly for good.

And whether there is one parent or two parents in the home, whether they are Christian or non-Christian, one of the most important things you can do is to get to know them. Knowing the parents will probably give you more insight into the kids than anything else you do. Let them get to know you and the fact that you aren't in the business of replacing them.

10. Keep a secret . . . hold a confidence
Confidentiality is important in counseling. If a kids asks you to keep a matter secret,

do so. If the "secret" is something that a parent or the legal authorities should know, reason with the young person about sharing it with them (volunteer to go along to lend support). If the teenager refuses to share it with anyone and yet you know you must, inform him or her before you take it to another person. Rule one is hold a confidence. If you feel you must pass on the information, rule two is—go to them with your decision before you go to someone else with the secret.

11. Walk with them through the crisis
You can't bear ultimate responsibility for a mistake nor can you take the place of a kid, but you can help them walk through the crisis. For example, if the young person has been guilty of shoplifting, you can go with them to the store when the young person must confess his/her actions and make restitution.

You do not have to keep professional distance. You are not a professional. You are a caring friend. Help them negotiate through the rough waters of life.

12. Get some help
When you realize a situation is potentially very dangerous—the person has a real desire to commit suicide, a strong bent toward violence, a definite predisposition toward psychological illness—get some help. Even before trouble strikes, develop some resources—a professional counselor, a doctor, etc. Making a referral to someone more competent to handle THE BIG ONE (and then walking with your friend through the crisis) is a wise move. It protects you from wrongfully handling the situation and provides the young person with greater resources.

Leader: Discuss the material. Ask for examples that support the principles. See who has questions. Work with the content until team members are clear and convinced of the principles of counseling.

GROUP SHARING
Groups of 4 to 8/15-20 Minutes

Five Questions

Leader: As a group discuss the following questions.

1. Who did you go to for "counseling" when you were in junior high and high school? Why did you go to that person?

2. As an adult, who do you seek out for advice or help? Why that person?

3. Of the dozen counseling principles mentioned, which one do you think is your greatest strength? Which one will you have to concentrate on the most to improve?

4. What kind of problems do you think kids will bring to YMT members for help? What biblical truths could be applied to these problems?

5. Who could we contact as possible resource people for referrals?

WRAP-UP
All Together/10-15 Minutes

What I Learned

Leader: Conclude this session by having each person fill out the open-ended sentences. Then have a few volunteers read their comments.

☐ As a counselor, I want to be . . . .

☐ Today, I learned . . . (three things)

Leader: Close in prayer after taking care of any unfinished business. Remind the group that next week will be "commitment time" when each person decides whether or not they want to be a member of the YMT.

session **6**

TEAM MINISTRY:
Where do I fit in?

Objective: To review the biblical concept of "gifts"; to discover where each team member is gifted and to affirm these gifts; to make a commitment to the YMT; to assign ongoing responsibilities to YMT.

Materials required: Leader's Guide, pencils, and BIBLES for everyone, plus a Bible Dictionary.

Leadership: During the week, the youth leader should contact each prospective member of the YMT to determine if he/she wants to be involved on a continuing basis on the YMT.

End result: At the conclusion of this session, team members should: (1) understand the biblical concept of gifts, (2) know some of their own gifts (3) know their role on the YMT, and (4) be enthusiastic about it.

GROUP BUILDING GAME
Groups of 4 to 8/20-30 Minutes

Collision

Rationale: Specific responsibilities for youth ministry should grow out of the gifts of individual team members; to help discover and be affirmed in their gifts, members will get involved with "Collision."

Instructions:
1. Step One: Look at the "Collision" picture carefully and decide which character best represents you. Write

your name beside that character on the drawing. Then write in the names of the other team members next to the character they most closely represent. (You can have more than one name per character.)

2. Step Two: One person sits in silence while each member of the group explains where they put this person on their picture and why. When everyone has told where they put Person One, Person One is given a chance to respond.

3. Person Two goes through the same process. The "Collision" experience continues until everyone has been "affirmed" in this way.

CONTENT
All Together/25-30 Minutes

Finding My Gift

Leader: Guide the group through the various steps. PASS OUT BIBLES TO EVERYONE.

To gain a better understanding of what it means to be gifted, move through the following steps:

1. *Everyone* is gifted! That's biblical. Read aloud 1 Corinthians 12:11.

2. Major New Testament passages that focus on spiritual gifts are Romans 12:1-11; 1 Corinthians 12; Ephesians 4:11-13. Read aloud all three.

3. But in other passages in the Bible (especially in the Old Testament) special people are called forth with special gifts for special jobs—craftsmen, musicians, speakers, leaders, prophets, judges, etc.

4. SOLO: Focusing on Romans 12:1-11, answer the following questions:

a. What is the basic preparation for the use of gifts? (12:1-2)

b. Are you prepared? _____

c. What is the basic attitudes regarding gifts? (12:3-6a)

d. What is your attitude? _____

e. What gifts are mentioned in Romans 12:6b-11? What do they mean to you? In the left column, jot down the 7 gifts mentioned in this passage. In the middle column, jot down what each means. In the right column, jot down the character in the game "Collision" that best personifies this gift.

GIFT	MEANING	CHARACTER
prophecy	One who speaks God's Word to a specific situation.	head waiter

Leader: When everyone has finished the chart above, discuss their conclusions. If you're not familiar with the gifts and their meanings, it would be good to do a word study on the gifts in preparation for session 6.

5. SOLO: Complete the following sentences:

From this list, I believe I have the following gifts:

[ ]

Other gift(s) I have include:

[ ]

GROUP SHARING
All Together/25-30 Minutes

Sharing My Gift

Leader: Ask each person to complete the following two sentences before moving to group sharing.

- ☐ From "Collision" I learned . . . .
- ☐ From the study in Romans 12:1-11, I learned . . . .

Leader: As a group, encourage sharing on what various individuals learned. If some were having trouble discovering their gifts, brainstorm on ways a person could discover their gifts. Some suggestions: ask God to show you, ask friends what they think your gifts are, determine your interests and what you've enjoyed doing in the past, experiment with various gifts.

As a group, go over functions and roles that will be needed by the YMT. Ask members where they feel their gifts would best fit. Encourage everyone to help one another determine gifts and roles.

- ☐ C-Group Leaders (one for each 3-7 kids)
- ☐ Recreation Coordinator (if you're planning on doing crowd breakers or having special-event nights)

- ☐ Retreat Coordinator (for the one retreat/camp during the 7-week course)
- ☐ Music Coordinator (if you're going to use music)
- ☐ Meals Coordinator (if you're going to have meals at the weekly meetings)
- ☐ Transportation Coordinator
- ☐ Outreach Coordinator (for events of an outreach nature or for contacting nonchurched kids)
- ☐ Contact Work Coordinator (person who makes sure some members of the YMT are attending major school events—games, drama presentations, concerts, etc., to be with the kids).
- ☐ Other: _____

NOTE: You may not need all these roles; you may need more. One person could fill two roles or each C-Group could alternate on meal preparation, etc. Determine how you want to do it and assign roles.

Leader: When the functions and roles have been decided based on the gifts God has given to the team, move to the Wrap-up and Commitment time.

WRAP-UP/COMMITMENT
All Together/10-15 Minutes

Hour of Decision

For six weeks you have hung in together, learning about each other and youth ministry. Now it's time to fish or cut bait. Will you become part of the YMT and make the commitment to God, yourself, the kids, and the rest of the team? You have been thinking about it; now it's decision time. Remember, the commitment involves:

- ☐ Weekly team meetings to share and go over the game plan.
- ☐ Weekly youth meetings
- ☐ Special events (retreats, activity nights, etc.)
- ☐ Contact work . . . caring for kids.

If you're ready, fill out the Commitment Contract below.

> **I am committed to Jesus Christ, to kids, and to this team. I commit to attend and participate in the weekly team meeting, the regular youth meeting, special events, and to care for the kids God has entrusted to me.**

☐ Signed _____

Leader: After everyone has signed the Commitment Contract, join hands as a group and pray for one another.

Set the meeting time for the next meeting. Take care of any unfinished business and dismiss the group.

Name _____ Name _____

Address _____ Address _____

City _____ Zip _____ City _____ Zip _____

Phone _____ Phone _____

Name _____ Name _____

Address _____ Address _____

City _____ Zip _____ City _____ Zip _____

Phone _____ Phone _____

Name _____ Name _____

Address _____ Address _____

City _____ Zip _____ City _____ Zip _____

Phone _____ Phone _____

Name _____ Name _____

Address _____ Address _____

City _____ Zip _____ City _____ Zip _____

Phone _____ Phone _____

Name _____ Name _____

Address _____ Address _____

City _____ Zip _____ City _____ Zip _____

Phone _____ Phone _____

YOUTH MINISTRY TEAM ROSTER

Name ______________________
Address ______________________
City ______________ Zip ______
Phone ______________________

Name ______________________
Address ______________________
City ______________ Zip ______
Phone ______________________

Name ______________________
Address ______________________
City ______________ Zip ______
Phone ______________________

Name ______________________
Address ______________________
City ______________ Zip ______
Phone ______________________

Name ______________________
Address ______________________
City ______________ Zip ______
Phone ______________________

Name ______________________
Address ______________________
City ______________ Zip ______
Phone ______________________

Name ______________________
Address ______________________
City ______________ Zip ______
Phone ______________________

Name ______________________
Address ______________________
City ______________ Zip ______
Phone ______________________

Name ______________________
Address ______________________
City ______________ Zip ______
Phone ______________________

Name ______________________
Address ______________________
City ______________ Zip ______
Phone ______________________

About Lyman Coleman

I grew up in an old-fashioned, shouting Methodist Church in the South, with an "Amen corner," summer revival meetings, and 17 verses of "Just As I Am" to get the wayward to the altar. The Bible was the center of our life at home. We read through the Bible together every year—from cover to cover, including the notes. (Daddy thought the notes were inspired too.) We didn't have much money. In fact, I can still remember the hand-me-down clothes, the paper-sole shoes, and the feed-sack shirts. But we had the Bible, a strong family, and a great church with a great youth program.

When I went off to college, I strayed from God, but I could not get away from the family roots. The cornbread, mustard greens, and Bible diet is hard to forget. Finally, the Navigators (a gung-ho, marine sergeant kind of approach to discipleship training) attracted me while I was floundering in psychology and philosophy. They taught me how to study the Bible for myself, and gave me a vision to make the church into a discipleship training institution.

While in seminary, I specialized in small-group technology and practiced on my Young Life kids when I was a club leader. Back in the 50s when I was in school, there was very little written about small groups—especially for church groups. I had to get most of my ideas from the secular world—from Alcoholics Anonymous and the "sensitivity" group movement.

In graduate school, they had a very effective device for helping people say "hello" in groups. They gave you an egg timer that lasted three minutes, and told you to "keep talking" until the three minutes were up. If you ran out of something to say, you had to go back to the beginning, give your name again, and start over.

In those sessions, the "serendipity" idea was born. As I sat there, with my knees knocking, my armpits dripping, and my mouth as dry as sawdust, I came to the conclusion . . . there must be a better way for shy people like me to say "hello."

I called the approach "serendipity" (meaning surprise) to distinguish it from sensitivity. And in place of the cold-turkey, "confrontation" model, I started writing simple "storytelling" approaches in Scripture that allow a group to go through six or seven stages in getting to know each other:

☐ Hello. . . . Is there anybody home?

☐ How are you? How ya feeling?

☐ Where ya been? What are your roots, heritage, and the significant watering holes in your past?

☐ What's happening? Where's it at right now with you—at work, school, family, etc.?

☐ What's the matter? Where are you hurting? Itching? Scratching?

☐ Where're ya going? What's the next step in your journey with Christ?

I have been working on this "serendipity" model for twenty years now, trying to integrate the "group building" process into a Bible-centered youth program. This Encyclopedia is a composite of my work.

ACKNOWLEDGEMENTS

I need to thank a lot of people who have shared with me in youth ministry over the years and directly or indirectly contributed to this Encyclopedia: □ **Robert Coleman,** my brother, for starting me off in writing Bible study material. □ **Frank Hart (Pogo) Smith** who was my youth director when I was a student at Baylor. □ **Young Life** for giving me a chance to run a club at Sunset High School in Dallas while I was in Seminary. □ **The Navigators** for teaching me how to study the Bible for myself. □ **Howie Hendricks** and **Robert Traina** for encouraging me in creative Bible study approaches while I was in seminary. □ **Faith At Work** for giving me a chance to travel with their conferences and try out some of my radical ideas in "group building." □ **The Fellowship of Christian Athletes** for originally commissioning the Bible study programs that appear in the colored sections of this Encyclopedia. □ **Father Don Kimball** for helping me to write these Bible studies. □ **Dave Stone** for assisting in the research and the fun of putting on the Serendipity Workshops in the 70's. □ **Denny Rydberg** for helping me write the new Youth Bible Study Series in the 80's. □ **Dick Schultz** and **Hayes Button** of Young Life and **Skip Stogsdill** of the Fellowship of Christian Athletes, and **Jim Whitmer,** a freelance photographer from Wheaton, Illinois, for all of the photographs in this book. □ **Tom Hershberger** of tom/ design graphics for the design and layout. □ **The Mennonite Publishing House** for the typesetting and printing. □ The **American Bible Society** for permission to use the Good News Bible, © 1976, American Bible Society. □ **Zondervan Bible Publishers** and the New York International Bible Society for permission to use the New International Version of the Bible, © 1973, 1978, by the New York International Bible Society.

And most of all, I want to thank my wife, **Margaret,** and my three children, **Tudor, Anna,** and **Kevin,** and the thousands of youth leaders who have encouraged me over the years to stay young, and keep plugging away at providing resources for youth leaders.

I especially want to acknowledge **YOUTH SPECIALTIES** for permission to use 25 games from their book *Fun-n-games.* **YOUTH SPECIALTIES** is a great source for youth resources, and we highly recommend their products.